ANZANIA

Kilwa
Rovuma R.
Ngomano
COMORO Is.
Ibo I.
Lujenda R.
Johanna I.
MOZAMBIQUE
SENA
MT. MORAMBALA
Mutu R.
Shupanga
Mazaro
Kongone

LIVINGSTONE'S RIVER

A History of the Zambezi Expedition 1858–1864

by

GEORGE MARTELLI

SIMON AND SCHUSTER · NEW YORK

Published by Simon and Schuster
Rockefeller Center, 630 Fifth Avenue
New York, New York 10020

First U.S. printing

SBN 671-20466-1
Library of Congress Catalog Card Number 71-101881
Designed by Edith Fowler
Manufactured in the United States of America

Frontispiece courtesy of Radio Times Hulton Picture Library

Contents

Foreword

Dr. David Livingstone, the Scottish medical missionary, is known to history as the greatest explorer of his age and a dedicated humanitarian who devoted his life to the eradication of the African slave trade. He was a national hero to his contemporaries and time has confirmed his reputation as one of the greatest, if not *the* greatest, of the eminent Victorians, both in his achievement and in his influence. It was thanks mainly to his discoveries and his writings that the most primitive regions of Central Africa were opened up to civilization in the second half of the last century, the slave trade finally was abolished, and the foundations were laid for the colonization of African countries by the European Powers; and it is no exaggeration to say that the map of Africa south of the Sahara is today largely the result of this one man's travels and his teaching.

There have been many books about Livingstone and many volumes of his own published and unpublished writings, such as letters, diaries, etc. Most of his biographers, however, have been either hero-worshipers or clergymen, the latter concerned mainly with the religious aspect of their idol, while the letters and diaries, which form by far the most interesting part of his own enormous literary output, are too voluminous to be read by any but specialists. In consequence it was felt there was room for another book about Livingstone, free of the excessive adulation which has characterized its predecessors and intended for both the general public and students.

The subject chosen for this work is the Zambezi Expedition, 1858–1864. This was the second in time of Livingstone's three great exploits, the other two being the Transcontinental Journey (1852–1856) and the Last Journey (1866–1873). It was the least successful and in consequence the least publicized of the three; in fact it was a failure—or so regarded at the time—and for this reason has been glossed over by most of Livingstone's biographers.

To the modern reader, however—and partly for this very reason—it is perhaps the most interesting chapter in Livingstone's career, certainly the most revealing of his strange character. For whereas in his previous and subsequent adventures he was on his own, in this he was accompanied and observed by other white men. He is no longer the lone explorer whose only human contacts are with his Negro porters or natives met on the way, but the leader of a large expedition, between the members of which and himself there is a constant play of personalities. Moreover, instead of having to rely exclusively on his own account of events, here we have the evidence of a dozen eyewitnesses. (Some of this, incidentally, has only recently become available and so was unknown to earlier biographers.)

Apart from its intrinsic interest as a tale of daring and endurance, the fascination of the story lies in the light it throws on Livingstone. The selfless—and self-made—Scottish evangelist, the humble man of God, champion of the oppressed, who endeared himself to the British nation—as few men have done to such a degree before or since—by his physical courage, modesty and idealism, is shown here as all that, but much more besides: ruthless in pursuit of his goal; unimaginative to the point of callousness as regards the feelings of others (except when they happened to be Africans); authoritarian and secretive; spiteful and vindictive; as much mistrusted by whites as worshiped by blacks; jealous of his glory, deceitful and even capable of double-dealing.

None of which, it may seem curious, detracts from the stature of the man. On the contrary, with all his faults uncovered he somehow manages to emerge, if less likable than his popular image, even larger as a man than before: more indomitable in face of reverses, more resourceful in crisis and more single-minded in his chosen path of service to mankind. Like other men of outstanding genius he had the defects of his virtues. By displaying them we make him more credible as a human being, and perhaps his legend—when it is no longer seen as too good to be true—may in consequence become more acceptable to today's skeptical generation.

Finally a word is necessary on the spelling of native names. This is always a problem and the rules are arbitrary. Generally I have adhered to the most common usage, but I have followed Coupland and others in adopting Livingstone's spelling of Nyassa and Rovuma as preferable to the more usual Nyasa and Ruvuma. Where, however, native names appear in quoted passages I have naturally left them as they were written, e.g., Tette for Tete, Senna for Sena, Zambesi for Zambezi, etc.

G.M.
Wooth, 1969

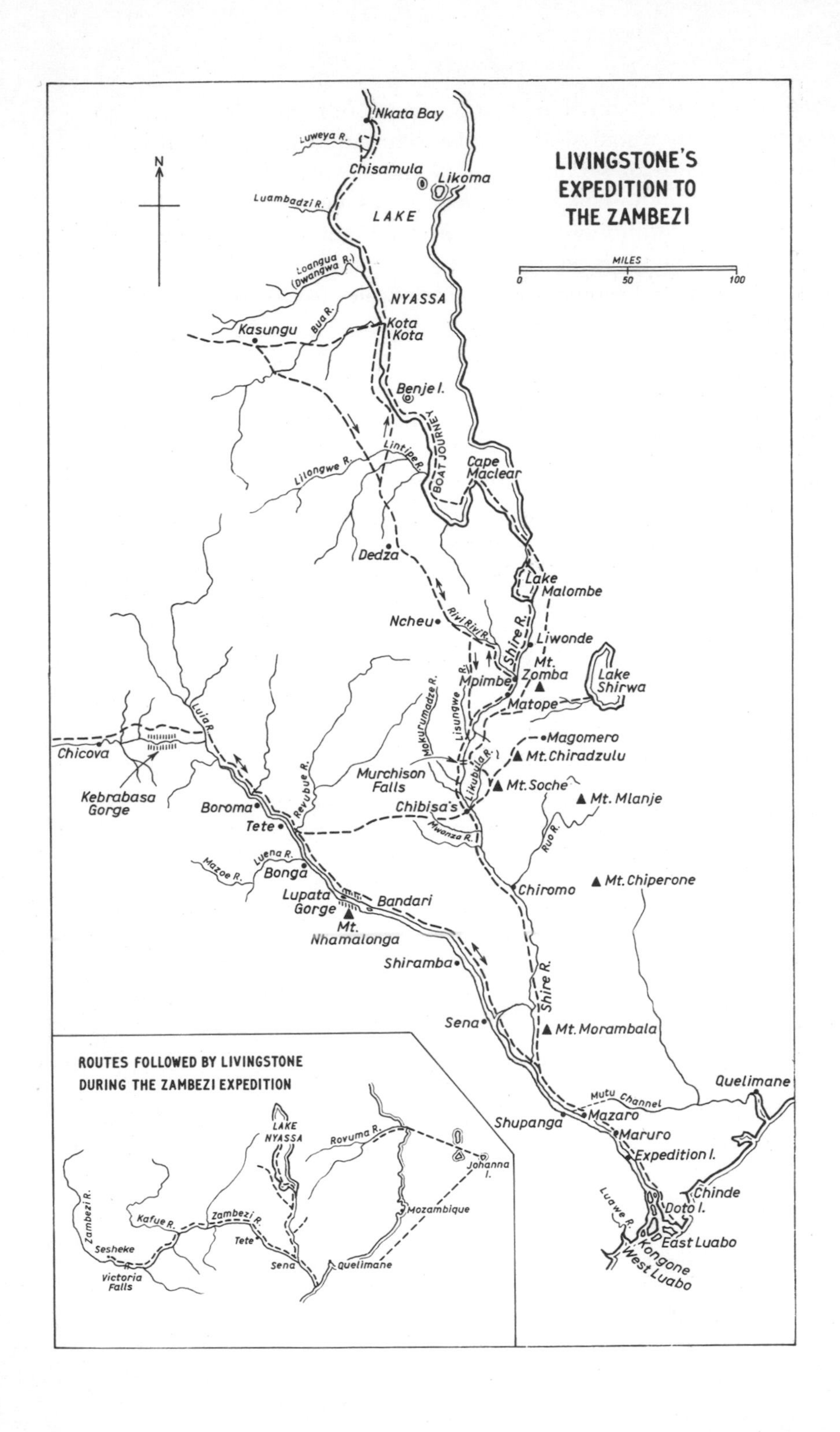
LIVINGSTONE'S EXPEDITION TO THE ZAMBEZI
MILES
0
50
100
N
Nkata Bay
Luweya R.
Chisamula
Likoma
Luambadzi R.
LAKE
Loangua (Dwangwa R.)
NYASSA
Kasungu
Bua R.
Kota Kota
Benje I.
BOAT JOURNEY
Lintipe R.
Lilongwe R.
Cape Maclear
Dedza
Lake Malombe
Ncheu
Rivi Rivi R.
Shire R.
Liwonde
Mt. Zomba
Lake Shirwa
Mpimbe
Matope
Mokurumadze R.
Lisungwe R.
Magomero
Mt. Chiradzulu
Likubula R.
Murchison Falls
Mt. Soche
Mt. Mlanje
Lujia R.
Chicova
Kebrabasa Gorge
Boroma
Revubue R.
Chibisa's
Tete
Mwanza R.
Ruo R.
Luena R.
Mazoe R.
Bonga
Chiromo
Mt. Chiperone
Lupata Gorge
Bandari
Mt. Nhamalonga
Shiramba
Shire R.
Sena
Mt. Morambala
Quelimane
Mutu Channel
Shupanga
Mazaro
Maruro
Expedition I.
Luawe R.
Chinde
Doto I.
East Luabo
Kongone
West Luabo
ROUTES FOLLOWED BY LIVINGSTONE DURING THE ZAMBEZI EXPEDITION
LAKE NYASSA
Rovuma R.
Johanna I.
Zambezi R.
Kafue R.
Zambezi R.
Mozambique
Tete
Sesheke
Victoria Falls
Sena
Quelimane

1
God's Highway

On May 14, 1858, the screw steamer *Pearl,* two months out from Liverpool, with the members of the Zambezi Expedition on board, dropped anchor off the mouth of the Luawe. This was an unimportant river flowing into the Indian Ocean from what was then known as Portuguese East Africa and is today the Portuguese province of Mozambique.

From the ship the land appeared to Dr. John Kirk, botanist and medical officer of the Expedition, as a line of "very low banks covered for the most part with mangrove, at others bare." There was no sign of any human habitation. Water was breaking over the bar at the mouth of the river, and also alongside the ship as she lay in a heavy swell in five fathoms.

For the members of the Expedition, and especially its leader, their arrival at this deserted spot, whence they were to launch on their great adventure, should have been a dramatic moment. But Livingstone was in no mood to appreciate its drama. He had been up all night with an acute attack of diarrhea while the vessel "rolled terribly," and noted in his journal that "nothing can exceed the discomfort and pain when one is obliged to hold on with all his might to prevent being pitched off the closet."

However, neither pain nor discomfort, which were to continue for several days more while Kirk treated him ineffectively with

"Jalap III," plumb opiate and morphia, prevented the patient from exercising his legendary powers of observation. After watching flotsam borne by the current floating past the ship, he recorded that "fishes under wreck screen themselves from birds of prey."

The bar looked so forbidding that naval officers on board the *Pearl*, with their usual ingrained caution, advised against any attempt to cross it. But the steamer's master, Captain Duncan of the merchant service, described by Livingstone as a "well-mannered agreeable gentleman" and a very competent seaman, was of a different opinion. He had observed that the bar was still covered at low water, and since there was a tidal rise of twelve feet and the *Pearl* only drew nine feet, he rightly concluded that she could pass over it at high water. He therefore "went at it," in the words of Kirk, "keeping the lead going and a good look out. We were so lucky as at first to hit upon a good channel, passed through the breakers and got fairly inside the bar to smooth water."

Here the *Pearl* anchored again, having safely reached, as it was thought, her destination. Actually she had entered the wrong river, mistaken for the Zambezi, but this was not discovered till more than a week later.

The next day being Sunday would normally have been observed as a day of rest and religious devotion, with morning and evening service conducted by Livingstone. However, apart from the fact, as Kirk tells us, that his "stock of sermons was run out," the leader of the Expedition was in a hurry to leave the unhealthy malarial coast and proceed up the river to the more salubrious interior. He therefore prevailed on Captain Duncan to set the crew to work on launching and putting together the separate parts of the paddle boat, always referred to by Livingstone as "the launch," which had been brought from England on the deck of the *Pearl*. This was the famous *Ma Robert*, so called after the native name for Mrs. Livingstone ("mother of Robert," her eldest son), and especially designed for navigating the Zambezi River.

"I did not wish," wrote Livingstone, "to wound the conscience of anyone, so asked the Captain to enquire if any man objected to the plan of working on that day, and if they had we should have remained idle. The engineer dressed himself on Sunday and stood all day in his best clothes, although this was the only Sunday he had ever done it since we left Liverpool. He never came near our worship."[1]

Except for this solitary protest against the breaking of the Sabbath, the work proceeded well and by sundown all the pieces of the paddle boat were in the water and two of them were joined together.

Here for a moment we must leave the *Pearl* and her passengers in order to explain how they came to be there.

In the year 1858, at the age of forty-five, David Livingstone was probably the most famous person in Britain. He had made his name a few years before by a spectacular journey, made mostly on foot or riding on oxback, from the northern border of Bechuanaland (now Botswana), which he himself had discovered on previous journeys, to Luanda on the Atlantic shore of Portuguese Angola, and thence across the continent to Quelimane, on the Indian Ocean, a distance of nearly 4,000 miles, of which all but the last few hundreds were through unexplored territory. Even before he set out on the second part of the journey, he had been awarded the Gold Medal of the Royal Geographical Society, the highest honor it had to bestow, and was being acclaimed as the greatest traveler of his age. His safe arrival on the other side four years after leaving Cape Town, as the first white man supposedly* to traverse Africa from coast to coast, put that title beyond question.

However, it was not simply the feat of exploration which impressed itself on the minds of his contemporaries. There was something in the man himself that gripped their imagination and transformed him on his return to England into a national hero. It has often been observed that to become such a hero a man must embody all the virtues which a nation likes to see as peculiarly its own. In the case of Britain these are pre-eminently physical courage, endurance, humanity and modesty. In addition the Victorians demanded at least a show of religious conviction (but not Roman Catholic), strict morality, sobriety and complete integrity. All

* In fact he was not the first white man to do so. The feat had been performed a few years earlier by the Portuguese trader Silva Porto. See *Journal of the Royal Geographical Society,* Vol. 30.

these Livingstone possessed in full measure. Thus he was utterly fearless—perhaps the main reason for his ascendancy over primitive peoples—and endowed with extraordinary powers of resistance, self-discipline and tenacity. He had a simple but passionately held Christian faith and a single-minded dedication to the service of God. His idealism, revealed in private but never paraded before the public, was untainted by sentimentality or by cant. It was combined, moreover, with a keen intelligence and acute practical sense: the vision and imagination which conceived the immense changes in Africa that his own largely unaided efforts were to be instrumental in bringing about went hand in hand with the professional competence shown in everything he set his hand to, from repairing a rifle or building a house to astronomy and navigation. There was finally his unique gift for understanding and dealing with Africans, deriving both from the deep compassion he felt for people whom he often described as the "most degraded" on earth and from the trouble he had taken to learn their language. As a result we can discover more about primitive Africans, and how they think and feel and behave, from one volume of Livingstone's letters or journals than from all the other literature on the subject put together.

Then again all his circumstances endeared him to the British public, and especially to the new middle classes, who liked a self-made man: the humble birth of "poor but honest" parents; the grinding childhood spent working fourteen hours a day in a Lanarkshire cotton mill; the sheer grit which enabled him to fight his way out of this hopeless environment and become a qualified doctor and ordained minister of the Church; even his happy marriage and devotion to his young family.

This was the popular image and it has endured to the present day. Were it the whole story Livingstone would emerge as a man of unquestionable moral grandeur, yes, but also as a humorless fanatic and a bit of a prig. Fortunately it is not the whole story. If a sense of humor in the modern sense of being able to laugh at oneself was not his strongest point, he was no prig, with a keen appreciation of the comic and a caustic wit. While respecting the conventions of his time, for instance, in referring to his trousers as "inexpressibles" or "unmentionables," he would discourse robustly to a man friend about his "barebummed ancestors." He chose his wife, whom he described to a friend as "not romantic but a matter-of-fact lady, a little thick, black-haired girl, sturdy and all that I want," because she was a suitable helpmeet, but fell in love with her afterward. On their first separation—he to set out on his trans-continental journey, she to return with the children to England—he wrote to her:

I never show all my feelings, but I can say truly my dearest, that I loved you when I married you, and the longer I lived with you, I loved you the better.[2]

And although it was probably his neglect of her that drove her to drink in desperation, after her death on a bank of the Zambezi he entered this in his journal:

The loss of my ever dear Mary lies like a heavy weight on my heart. In our intercourse in private there was more than what would be thought by some a decorous amount of merriment and play. I said to her a few days before her fatal illness; "We old bodies ought now to be more sober, and not play so much." "Oh, no," said she, "you must always be as playful as you have already been. I would not like you to be so grave as some folks I have seen." This led me to feel what I have always believed to be the true way, to let the head grow wise, but keep the heart always young and cheerful.[3]

The portraits of Livingstone suggest that he was a man who did not often smile. But the severity of his expression was not the reflection of Calvinist gloom and repression; it was the mark of suffering seen and experienced by a sensitive man over many years of solitary exploration, when abandoned to his own resources in the midst of savagery. He himself would describe the hardships of African travel—sleeping on the ground, living off a diet of manioc or millet meal, interminable marching under a tropical sun, frequent soakings from wading through swamps or streams, repeated attacks of malaria and dysentery, not to mention the constant risking of life or limb—as daunting only to those who were "fastidious over trifles." But in fact they undermined his health and in the end killed him.

We have very few descriptions of Livingstone physically; one of them is from an anonymous newspaper correspondent who attended a lecture given by the explorer in 1858. It is quoted by Seaver in his biography.

A foreign looking person, plainly and rather carelessly dressed, of middle height, bony frame, and Gaelic countenance, with short cropped hair and moustachios, and generally plain exterior, rises to address the meeting. He appears to be about 40 years of age. His face is deeply furrowed and pretty well tanned. Unanimated its most characteristic expression is that of severity; when excited a varied expression of earnest and benevolent feeling, and remarkable enjoyment of the ludicrous in circumstances and character, passes over it.[4]

Like other dedicated men Livingstone was indifferent to money, or rather he was only interested in it inasmuch as it could further his plans for helping mankind. His salary from the London Missionary Society was £100 a year, out of which he not only supported his wife and four children but also financed his journeys of discovery, being usually overdrawn for several years in advance. Unlike most other explorers of his time, who either possessed private means or were subsidized by Governments or institutions, Livingstone until he became famous had only his miserable stipend and conducted his earlier exploits "on a shoe string." While his rivals set out with large caravans of porters, carrying bundles of cloth, beads and other articles which were needed as barter to exchange for food or for buying permission from native chiefs to cross their territories, Livingstone was usually accompanied by either his family or one companion; and he made the first stage of his transcontinental journey, from Barotseland to Angola, without any of the usual preparations, with barely the means to pay his way, and escorted only by some Makololo tribesmen, lent him for the journey by their friendly chief, Sekeletu.

Even when practically penniless he was prepared to help his impoverished parents to emigrate; and when he did make some money from the sale of his book *Missionary Travels,* the first thing he did with it, after providing for his widowed mother and the education of his family, was to offer the sum of £500 to his brother-in-law, John Moffat, with a promise to pay him £150 a year for as long as he lived, on condition that Moffat went as a missionary to the Makololo or Matabele. The offer was accepted and Livingstone promptly carried out his side of the bargain. As the first white man to reach the elephant country of the Zambezi valley he could have made his fortune as a trader in ivory; alternatively he could have earned a good living as a doctor in the Cape Colony. But when his canny Scottish relatives wanted to know why he stuck to his ill-paid job he proudly put them in their place.

You may tell those who interrogate you that if I did not love my employment I could easily quit it. I am not in the position of a half-starved Scotch dominie or Independent minister. I could become a merchant tomorrow with a fair chance of making a fortune . . . the people would prefer trading with one who knows the language; and I have been confidentially recommended by some Natives who loved me to give up preaching and praying, for that only bothered them, and become a trader, for though I cheated them they would much prefer the cheating to the bothering. . . . If I liked filthy lucre better than the work of Christ I could make £500 every trip.[5]

Although reduced more than once to near destitution by the expenses incurred on his journeys, and only rescued from begging by his good friend Oswell, he never allowed poverty to deflect him from his purpose and could make a joke of being treated meanly. For the discovery of Lake Ngami—his earliest feat of exploration—which probably cost him a year's salary, the Royal Geographical Society awarded him the princely sum of twenty-five guineas, presented by the Queen. On which he wrote to his parents:

It is from the Queen. You must be very loyal, all of you. Next time she comes your way shout till you are hoarse (fear she forgot to put an o to the sum—250!) O you radicals, don't be thinking it came out of your pockets. Long live Victoria.[6]

And to a friend, when telling him the news, he added: "I shall try and render her twenty-five guineas' worth of loyalty."

Like all men of genius Livingstone was a complex character, and although no one had more true compassion for the weak and oppressed, he did not suffer fools gladly. During his time in South Africa he quarreled with most of his fellow missionaries, who accused him of neglecting his duties and sacrificing his family—on two of the journeys they made together his wife was taken ill and became partly paralyzed, also losing a baby—in order to satisfy his personal ambition. This worried him for a time, but after searching his conscience he concluded that he was in the right path.

"Some of the brethren," he wrote to Tidman, Secretary of the London Missionary Society, "do not hesitate to tell the natives that my object is to obtain the applause of men. This bothers me for I sometimes suspect my own motives. . . . On the other hand I am conscious that though there is much impurity in my motives, they are in the main for the glory of Him to whom I have dedicated my all."[7]

He was also often at loggerheads with the Directors of the L.M.S., who had to put up with long tirades teaching them their business, and it is a tribute to their wisdom that they recognized the originality of Livingstone and bore with his forthrightness patiently.

To those who enjoyed his confidence on the other hand he was a loyal and affectionate friend, and poured out his heart in a tireless correspondence. Chief among them was his father-in-law, Robert Moffat, the most distinguished of the South African missionaries, author of the first translation of the Bible into native dialect, friend of Mosilikatse, the renowned chief of the Matabele, and himself a pioneer of African travel. Another was William Cotton Oswell, a wealthy and generous sportsman who was with Livingstone when he first gazed on the waters of the Zambezi. For Livingstone, himself a "man of the people," Oswell was all that an English gentleman should be, and he had a great admiration for the type. To behave like a gentleman, he thought, was essential in dealing with the natives, and by this he meant that one should be patient, considerate and understanding, but also fearless, dignified and quietly firm in face of impudence, duplicity or threats. Unfortunately he was less happy, unless they were friends, in dealing with his own kind and this was to prove a serious handicap to him as leader of the Zambezi Expedition.

Although consistently modest about his own achievements, both in public and private, he knew their true worth and was annoyed if people belittled them or questioned his claim to prior discovery. This was something he never forgave the Portuguese, who had in fact traveled far into the interior of South Central Africa long before Livingstone—the earliest of them 400 years before—but never took the trouble, or lacked the means, to map their journeys with the accuracy which made him such an efficient geographer, and also published their accounts in books which were unread outside Portugal.

Much that we know about Livingstone today could not, of course, be known by his contemporaries, who had not read his private diaries or his correspondence, and could only judge him by his exploits, his published works and public appearances. Nevertheless they instinctively recognized the exceptional quality of the man. There was, however, another side to the medal, of which also they were unaware, and this will emerge in the following chapters.

To become a national hero a man must not only excel in something, he must also arrive at the right hour. The almost hysterical enthusiasm aroused by Sir Francis Chichester's voyage of circumnavigation was that of an England down in the dumps on whom it acted as a tonic; the excitement would not have been so frantic at a period of greater national confidence. Livingstone similarly profited by a particular, though different, national mood. At the time of his birth, in the year 1813, the interest first aroused in Africa at the end of the previous century by Wilberforce's campaign for the abolition of slavery was still running strongly, and there was no cause to which the British public, in one of its recurrent moods of moral fervor, was more passionately attached. The British, as the principal maritime nation, had made more money out of the slave trade than any other; they had, also, perhaps in consequence of this, the strongest sense of guilt and the keenest desire to make amends. Nor did they intend to be the only "good boys"; in any case unilateral action would have been ineffectual. Waterloo and unchallenged sea power had made Britain the strongest power in Europe, and she used the position to further not only her own interests but what she believed to be right. Having herself abolished slavery by an Act of Parliament in 1807, she proceeded to impose the same reform on other countries both by treaty and by force. Warships of the Royal Navy patrolled the West Coast of Africa, the principal source of supply to the Americas and West Indies, with orders to seize any ship engaged in the slave trade. As a result by the middle of the century the West Coast traffic had almost dried up.

This, however, was only a first step. In the interior the traffic continued unabated, and the shipment of slaves from the East Coast, mainly by Arab traders, was if anything on the increase. It was realized by the abolitionists that the only way to stop the trade was to make it unprofitable to the African chiefs who sold the slaves by offering them an alternative and better source of income. The chiefs sold slaves because these were the only goods accepted by the traders in exchange for the firearms, cloth and beads which the Africans coveted. If, however, the latter could be persuaded and taught to exploit their natural resources and were given the opportunity to sell the products of their soil, then the motive for engaging in the slave trade would disappear as it was replaced by "legitimate commerce," and the horrible traffic in human lives would die a natural death. Moreover, England too would benefit by the exchange of her manufactures for the primary products of Africa—ivory, cotton, sugar, indigo, palm oil. New markets would be opened and new sources of raw materials would be made available. Thus the seeds of nineteenth-century imperialism—or "philanthropy plus five per cent"—were sown by humanitarians who were shrewd enough to appeal both to the charity and the business instinct of their countrymen.

These ideas were given wide circulation in a book by T. F. Buxton entitled *The African Slave Trade and Its Remedy,* which was published in 1840. Buxton had succeeded Wilberforce as champion of the oppressed, and his plan was received with enthusiasm. A new society was formed, called the Society for the Extinction of the Slave Trade and for the Civilization of Africa, but better known as the African Civilization Society, and held its first meeting at Exeter Hall under the chairmanship of the Prince Consort. Its aims were ambitious.

The Society was to promote every practicable means of civilizing Africa which were not already, like missionary work, in the charge of competent bodies. The languages of West and Central Africa were to be studied and reduced to writing. Medical science was summoned to do battle with tropical disease for the benefit of the natives and of the white men who went out to help them. Engineering likewise was to play its part; irrigation and drainage were to be undertaken; a chain of roads was to be constructed. The natives were also to be taught the best methods of agriculture and the products most required in Britain and tools and seeds were to be provided for them. And finally "the manufacture of paper and the use of the printing press, if once established in Africa, will be amongst the most peaceful auxilliaries in the dispersion of ignorance and the destruction of barbarism."[8]

Here was the Brave New World of Victorian liberalism with a vengeance, a blueprint for the civilization of Africa inspired by altruism, optimism and a sublime confidence in the mutual benefits of free trade and science. Carried forward by a new wave of national idealism, the Society's scheme caught the imagination of the public and Lord Melbourne's Government promised to support it. The immediate result was the dispatch of the Niger Expedition, consisting of three iron steamships under the command of Captain Trotter, R.N., and carrying a cargo of technicians—that is, a botanist, a mineralogist, a geologist, a draftsman and a practical gardener—as well as two missionaries and eight doctors. The Expedition was to ascend the river Niger, make treaties with the chiefs along its banks, examine the economic capacities of the adjacent country and prepare the way for commercial enterprise.

The sequel was disastrous. Little was achieved and the mortality was appalling. Of 193 white men who had ascended the fatal river, forty-one died of fever, including Commander Bird Allen of the *Soudan*.

The costly failure of the Niger Expedition caused a revulsion of public opinion. The press denounced the philanthropists for sending men to their death, and the Government was blamed for exposing them to such dangers in what was known to be "the white man's grave." Bowing to the storm the African Civilization Society was dissolved, and two years later its founder, Buxton, died of a broken heart. Traders and missionaries continued to risk their lives in the malarial deathtraps of the West African coast, but all attempts to penetrate the interior were abandoned and fine plans for civilizing Africa were soon forgotten.

But there was one man who did not forget. Eighteen forty was the year in which Livingstone left England to embark on his career as a missionary in South Africa and earlier in the year he attended the inaugural meeting of the African Civilization Society at Exeter Hall. It made a lasting impression on him. Previously he had wanted to be sent to China, but this was prevented by the Opium War, and a chance meeting with another missionary, his future father-in-law, Robert Moffat, who was in England lecturing about his work in South Africa, made up his mind to apply to the London Missionary Society to be sent there. Henceforward, the whole of his life was devoted to putting into practice the ideas of Buxton as he had heard them expounded in the Prince Consort's speech. They were not his own ideas originally, but they were in the air when he was looking for a way to carry out the decision which he had taken at the age of twenty, after a spiritual revelation, and which he described in the opening chapter of *Missionary Travels.*

In the glow of love which Christianity inspires, I soon resolved to devote my life to the alleviation of human misery . . . and therefore set myself to obtain a medical education, in order to be qualified for that enterprise.

They were ideas which subsequently he was to make peculiarly his own and which inspired all his exploits, including the Zambezi Expedition, and he saw them as the means by which he could achieve the supreme aim of his life—*the alleviation of human misery.* Unless this is understood, nothing he did makes sense. To attain the goal he had set himself he was prepared to sacrifice comfort, financial security, his own family, his health and finally his life.

For although the greatest explorer of his age Livingstone was not primarily interested in discovery. As he wrote after the completion of his first great journey, "the end of the geographical feat is but the beginning of the missionary enterprise." In all his wanderings he had the same purpose: to open up a route to the interior and establish communications with the coast which would make possible the development of "legitimate commerce," the extinction of the slave trade, the spread of civilization and the establishment of missions to preach Christianity. And it was in this order—commerce, civilization, conversion—that he saw the redemptive purpose taking place.

When he first arrived in South Africa, in the spring of 1841, the farthest outpoint of civilization was at Kuruman, 600 miles from Cape Town by wagon, where Moffat had established a flourishing mission station. Between there and the Sahara, 3,000 miles away, the map was a blank, on which only the Portuguese settlements on the West and East coasts were marked. To Livingstone this was a challenge which he accepted within a few weeks of his arrival in Bechuanaland. "I shall proceed to the Northward," he wrote to a friend in Scotland, "and live excluded from all European Society."[9] During the next ten years he was to be constantly on the move, as he restlessly probed ever farther into the interior.

As he perceived himself in moments of illumination, Livingstone's motives in choosing a life of adventure and danger, rather than settling down in one spot like other missionaries, were mixed. To his employers, the Directors of the London Missionary Society, he justified his action on the grounds that there were too many missionaries concentrated in too small an area and that the need was to spread the Gospel much farther afield. He believed that the conversion of the heathen should largely be left to native preachers who understood their own people, and that the missionaries would be better employed expanding the area of operations and opening new stations among the remoter populations. He also thought that the "Hottentot" churches should be independent—i.e., self-supporting. Since this was a threat to the livelihood of the missionaries who ran them, they naturally resented it.

But there were also other reasons. In the first place he was much too ambitious to be content with the static life of a missionary—building his church, cultivating his garden and ministering to his little community. Then again he loved the open-air life, the long journeys by ox wagon, the campfire evenings, and he was much happier traveling alone or with a handful of native attendants than he was in the society of other white men. Furthermore—and perhaps this was the crux of the matter—he was, by normal criteria, a failure as a missionary. During his ten-year residence in Bechuanaland he made only one convert, the Bakwena chief, Sechele, who relapsed into the sin of adultery within six months of his baptism and was punished by Livingstone with excommunication. Considering that Sechele's crime was to have slept with one of his former wives, "whom, in consequence of her having a young child and no parents, he had found impossible to send away with the others," and that he freely confessed it, the penalty paid might seem somewhat excessive. After he had finally abandoned the Bakwena in 1851, Livingstone wrote to Tidman, Secretary of the L.M.S., that they had "wilfully rejected the gospel."[10] This was to imply that his failure was due not to any fault of his own, but to the hardness of the people's hearts. But it may also have been, as Schapera considers, that he was "too impatient and was not prepared to remain indefinitely and work steadily with any one group of people."[11]

The truth is—and it has an important bearing on the Zambezi Expedition—that after trying it for a decade he was thoroughly disillusioned, not only with his own efforts but with mission work in general, as it was then understood. "The whole of this country is in confusion," he wrote to his sister in 1851. "Not a single missionary station can tell of the least success. The English Government is at loggerheads with all the Native tribes. The Caffres are at war with us and they have been joined by the Hottentots."

The trouble was that in the eyes of the natives Christianity tended to be identified with aggressive colonialism. Livingstone put his finger on it when he wrote in the same letter:

> I don't think it is right that lands should lie waste which were intended by Providence for the sons of men, but justice should be done to all who have claims upon these lands. The Natives always become much worse somehow after contact with Europeans, and they cannot stand against the white men. It seems as if they must go to the wall, for they do not generally appreciate our instruction and friendship. Sechele has gone quite back again, and ten to one will be driven away by the Boers . . .[12]

The worst offenders against the justice which Livingstone was demanding were, of course, the Boers, who had conquered the Transvaal and were brutally suppressing all native opposition. They hated and feared Livingstone for his influence with Africans, and were in turn heartily disliked by him, even before they raided and plundered his house at Kolobeng. It was their presence to the east which prevented him expanding his mission in that direction and drove him to seek a new field in the north.

The other great obstacle to Christianity, then as now, was the native practice of polygamy. No white man was more loved and respected by Africans than Livingstone and they would do anything for him—except listen to his sermons. Sekeletu, chief of the Makololo, whose help made possible his transcontinental journey, and who on one occasion gave up his own blanket to protect him from a rainstorm, refused to be taught to read by Livingstone "lest it should change his heart and make him content with one wife."[13] And Sechele, the solitary convert and till then a venerated chief, was afterward regarded by his own people as "a renegade among them; the betrayer of all their ancestral institutions."[14]

It was not that Livingstone had lost his faith in the value of the Christian message. At the moment of greatest disillusionment he could still write:

> Our duty seems to be to preach the good tidings to all, whether they will hear or whether they will forbear. We can vindicate the character of God among the heathen. He *is* a God of love and justice, though they think differently of him.[15]

He realized, however, that some prior conditions were necessary to make Christian teaching, and the revolutionary changes it demanded in their way of life, acceptable to African tribesmen. Thus he found excuses for the Bakwena—and for himself—in the facts that they were "pinched by hunger and badgered by the Boers"; and to his brother Charles, also a clergyman, he wrote: "A certain measure of bodily comfort and security seems necessary before a people will attend to teaching. Without food, as our people are, there is little curiosity."[16] Moreover, he believed that the "wide diffusion of better principles" was more important than conversions, and that it was the moral influence of a missionary that counted: the example he gave of charity, honesty and industry, and the benefits he could bring to the people by teaching them the arts of civilization, such as agriculture, irrigation, hygiene and reading. It was by these means, together with his knowledge of medicine, and not by preaching, that he himself exercised so great an influence with Africans.

Thus it was not only ambition to blaze new trails and the spirit of adventure which drove him on, but the desire to find some place where he could live in peace with himself and his flock, away from the bickerings of his brethren, the carping criticism of settlers, the indifference of colonial officials and the corrupting influence of traders. Above all he had to escape from the Boers, whose rapacity and hostility had made his position impossible and placed him in danger of his life.

Immediately to the north of his last outpost at Kolobeng was the Kalahari Desert, 400 miles of waterless waste inhabited by a few Bushmen, which he had already crossed twice on his journeys to Lake Ngami. But beyond that, he knew, lay a well-watered and fertile country, the country of Sebituane,* chief of the Makololo and ruler of Barotseland (today part of Zambia), and this now became his goal. But while his main object was to found a new mission out of reach of his enemies, the idea was already forming in his mind of finding "a passage to the sea on either the Eastern or Western coasts."[17]

Setting out with his family and his friend Oswell in the spring of 1851, he arrived in June at the Chobe River, southern limit of Sebituane's domains, and was well received by the chief. A few days later, unfortunately, Sebituane died suddenly of pneumonia, and Livingstone had to wait several weeks before being allowed to proceed to the Zambezi, which he reached a little way above and without visiting the waterfalls which he was to discover five years later and name after Queen Victoria. Of more interest to him, however, than the sight of the great river, 500 yards broad even in the dry season and with "waves of considerable size," was the discovery of a flourishing slave trade between the Makololo and Portuguese half-castes coming from Angola,

* Father of Sekeletu, who succeeded him on his death.

who exchanged guns, baize and calico for boys of fourteen, at the rate of one ancient musket or nine yards of cloth for one boy. More sinister was the presence of some Arab dealers, who had come all the way from Zanzibar, off the East Coast, to purchase slaves. He now saw it as his primary duty to try to stop this traffic and divulged his plans for doing so in a letter to Tidman.

When we reached Sebituane's country, we were much pleased to see so many wearing European articles of clothing. And since our country's manufactures are so highly valued in the very middle of Africa it is a pity the market cannot be supplied by legitimate commerce. The Makololo purchased eagerly and though they promised to refrain from traffic in slaves the only effectual means of stopping the trade would be by supplying the market with English goods in exchange for the produce of the country. Since it is found profitable for those engaged in the coast trade to pass along picking up ivory, bees wax etc., would it not be much more advantageous to come up the Zambezi and receive those articles from the producers themselves? I feel assured if our merchants could establish a legitimate commerce on the Zambezi, they would soon drive the slave dealer from the market and be besides great gainers in the end.[18]

Here we see for the first time the genesis of the grand strategy that was to inspire the Zambezi Expedition. If there was a river 500 yards wide in the very center of Africa, 1,000 miles from the sea, there could surely be no difficulty in bringing goods up it, exchanging them for the local produce—but not slaves—and carrying it down to the sea.

As for Livingstone's own role in this scheme of things, although he had already "undergone much fatigue and manual labour" in raising three mission stations, all of which he had abandoned, he would cheerfully undergo much more to raise another "if it should prove a sanatorium for more unhealthy districts," since once it was found that "Christian missionaries and Christian merchants can remain throughout the year in the interior of the continent, in ten years the slave dealer will be driven out of the market."[19]

It was agreed that Oswell should explore the Zambezi downstream in the hope of finding a way to the coast, while Livingstone remained with the Makololo "in pursuit of my objects as a missionary." But impassable marshes and the prevalence of the tsetse fly obstructed Oswell, while Livingstone was soon anxious to return to his family, left behind on the Chobe River. In any case he had decided that the Barotseland swamps were too unhealthy a locality for his wife and children, and that he would need to be separated from them while he looked for a more salubrious area to settle in. He therefore reluctantly abandoned his project for the time being and wrote to the London Missionary Society proposing that he should send his young family back to England to be educated and spend the next two years by himself prospecting for a healthy mission site beyond the Barotse, and finding a passage, east or west, to the sea. This was agreed to by the Directors, and in April 1852 Livingstone said goodbye to his family in Cape Town before setting out once again for the north.

After being much delayed on the way—partly by fear of interception by the Boers, who had raided his home at Kolobeng in his absence, removed his belongings and destroyed his books and papers—he arrived back in Barotseland a year later. The deceased chief of the Makololo, Sebituane, had been succeeded by his son, Sekeletu, who was equally friendly. With his help Livingstone spent some time exploring the upper Zambezi, but he was no more successful than before in locating a healthy site for a mission station.

He then turned to his second objective: the finding of a way to the coast. This was a turning point in his career: the point at which, whatever he said to the contrary, the explorer and reformer took over from the missionary. Being almost exactly in the center of Africa and equidistant from the Atlantic and the Indian oceans, he could have gone either east or west, but decided to go west, to Luanda in Angola, because there were English people living there.

In opting for the west he may also have been influenced by a meeting with Silva Porto, the famous Portuguese trader and traveler, who was in Linyanti, Sekeletu's capital, at the same time as Livingstone and entertained his fellow white man to a sumptuous dinner, served with Portuguese wine. Silva Porto came from Bié in Angola and was returning with a chain gang of slaves, which he had recently purchased from the Makololo. Knowing that Livingstone wanted to visit the coast, he proposed that they should travel together.

Had Livingstone accepted the invitation he would have saved himself a great deal of trouble and discomfort, but he would have got no credit for a journey made more or less as the guest and under the protection of the Portuguese. However, his main reason for declining was dislike of being seen in such compromising company.

"The Portuguese are carried in hammocks slung on poles," he told Tidman. "Two slaves carry a man—it does not look well."[20] And to his family he wrote: "I was so disgusted with the sight of poor gangs of wretches in chains I have decided to travel alone."[21]

He therefore set out with a party of Makololo, the bare minimum of provisions and beads for bartering, half a dozen firearms and a magic lantern "to convey the elementary truths of the Bible."

The hardships and dangers of the six-month journey to Luanda, which left him a physical wreck but made him famous overnight, convinced Livingstone that the route to the west was impracticable and that he must try the one to the east. This meant retracing his footsteps for more than 1,000 miles, then following the Zambezi down to its mouth for nearly another 1,000 miles. Leaving Luanda in September 1854, he was back in Linyanti a year later and reached the coast at Quelimane in another eight months, to be exact, on May 20, 1856, having discovered the Victoria Falls on the way. Although following the river for most of the time, he had left it to strike inland for the last stage before arriving at the Portuguese outpost of Tete. As a result he missed seeing the Kebrabasa Rapids, which formed an impassable barrier to navigation above Tete, and thus was able to convince himself erroneously that, as he had hoped, the Zambezi was in truth "God's Highway" to the interior, through which legitimate commerce, civilization and Christianity would enter to rescue Africa from slavery and degradation. He had also discovered, on the Batoka Plateau north of the Zambezi, the healthy locality for a settlement that he had been seeking.

It will be gratifying for you to hear [he reported to Tidman from Tete] that I have been able to follow up without swerving my original plan of opening up a way to the sea on either the East or West Coast from a healthy locality in the Interior of the continent. And I can announce not only a shorter path for our use but if not egregiously mistaken a decidedly healthy locality. By this fine river flowing through a fine fertile country we have water conveyance to within 1° or 2° of the Makololo. The only impediments I know of being one or two rapids (not cataracts) and the people in some parts who are robbers.[22]

In other words he had proved his point—at least to his own satisfaction—and it only remained to hurry home and plan the next move.

2
The Expedition Prepares

WHAT THIS NEXT step must be Livingstone had decided in his mind long before the end of his journey. It was to "rest myself a month or two in England and come back to do some good in Africa before I die."[1] He had achieved the two objects he had in view when leaving Cape Town four years before: the discovery on the Batoka Plateau of a healthy site for a mission in the center of Africa and the discovery (as he thought) of a route, the Zambezi, connecting this locality with the sea. But his motives for establishing the mission and opening the route were now much stronger: he had seen for the first time with his own eyes the slave trade operating in all its grimness, the chain gangs of women and boys, the guards with their whips, and was more than ever convinced that his solution for ending it, by the introduction of "legitimate commerce," was the right one, and the sooner the better.

"It being absolutely necessary," he wrote to Tidman, "to get through this delta during either April, May, June, or July, on account of its well-known insalubrity, and also because I have a number of Sekeletu's people waiting for me at Tete, my stay in England must be extremely short."[2] "Sekeletu's people" were the 120 Makololo tribesmen who had accompanied Livingstone as porters and escorts on his journey down the Zambezi. He had left them at Tete in care of the friendly Portuguese commandant, Major Sicard, with a promise to return as soon as possible and conduct them back to their homeland, 600 miles away. Another reason for hurry, revealed only in a letter to a Portuguese friend at Quelimane written on the voyage home, was his desire not to be forestalled by the East African expedition of Burton and Speke which the Government had just approved.[3] For although, as he often explained, exploration for Livingstone was only a means to an end, he still liked to be the first man there.

Shortly before sailing for England, however, he received a letter from the London Missionary Society which threw a cold douche on all his future plans. "The Directors," it said, "while yielding to none in their appreciation of the objects upon which, for some years past, your energies have been concentrated, or in admiration of the zeal, intrepidity and success with which they have been carried out, are nevertheless restricted in their power of aiding plans connected only remotely with the Gospel"; and it concluded with the statement that even if the obstacles, such as fever, tsetse, etc., proved surmountable, "the financial circumstances of the Society are not such as to afford any ground of hope that it would be in a position within any definite period to undertake untried, remote and difficult fields of labour."[4] To make the douche a little colder, the letter was accompanied by a reminder that he owed the Society money.

Livingstone's reaction to this was the indignation of a man who has repeatedly risked his life and endured extreme hardship, besides spending his last penny, in performing what he believed to be his duty, only to be told that he was not really doing his job. It was to leave him with a bitter resentment against the Society which all their subsequent efforts to make amends never removed.

I had imagined in my simplicity [he wrote to a fellow missionary] that both my preaching, conversation and travel were as near connected with the spread of the Gospel as the Boers would allow them to be. The plan of opening up a path from either the East or West coast for the teeming population of the interior, was submitted to their judgement and secured their formal approbation. I have been seven times in peril of my life from savage men, while laboriously, and without swerving, pursuing that plan, and never doubted but that I was in the path of duty. Indeed so clearly did I perceive that I was performing good service to the cause of Christ I wrote my brother that I would perish rather than fail in the enterprise. I shall not boast of what I have done, but the wonderful mercies I have received will constrain me to follow out the work in spite of the veto of the Board. If it is according to the Will of God means will be provided from other quarters.[5]

It was not only the Directors of the London Missionary Society who were wondering what Livingstone's travels, and his plans for introducing legitimate commerce in the interior of Africa, had to do with mission work. His letters to his parents at about this time make it clear that they and some of their canny churchgoing neighbors had serious doubts of what he was up to, suspecting that he was neglecting the saving of souls, or alternatively the chances of making money, for the sake of winning fame as an explorer. He answered them by suggesting with gentle irony that the award of the Gold Medal of the R.G.S. and an honorary LL.D. from Glasgow University were better than if they "had heard he had been hanged for sheep stealing."[6]

The realization of how little the significance of his achievement was understood by the simple folks at home, who could only conceive of the spreading of the Gospel in strictly literal terms, may have hastened his decision to break with the L.M.S. In any case he had now outgrown the Society. He was no longer the eccentric missionary always at war with the authorities, but a man whose feats were universally acclaimed and who could dictate his own terms. While still at Quelimane awaiting a ship to take him home he already had a foretaste of the reception he was to meet with in England. "It may be agreeable to you to hear," he wrote to his parents, "that a ship of war was sent expressly to Quelimane with letters and orders to take me wherever I chose. . . . The great folks are well pleased with my efforts and laying down the positions of places referred to with some degree of astronomical accuracy."[7] Although the last person to have his head turned by it, Livingstone would not have been human if he had not enjoyed his success. But he saw in it above all a means of pursuing his purpose independently, of becoming his own master, free to follow his bent. He would still be a missionary, but in his own way:

not as a "dumpy sort of person with a bible under his arm," but one who was "serving Christ when shooting a buffalo for my men or taking an observation or writing to one of his children," even if there were some who "will consider it not sufficiently or even at all *missionary*."[8]

His reception in England, where he arrived in December 1856 (having narrowly escaped shipwreck on the way), was in fact more enthusiastic than anything he could have imagined. Learned and philanthropic societies, universities, chambers of commerce and the cities of London, Manchester, Glasgow and Edinburgh competed in showering honors upon him, culminating in his election as a Fellow of the Royal Society. To add the final leaf to his laurels he was summoned to a private interview with Queen Victoria, and made Her Majesty laugh by telling her the story of the African chief who, on being informed by Livingstone that *his* chief was very rich, asked him how many cows she possessed.

Requests to hear the explorer speak came from all over the country, but before embarking on a lecture tour he had to sit down and write his book. This had been suggested by John Murray, the enterprising publisher who wrote to Livingstone while he was still in Africa offering him two-thirds of the profits on every edition; and he had agreed to do it, although it meant delaying his return to Africa. Since he had received an assurance that his Makololo would be looked after by the Portuguese, this was now less urgent, while the book, besides earning some money for him, would also further his cause. He therefore wrote to his young friend José Nunes, nephew of the Governor of Quelimane and British Vice-Consul there, asking him to detain the men until June or even later.

> Tell my head cook Kanyata that he is to speak to all the others to have patience . . . I have been invited to a great many places to lecture, and might make much money by going, but always refuse, as I have made a promise to my men and will if possible fulfill it.[9]

By lifting large extracts from his journals and paying little heed to style or construction (for which the book was all the better), he was able to complete the 600-odd pages of *Missionary Travels and Researches in South Africa* in a bare six months; and its appearance only three months later, in November 1857, was almost an equal tour de force on the part of the publisher. The book was an instant success and, besides making a small fortune for the author, established with the general public the reputation he already enjoyed with the *cognoscenti* as an accomplished and intrepid explorer and great humanitarian, with a gift for keen observation and a vivid descriptive style. It also had immense influence in arousing interest in Africa. After its publication there was almost nothing that Livingstone might ask which could be refused by an admiring public or a Government anxious to show their appreciation of such a man. It was rather a case of *their* asking what *he* wanted.

It was in this atmosphere of euphoria for a national hero that the Zambezi Expedition was planned and mounted, and it explains much that subsequently went wrong. Had Livingstone not been elevated to so high a pinnacle he would not have felt his failure so keenly, or striven so desperately and for so long to retrieve it.

The idea for the Expedition originated with Sir Roderick Murchison, the bossy President of the Royal Geographical Society and a valued friend and patron of Livingstone's. Murchison was one of the speakers at a Mansion House meeting held on January 5, 1857, to consider the form of a testimonial to Livingstone from the City of London; and on the same night he wrote to the Earl of Clarendon, the Foreign Secretary, giving the substance of his speech, in which he had expressed the hope "that you might make good use of the man who knows more African languages than any other European, and who seemed to have such a happy way of carrying on an intercourse with the natives along our frontiers."[10] He also suggested that Livingstone should write to Clarendon.

Although determined to do so if necessary to carry out his plans "as a private Christian," Livingstone had not yet resigned from the London Missionary Society, which was still his only means of livelihood. The salary of £100 a year was "bare subsistence," but there was "in addition the certainty of education for our family and some provision for our widows," so that the prospect of leaving the Society without any alternative source of income was, as he told Murchison, "rather trying."[11] He may already have been thinking of applying to the Government for support when he wrote from Quelimane that "if it is according to the Will of God means will be provided from other quarters." At all events he now jumped at the opportunity put in his way by Murchison and on January 26, from the lodgings in Sloane Street where he was living with his family, wrote a long memorandum which was forwarded by Murchison to Clarendon.

After explaining that his differences with the L.M.S. were due to "nothing of a disagreeable nature," but to a divergence of view as to the best method of propagating the Gospel in Central Africa, and also that "an affection of the throat rendered much exertion in preaching impossible," the memorandum went on to say that his intention was to devote a portion of his life "to the special development of the commercial resources of the country drained by the Zambesi," and then proceeded to justify that intention.

In proposing this work to myself I must bear the imputation in the minds of some that I have forsaken missionary labour for the sake of 'filthy lucre' but am fully convinced that viewing the subject on a large scale I should be performing a work which would effect a much larger amount of good than I could do by settling down for the remaining portion of my life with any one of the small tribes which are dotted over the country. Legitimate commerce breaks up the isolation engendered by heathenism and the slave trade, and surely if we take advantage of the very striking peculiarity of the African character (i.e., their fondness for barter and agriculture) we shall eventually bring this people within the sphere of Christian sympathy and the scope of missionary operations.[12]

The Government, already primed by the publicity given to Livingstone's view in various speeches since his return, were not indifferent. In spite of the tragic debacle of 1841, there had been a second expedition to the Niger in 1854 and a third was about to be dispatched. Official approval had also been given to the Royal Geographical Society's sponsoring of the East African expedition of Richard Burton and J. H. Speke, which was to result in the discovery of Lakes Tanganyika and Victoria Nyanza. African exploration was the order of the day, and Livingstone's plan in addition to exploration included other objects equally desirable: the development of trade and the spread of Christianity. For the Liberal politicians of the first Palmerston Ministry it seemed eminently deserving of support.

Early in March Livingstone went with Murchison to the Foreign Office for an interview with Clarendon. The Foreign Secretary listened with sympathy to his visitor and invited him to submit a formal statement on his aims and requirements. This was done in a letter dated March 19, also from Sloane Street. The main objects, Livingstone wrote, were to use the Zambezi to introduce commerce into the interior and thus end the slave trade. Advantage would be taken of the natives' love of barter and they would be encouraged to grow cotton by a distribution of cotton seeds (provided by the Manchester cotton merchants). Further to assist them he proposed to take out with him "2 or 3 cotton gins of the simplest construction, 2 or 3 strong malleable iron ploughs, 2 presses for extraction of oil from groundnuts, and 2 small pairs of rollers for extracting juice from sugar cane." As for the Portuguese, who controlled the outlets on both sides of the continent, while in Angola they were firmly established, in East Africa "no vestige of their ancient authority remained" and they would "gladly co-operate in developing the resources of a fertile country from which they derive no benefit. Both countries, Britain and Portugal, could then go forward together."

Apart from a bare acknowledgment, no reply to this was made by Clarendon, and it is probable, as Seaver suggests, that the Foreign Secretary was still hesitating for fear of offending the Portuguese by encroaching on their rights.

Meanwhile Livingstone had not yet severed his connection with the L.M.S., and, as he told his friends, although he had made up his mind for the break, was too cautious to be quite "off" with them until he was quite "on" with the Government. On their side the Society were much more willing to consider his plans favorably now that he was a national hero; after "basking in the sunshine of his popularity" they were ready to reverse their decision not to venture into "untried, remote and difficult fields of labour" and to give him practically a free hand. Unfortunately—or perhaps fortunately—it was now too late. They had offended him deeply and he could not forget or forgive the injury.

One of his first engagements, after the public receptions, was to attend a special meeting convened by the Directors to discuss his plans, and particularly his proposal for establishing two new missions respectively to the Makololo and the Matabele. Livingstone had urged Sekeletu, the Makololo chief, to move the tribe from the unhealthy Barotseland swamps to higher ground north of the Zambezi, promising that if he did so missionaries would come and settle with him. Sekeletu had demurred on the grounds that by moving he would expose himself to attack by the Matabele, a powerful and warlike tribe inhabiting part of what is now Rhodesia, who lived by plundering their weaker neighbors. If, however, the Livingstones came to live with him, he would then feel safe, the reason being that Robert Moffat, Livingstone's father-in-law, had made a friend of Mosilikatse, the redoubtable chief of the Matabele, and the latter would never molest a tribe where a daughter of Moffat was residing.[13] Livingstone had agreed at the time, and in a letter to Tidman written at Linyanti, Sekeletu's capital, in October 1855, had said that while he could not speak for his children "without their own intelligent self-dedication," he and his wife would go to the Makololo "whoever remains behind."[14]

But that was fifteen months ago and in the meantime he had become famous. Much wider vistas had now opened for him, and he could not see himself, at any rate at the moment, settling down as a missionary in one spot for the rest of his life. Instead he proposed to send others in his place, reasoning that if missions could be established with both the Makololo and the Matabele, whether or not they included members of the Moffat family, they would be able through their influence to maintain peace between the two tribes and thus enable the Makololo to move to a healthier region. While agreeing in principle to establish the two missions, the Directors of the L.M.S. were not convinced that the scheme would work unless Livingstone took an active part in it. They therefore added a rider to the effect that "the success of the mission to the Makololo would be promoted by the residence of Doctor and Mrs. Livingstone among them." Whereupon Livingstone promptly made it clear that he had no such intention: he had agreed only to help in organizing the mission and would not commit himself to anything more, a position which it seems the

Directors accepted, without, however, fully appreciating its implications.[15]

This attitude, and the misunderstanding following from it, which was to have tragic consequences and to cast a blight over the Zambezi Expedition, comes out still more clearly in some correspondence now in the archives of the L.M.S. Shortly before sailing with the Expedition, Livingstone wrote to Tidman to inquire "when it is likely that the young missionaries who are expected to commence the Zambezi mission will take their departure from this country." Having received Tidman's reply he then wrote to him again as follows:

I am also very much gratified by finding from your obliging note of the 27th February that the young men are to leave in May, and I may repeat that the only thing that could have come under discussion had a meeting taken place [is] that should they come through Mosilikatse's country to the Zambesi to a point below the Victoria Falls where our steam launch will be of any service to them, my companions will readily lend their aid in crossing the river and otherwise . . .[16]

From this it can be deduced that Tidman had expressed some regret that amidst all his other preoccupations Livingstone had not found time to meet the new missionaries and give them the benefit of his advice and experience, all the more so since they were being sent out to a part of Africa of which he was the only person with any knowledge and as a result of a proposal first put forward and strongly advocated by himself. All that he was prepared to offer was a promise of assistance if they ever reached the Zambezi and his steam launch happened to be there at the time. Otherwise they could fend for themselves, as he had, which was not very encouraging either for the Society or for the completely inexperienced young men they had engaged at Livingstone's instigation. In any other man such deliberate offhandedness would be seen simply as "bloody-minded," and as we shall see its effects were to be disastrous.

It is true that by this time Livingstone had resigned from the Society and no longer felt under any obligation toward it. All the same he was largely responsible for what they were now doing and could not decently wash his hands of it. He seems, however, to have carried his resentment against the Directors into a deep distrust, which increased when he suspected that they were not in earnest about the two new missions. (There was, in fact, some delay, but it was probably due to the need to raise funds.) This was his main reason for offering to finance his brother-in-law, John Moffat, who was engaged to be married, to go out with his wife on their own as missionaries to the Makololo or the Matabele. In the letter containing the offer—£500 down, the gift of an ox wagon and £150 a year during Livingstone's life—he wrote:

Both Mary and I had the same thought; only as you had received education from the Society, we did not like to make the proposition. Now, however, as the conduct of the Directors is merely trifling, and it involves trifling with the affections of your wife, the most sacred thing in the world, I make it in all seriousness and beg you will accept the offer.[17]

If this was not an encouragement to young Moffat to make himself independent of the Society, it would be difficult to see what further inducement was needed. When, however, as much was hinted at by Tidman, Livingstone was immediately up in arms and, as always at the least criticism, was righteously indignant.

You take the opportunity of the note to state your belief that Mr. Moffat separated himself from the Society by my advice—this belief was no doubt founded on what you felt to be trustworthy evidence. You have been misled and as Mr. Moffat is quite of age to judge and act for himself the statements to me with respect to him might without any impropriety have been left unsaid. I believe that Mr. Moffat sympathises with me in my affectionate respect and esteem for the great body of the Directors throughout the country, but you will agree with me that I cannot be mixed up with differences between small portions of the Directors and the agents of the Society.[18]

This was the last bitter exchange across the rift which had been widening between Livingstone and the Society ever since his return to England and was never subsequently to be healed—it must be said as much by his own fault as theirs. Livingstone's ideas on the true nature of mission work were completely sound, but they were also completely revolutionary in his day, and his former employers can be forgiven for failing to grasp the connection of cotton gins, iron plows and the promotion of trade with the teaching of the Gospel. His resignation from the Society marked to all intents and purposes the end of his career as an orthodox missionary, although not the end of his religious vocation. We may therefore now leave Livingstone's dealings with the Society and return to his negotiations with the British Government.

No answer, as we have seen, having been received to his letter of March 19, Livingstone, again at the suggestion of Murchison, wrote another letter to Clarendon at the beginning of May. The crucial question was his future income, for although he cared nothing for money, he still had to provide for himself, his wife and their four surviving children, soon to be increased to five. As is clear from his covering letter to the Foreign Secretary, it was Murchison who had the idea of appointing the explorer as British Consul and suggested £500 a year as an appropriate salary. Livingstone himself left the decision to the Government.

Should your Lordship wish to aid me in my efforts, in adopting a line of policy which would give no offence to our allies the Portuguese, to support me in my enterprise, by appointing me an agent of H.M. for the promotion of commerce and civilization with a view to the extinction of the slave trade—I beg to solicit such salary as may be deemed suitable. I do not intend to accept any gratuity from my former employers, the London Missionary Society.[19]

In a further letter to Clarendon, dated May 17, Murchison ventilated some ideas which he must have discussed with Livingstone and which throw a somewhat startling light on the longer-term objects which they both had in view when pressing for the Zambezi Expedition. After referring to a suggestion of the Prince Consort that Livingstone should visit Lisbon in order to obtain the support of the King of Portugal, Murchison goes on to reveal what is really in his mind.

Now Livingstone was never treated with suspicion by the Portuguese, but on the contrary with all civility and hospitality. He is therefore precisely the person who, by his profound acquaintance with the natives and their languages and his possession of the confidence of the Portuguese, may be the means of introducing British commerce to lands where fertility is sufficient to supply us with all those elements of our own manufacturing power for which we are now dependent on foreigners. Either England and her ally Portugal may be made one for this great object, or the latter country might readily part with her Colony of Quilimane and Tete, etc., useless to her, *but which in our hands might be rendered a paradise of wealth.**

Of the "elements," i.e., raw materials, of which Murchison was thinking, cotton was the most important. The chief source of supply was the American South, where it was grown with slave labor. This hurt the consciences of the manufacturers, and if an alternative source could be found using free labor and under British control, the prospect would be very tempting. If Portugal was prepared to cooperate well and good; if not she should be persuaded to hand over her colony to people who could make better use of it. No wonder the Portuguese, who had given Livingstone a warm welcome when he first emerged in their midst out of the bush, were soon to become highly suspicious of him!

No further action was taken until nearly the end of that year (1857), partly perhaps because the Government were fully occupied with the Indian Mutiny and the war in China. In any case Livingstone was up to his eyes in work, first writing his book and then on a lecture tour which took him all over the kingdom. It was in the course of this journey that he developed before a larger public, including businessmen, scientists and philanthropists, his ideas for the civilization of Central Africa which he had set out in his various memoranda to the Foreign Office, and that support for them from influential people grew. For example, it was after addressing the British Association in Dublin that one of its members, General Sabine, suggested that he should take a steamboat to the Zambezi and asked if he saw any objection.

---

* Author's italics.

I replied that the only objection I knew of might be raised by the Portuguese. He said, we can let them find out, and they resolved on sending a deputation to the Government.[20]

Interest in his plan was particularly marked in Manchester, where members of the Chamber of Commerce questioned him closely on the prospects of finding raw materials, especially cotton, in Central Africa. Livingstone replied by painting an alluring picture of exotic fruits, new kinds of oil, dyes, fibers, sheep that were "hairy but not fleeced," and valuable metals.[21]

The enthusiasm aroused both by the man and by his proposals was such that no government could have resisted it. In any case Clarendon was already convinced and had little difficulty in convincing his colleagues. When exactly the decision was taken in the Cabinet to back Livingstone there is no record, but at the beginning of December and on the invitation of the Foreign Secretary he once again committed his views to paper.

Realizing by this time that the only hesitation of the Government would come from fear of upsetting the Portuguese, he was at special pains to give the impression that he was well disposed toward "these ancient allies" and only wished to work with them. Thus he suggested that "it would be in accordance with the sentiments which have actuated the enlightened Governments of England and Portugal were they to unite in an attempt to open up South Central Africa to the commerce of the world." The establishment of new trading stations on the higher portions of the Zambezi should be a "combined effort" and would not interfere with those already existing nearer the coast. To give full effect to the intentions of the two Governments, however, the "river ought to be declared a free pathway for all nations," and "an entirely new system of free trade . . . must be commenced." The memorandum concluded with the statement that, if the objects proposed were secured,

great benefits will be conferred on English commerce, on the Portuguese settlements and on the Africans. After the very great kindness I have experienced from both Portuguese and Africans I should be most unworthy of it if I could not add that in these propositions I contemplate and can procure nothing but prosperity for all parties concerned.[22]

Livingstone was possibly sincere in his desire to cooperate with the Portuguese; but from a man who had already declared that in East Africa "no vestige of their ancient authority remained," his offer to do so was the equivalent of a proposal that 300 years of Portuguese colonization should be ignored and an entirely new start be made with Britain and Portugal going "forward together," presumably as equal partners, if that was possible considering the disparity between them. Could he really believe that Portugal would accept this position, or was he simply pulling wool over somebody's eyes? One can never tell with Livingstone, and one wonders, such were his powers of self-deception, whether he knew himself.

As for the Africans, after starting as the chief beneficiaries, by the end of the memorandum they are relegated to third place, behind "English commerce" and "the Portuguese settlements." This was not because Livingstone put them last; in his own mind they were always first; but he knew that when it came to voting money Parliament must have solider reasons than pure philanthropy. It had to be "philanthropy plus five per cent," and of this doctrine Livingstone, if not the inventor—which title should more justly go to Buxton—was the first practical exponent. He may thus be considered the father of nineteenth-century imperialism, although it is doubtful that he would have recognized some of his progeny.

On December 11, 1857, just before Parliament adjourned for the Christmas vacation, the Chancellor of the Exchequer announced the Government's decision to the House of Commons.

There is an object [he said] which we think of importance to the public and which it would be improper to attempt to accomplish without some notice to the House. It is doubtless within the knowledge of the Members of this House that important discoveries were made lately in Africa by Dr. Livingstone (cheers) and places which had hitherto been undiscovered have been described in the account of his travels lately published . . . It is now desired to furnish him with the means requisite for a voyage of discovery upon the river Zambesi (cheers). It is stated that such an exploration might lead to important commercial consequences, and that it is a district well fitted, among other things, for the cultivation of cotton . . . the cost of the expedition is not likely to exceed £5000. . . . It appears clear to me that the amount will not be objected to, and that the Government may consider themselves authorised to take that amount (cheers).[23]

"We managed your affair very nicely," Lord Palmerston remarked when he met Livingstone the next day at a reception of Lady Palmerston's. "Had we waited till the usual time when Parliament should be asked, it would have been too late."[24] There was in fact very little time if the Expedition was to leave in March, the latest date for arriving at the Zambezi in the healthy season. But once the decision was taken the Government machinery went into action with a speed and efficiency which would be the envy of any civil servant today, plagued by the telephone, the automobile and the typewriter. Around Whitehall the official letters, with their beautiful legible handwriting, circulated between the Foreign Office, the Treasury and the Admiralty, with an occasional diversion to Downing Street. Addressed to and signed by under-secretaries, they invariably began with the same formula: "I am directed by his Lordship [the Foreign Secretary] to request that you will move their Lordships [of the Treasury or Admiralty] to" etc., etc.; and back came the answer in the same sonorous style, but pat, brief, precise and to the point.

While the responsibility for the Expedition rested primarily with the Foreign Secretary, the Treasury had to approve of all expenditure, while the practical arrangements were left to the Admiralty, as having the most experience in such matters. Here the key man was Captain (afterward Admiral) Washington, R.N., who occupied the important position of Hydrographer of the Navy. He was a great admirer of Livingstone's and a firm supporter of the Expedition, besides enjoying the confidence of successive Foreign Secretaries who depended largely on his advice when taking decisions about it.

When first consulted, in the middle of December 1857, Washington drew up three alternative schemes, the most ambitious of which, based on the experience of the several Niger expeditions, would have employed a great many people, including naval personnel, and cost a great deal of money. The second was more modest, but still too cumbersome for Livingstone; and it was finally the third and least pretentious, proposed by himself, that was adopted. He set out the details in a letter to Clarendon dated January 7, 1858. Livingstone, of course, was to be the leader and the other personnel were to consist of a naval officer, Commander Norman Bedingfield, R.N.; a geologist, Richard Thornton; a botanist *cum* medical officer, Dr. John Kirk; a general assistant *cum* "moral agent," Charles Livingstone; an artist *cum* storekeeper, Thomas Baines; and a ship's engineer, George Rae. As crew for the boat twelve African Kroomen were to be recruited from Sierra Leone.

Livingstone had met Bedingfield briefly in Luanda, Angola, and had entrusted him with dispatches which were afterward lost in the wreck of the mail packet *Forerunner*. Bedingfield was a survivor from the wreck, in which he had distinguished himself by saving other lives. He had also been commended for his zeal in the suppression of the slave trade—a point that particularly appealed to Livingstone. What the latter may not have known at the time—although he was told later—was that Bedingfield had been twice court-martialed, and on one occasion dismissed from his ship for "contempt and quarrelsome conduct towards his superior officer." This would have been sufficient reason for the Admiralty to veto his appointment to the Expedition, but when subsequently taxed with failing to do so Washington excused himself on the grounds that Bedingfield had been publicly recommended in a speech by Murchison and this made it difficult to turn him down. Although he quarreled with Livingstone and left the Expedition under a cloud, Bedingfield rose to the rank of Vice-Admiral and retired at his own request in 1877. He could therefore scarcely have been the scoundrel that Livingstone later made him out.

Richard Thornton, the geologist, was not yet twenty, and as events were to show, his chief defects were youth and inexperience. The most brilliant student of his year at the School of Mines, he had not yet started his career and was waiting for an appointment as geologist to a Government survey in Australia when engaged by Livingstone on the strength of a very warm recommendation by Murchison, principal of the School and the leading geologist of his day.

Dr. John Kirk, aged twenty-five, who was to succeed as second-in-command of the Expedition after the departure of Bedingfield, was by far the best of the bunch; and his subsequent career, as British political agent at Zanzibar, was only less distinguished than Livingstone's in relation to the suppression of the slave trade.

Charles Livingstone was the leader's younger brother and a clergyman. He had gone to the United States as a penniless emigrant, supported himself while studying theology, become ordained and been appointed pastor of a parish in Lakeville, situated by a curious coincidence, in Livingstone County, N.Y. Livingstone had helped him with money out of his salary of £100 a year, and also recommended him to the London Missionary Society, which, however, would not engage him without an interview. Happening to return to England in 1857, he volunteered for the Expedition and was taken on by Livingstone, chiefly, one assumes, because he was his brother. Although heartily disliked by the other members, he stuck it out as long as any and must have had something in him.

Thomas Baines, thirty-eight, artist and storekeeper to the Expedition, and the most ill-starred of its members, was a gifted and likable man. A native of King's Lynn, he wanted to follow the sea, but had been apprenticed by his parents as an ornamental painter, and at the age of twenty-one emigrated to South Africa, where he made his living by traveling around with a sketchbook and selling his paintings. Between 1848 and 1851 he had accompanied the British Army as official artist in the Kaffir War. After returning to England he joined an expedition to Northern Australia and distinguished himself by sailing a longboat over 900 miles of coastal waters and open sea. Livingstone heard of him through the Royal Geographical Society, of which Baines was elected a Fellow in 1857 in recognition of his services to geography.

The last member of the team to be chosen was George Rae, the engineer, a Scotsman from Livingstone's native town, Blantyre. He was a competent man, "skilled in the working of wood and iron," hard-working and loyal, but moody, prone to melancholia and with a propensity to tell stories about his colleagues.

Such was the team that Livingstone got together. Individually, with the possible exception of his brother Charles, they were all men of character and ability, well qualified to serve the purpose of the Expedition. But like any team, to get the best out of them they needed a leader who could handle men, and Livingstone was not this person. Incomparable at the head of his devoted band of African porters, he had never commanded white men and lacked the "touch" necessary to do so successfully. Driving himself to the limit, he had no patience with weaker souls and was unable to make allowances for youth or inexperience, or even ordinary human failings, such as illness or exhaustion. Being himself incapable of relaxation he could not see why anybody else should need it, and not only disapproved but resented anything savoring of frivolity. Because he was uncertain of his authority he always had to assert it, and regarded any slackness or backsliding as a personal injury to himself, which would rancor with him for weeks afterward. It is thus scarcely surprising that he quarreled with half the members of the Expedition and was eventually deserted by the remainder. It is a tribute to his personality that they put up with him for so long.

After detailing the personnel Livingstone proceeded to outline his plan. The Expedition was to pass rapidly through the unhealthy area of the lower Zambezi, deposit its heavy baggage at Tete, visit the leading native chiefs above Tete, and proceed to the Kebrabasa Rapids to discover whether the steam launch would be able to get up there when the river was high, thus avoiding the necessity of taking it to pieces for porterage. Assuming this obstacle to be surmounted or by-passed, the Expedition would continue its journey inland until it reached a suitable healthy site above the confluence of the Zambezi and Kafue rivers. Here an iron house—to be taken out in sections—was then to be erected to serve as a central depot. This would be of great importance "for depositing collections and for its moral influence on the public mind of the country." Further explorations would be undertaken toward the source of the Zambezi and up the rivers flowing into it from the north, "in order to ascertain whether the network of waters reported by natives exist or not." Some members of the Expedition would, however, remain at the central depot to conduct experiments in agriculture and give religious instruction to the natives. At the end of two years Livingstone would return with the launch to the Kebrabasa Rapids to await further instructions. Any member of the Expedition would then have the option of returning to England.[25]

"This would be a cheap plan," Clarendon noted in the margin, "and much better than having anything more to do than we can help with the Expedition." By this time the Foreign Secretary was engaged in negotiations with the Portuguese and, perhaps as a result, may have started to get cold feet.

On paper the plan was delightfully simple, and doubtless this is how Livingstone meant it to appear. The suitable site above the confluence of the Zambezi and Kafue was the Batoka Plateau, which he had already recommended to the London Missionary Society as a healthy district for a mission station. The ground was high, the tribes were friendly, and there was plenty of produce for the purpose of "legitimate commerce." The only problem was getting there, and for this everything depended on whether the launch could navigate the rapids. Livingstone implied that if not, no matter; she could be taken to pieces and carried overland. But he must have known—or should have known—that this was impossible. The launch was made in three sections for shipping to Africa on the deck of a larger steamer, and although no section was supposed to weigh more than two tons, there were also the engines and the boiler. How could these be carried overland, when there was no road, no wheeled transport, and the only porterage was by canoe or on the backs of Negroes? In other words, Livingstone's plan was a gamble on finding the Kebrabasa Rapids navigable for his launch, which any local resident, or indeed any competent official in Lisbon, could have told him it was not. For example, in a note dated November 1858, Viscount Sá da Bandeira, the Portuguese Minister of Marine and Colonies, informed Mr. Howard, the British Minister in Lisbon, that native canoes conveying goods up or down the Zambezi were always unloaded at the Kebrabasa gorge and their cargoes conveyed overland. If this was the case, how could it be expected that an eighty-foot steam paddle boat drawing much more water than any canoe could possibly pass the rapids?

Perhaps Livingstone had an inkling of the risk he was taking inasmuch as the whole Expedition was doomed to failure from the start if his gamble failed to come off. But he was forced to accept it. He had not originally proposed to ascend the Zambezi by steam launch; the idea had been suggested to him at the Dublin meeting of the British Association. Later he spoke to the Manchester Chamber of Commerce and "they too," as he wrote to Lady Murchison, "resolved to recommend the Government to send out a steamer for the same purpose. . . . All without my asking for it, or even hinting that it ought to be done."[26] He might well have thought that it ought *not* to be done—at least until the river had been surveyed. But after painting the Zambezi in glowing colors as "God's Highway," how could he turn round now and tell his audience that he did not really know whether it was navigable? He had aroused such enthusiasm that he was now its prisoner, and was carried along like a man by a cheering mob, not necessarily in the direction he wants to go.

In any case the question of the launch was taken out of his hands. The Government had approved and it was too late to raise objections if he had any. The order for the vessel was placed on behalf of the Admiralty by Washington, the naval hydrographer, and she was built for the modest sum of £1,200 at the Birkenhead yard of Macgregor Laird. Laird had been with one of the Niger expeditions and designed the launch in the light of his experience there: she was to be constructed of a new and untried type of steel plating, only one-sixteenth of an inch thick, to be seventy-five feet long and eight feet in beam, and to draw two feet of water. There were three watertight compartments which could be taken apart or bolted together, a boiler designed to burn wood, a twelve-horsepower steam engine turning paddle wheels, masts and rigging for two sails, one large saloon and several cabins, and awnings fore and aft. With a displacement of thirty tons she was capable of carrying thirty-six men and ten to twelve tons of freight, and of steaming at a maximum speed of eight knots. In honor of Livingstone's wife she was named the *Ma Robert.* Completed in barely five weeks, the launch underwent trials on the Mersey in the first week of February, in the presence of Bedingfield, who pronounced himself satisfied with her performance. When later she failed to fulfill expectations, the engineer, Rae, who was not present at the trial, alleged that steam had been raised on that occasion not with wood as specified, but with coal; and this accusation prompted Livingstone, ever quick when things went wrong to blame anybody but himself, to deliver a bitter attack on Laird for "dishonesty." In fact it would have been quite in order, to save time, to start the furnace with coal, this being normal procedure with wood-burning boilers. The trials, of course, were carried out when the vessel was light, whereas after being launched on the Zambezi she was invariably overloaded and there was frequently not enough water in the river to float her.

After stores and provisions, including gifts for native chiefs, had been purchased for the Expedition, it only remained for the Government to issue its instructions. These were prepared for the Foreign Office by Washington on the basis of a draft written by Livingstone. They were, in fact, his own instructions addressed to himself: dated February 20, 1858, they were a repetition, in different form, of the plans already submitted by him in various memoranda. To make sure, moreover, that he retained a completely free hand, a paragraph was inserted stating that "you are yourself so experienced a traveller in these regions that it is hardly necessary to do more than state the general objects of the Expedition and leave it to you to carry them out in the manner most conducive to these results." In a further and more significant clause, of which full use was to be made by Livingstone later, it was laid down that "should any individual refuse to comply with your reasonable directions, you are fully authorised to send him home at the first opportunity, and his salary will cease from the day you find it necessary to discharge him." The instructions, which were signed by Clarendon, concluded with the words, which only a Livingstone could have put in the mouth of the Foreign Secretary: "I heartily commit you and the cause in which you are pioneers to the safe keeping of the Almighty Dispenser of Events."[27]

When all the preparations were complete Washington drew up an account showing that the expenses incurred, including the salaries of members of the Expedition for one year, amounted almost exactly to his original estimate of £5,000, which was the sum approved by Parliament. The only extra was Livingstone's own salary, which in view of his appointment as British Consul was to be paid out of the consular fund. It was fixed at the rate of £500 a year—the same amount that was paid to other British Consuls in Mozambique—and was regarded by Livingstone as quite inadequate, all the more since as Consul he was "restricted from engaging in commercial pursuits." At the time, he was too busy to argue, but later he wrote to the Foreign Secretary protesting and requesting a revision. Lord Malmesbury, who had succeeded Clarendon, made vague promises to review it, but in the event nothing more was done.

Whatever else might be said about it, the organization and preparation of the Expedition, including the construction of a special vessel, in the short space of three months between the moment when the go-ahead was given and its departure from England, was an astonishing feat of Government administration which would be quite inconceivable today.

3

The Portuguese and the Zambezi

In any official of the Foreign Office Livingstone's references to the Portuguese were bound to arouse some apprehension. It was after all their colony he was proposing to make free with, and however sincere his professions of friendship for them, they had reasons to fear his intervention. To understand what these were it is necessary briefly to trace the history of the colony.

The Portuguese connection with Southeast Africa dated from the year 1498, when Vasco da Gama stopped at the island of Mozambique on his voyage of discovery to India. In the following century their armies, clad in mail armor and armed with matchlocks and harquebuses, ascended the Zambezi to Sena and Tete, and fought the first battles between black and white to demonstrate the superiority of gunfire over bows and arrows. Subsequently their traders and missionaries penetrated as far into the interior as Zumbo, on the present frontier with Zambia, and Masapa, near what is now Mount Darwin in Rhodesia. Early in the seventeenth century a treaty with the Monomotapa, the most powerful of the African rulers, placed him under the protection of the King of Portugal, to whom he agreed to pay homage. For a brief period the enterprise looked like it was paying off.

But the search for gold, which had been the principal lure, proved illusory; and after the loss of its eastern empire to the

Dutch, British and French, Portugal lacked the means effectively to occupy, still less develop, its East African colony. Attempts at colonization were defeated by the climate, the difficulty of reaching the healthier interior, and the insecurity of the country, while the inadequate military garrisons, composed largely of *degradados*—that is, people who were shipped to the colonies as a punishment—were frequently in danger of being overrun by warring tribesmen.

Along the valley of the Zambezi the better land was parceled out in large estates, or *prazos*, which the first Portuguese settlers, soldiers of fortune or traders, had acquired by conquest or treaty with the Monomotapa. The *prazeros*, as they were called, were absolute masters in their domains, and lived by levying tribute on the native inhabitants, which they accepted either in kind (usually ivory) or in the form of slaves. Many of them amassed great wealth and, with their private armies and hordes of attendants, lived like feudal barons and with as little respect for central authority. Since they intermarried with Africans their successors were half-castes who felt little loyalty to Portugal and soon relapsed into a state of barbarism.

To correct this tendency and inject fresh Portuguese blood into the country, the Government in Lisbon, toward the end of the seventeenth century, introduced the system of *prazos da caroa*, which were leased to deserving subjects at a low rent on condition that they passed on the death of the holder to the eldest daughter and that she married a white Portuguese. The rule, however, was seldom observed—few white women could stand the climate—and the *prazos* remained the preserve of mulattoes, who continued to defy the Governor, even when troops were sent to subdue them. Constantly at war with their neighbors or with the African tribes, their lands depopulated by the slave trade and producing no crops, the *prazeros* hung tenaciously to their privileges, exacted at the point of the gun, and although outlawed in 1832 did not finally disappear until nearly the end of the nineteenth century.

Thus when Livingstone passed through it on his journey down the Zambezi, the country appeared to him in the last stages of decay. The reception given him by the Portuguese, both in Angola and East Africa, overwhelmed him by its kindness, of which he repeatedly expressed his appreciation. There is no reason therefore to suppose he was prejudiced in his description of the colony. At Zumbo, its most westerly outpost, which had been abandoned fifty years previously, he found the houses, fortress and church in a state of dilapidation. At Tete, where he was hospitably entertained by the Portuguese commandant, Major Sicard, there was still a church and a fort in use; but the place was in ruins as a result of native wars, with indigo growing wild in the streets, and only a handful of traders.

> All the rich villas adjacent, where the merchants lived luxuriously, are burned. And Sena is no better. There they are bothered by the real Caffres, here named Landeens.[1]
>
> The Governor says frankly that the cause of the decay of this Colony is undoubtedly the slave-trade, which withdrew the attention of the colonist from agriculture; and every other branch of agriculture—cotton, indigo, wheat, coffee, even gold—was neglected for the gambling gains of the hateful trade. And the ill-will of the natives was engendered as well.[2]

Livingstone estimated that in the whole colony there were not more than a few hundred white men. There was so little revenue that most of the Portuguese officers had not been paid for several years and could exist only by trading. Besides ivory and a little gold dust, the only profitable trade was in slaves.

Portugal had undertaken by treaty in 1836 to suppress the slave traffic, and in 1847 she agreed that British men-of-war should be allowed to operate against it off the mouths of rivers where there was no Portuguese authority. In the course of 1856, laws were passed liberating certain categories of slaves and decreeing that the children of all female slaves should be free. Finally in 1858 it was decreed that slavery in the colonies would cease altogether at the end of twenty years.[3] But in spite of these measures the trade continued, and the British Government suspected that it did so with the connivance of the local Portuguese officials. As the external pressure for abolition increased, the slaves were replaced by "free emigrants," who were brought in the old way from the interior, sold by dealers for thirty or forty dollars each and shipped to the French island of Réunion. Although they were ostensibly volunteers and were paid a small wage, the method by which they had been obtained did not differ from enslavement and their so-called freedom was at most relative.

In 1855 the Portuguese Government had agreed with Britain, against French opposition, to consider the free labor emigration system, as it was euphemistically called, as equivalent to the slave trade, and had given orders prohibiting it, which were repeated the following year. Furthermore, when informed by the British that the orders were being ignored, they took prompt action: the Governor General in Mozambique was summarily dismissed and a successor, Colonel J. d'Almeida, was sent out for the express purpose of enforcing the prohibition and otherwise suppression of the slave trade. D'Almeida acted with such energy against the free labor emigration system that within three weeks of his arrival he deeply offended France by seizing a French ship, the *Charles et Georges,* loaded with Negroes for Réunion. This was enough to provoke an international crisis. The French, who maintained that the system was legal, demanded the immediate release of the vessel; and after negotiations had failed to find an amicable solution, in spite of British diplomacy, two French warships were sent to the Tagus and the French Minister in Lisbon threatened to break off relations.[4] Britain, having persuaded Portugal to act in the first place, could not escape some responsibility for the consequences; but though willing to bully Portugal she was not prepared to quarrel with France, and without her support the Portuguese had no option but to climb down. For several more years the system was allowed to continue, until in 1864 Napoleon III himself abolished it, thereby earning the grateful acknowledgment of Livingstone that "of all the benefits which the reign of Napoleon III has conferred on his kind, none does more credit to his wisdom and humanity than his having stopped this wretched system."[5]

The incident showed that there was no lack of good intention in Lisbon, or of men on the spot capable of carrying out that intention. But it was not exactly encouraging to Portugal to be obliged to pay with her own humiliation the price of British liberalism.

Against this background the Portuguese could scarcely be expected to react with enthusiasm to Livingstone's project. It might well be true, as Livingstone asserted, that their authority in East Africa extended barely beyond the perimeter of their beleaguered garrisons and that they had to bribe the adjacent tribes not to attack them; that they had failed to develop the colony and derived no benefit from it; and that the only thriving trade was in slaves. But they were not particularly keen that these facts should be published abroad; nor did they welcome advice as to how to run a colony which had been part of their possession for more than 300 years. Livingstone had already written to King Pedro from Africa making various suggestions for improvements in Angola, such as the cultivation of crops, provision of roads and canals, importation of white women and "formation of a middle class of free labourers";[6] and his further communications were awaited in Lisbon with an uneasiness which Coupland has described.

They were aware, though they could scarcely be expected to admit it, that Portuguese East Africa had scarcely proved a model of colonial enterprise. . . . The first irruption, therefore, of a wandering British missionary into this particular area must have caused some little disquiet on official circles; and when Livingstone returned to England and opened his campaign the disquiet must have deepened. He was not, it seemed, merely an other worldly evangelist intent on nothing but conversions. He was a colonial politician full of ideas about trade and settlement; and he was making a public scandal of the Slave Trade. Apparently too he had caught the attention of the British public; and once the British public got excited about a question of that kind, it might run amok. . . . An attempt might even be made, in the last resort, to deprive Portugal of the colonies she cherished so deeply if only as the last concrete symbol of her imperial past.[7]

Of these anxieties Livingstone must have been aware since he was at pains to calm them before he started off. In suggesting that the Portuguese would "gladly cooperate in developing the resources of a fertile country from which they derive no benefit," he was thinking of the healthy central region (now part of Zambia) which lay between Angola and Portuguese East Africa.

Since Portugal had never officially laid claim to this territory he apparently assumed she would have no objection to his going there, indeed that he would be doing her a good turn by opening it up to trade from some of which she would benefit.

But if that was his supposition it was somewhat naïve. Livingstone was well aware of the repeated attempts made by Portuguese travelers prior to himself to discover a route between their colonies on the East and West coasts: De Lacerda in 1798, the *pombeiros** Amaro José and João Baptista between 1802 and 1811, Monteiro and Gamitto in 1831. He must also have realized that, had they succeeded, the opening up of the route would have been followed by territorial claims, as were in fact put forward thirty years later when the famous "Rose-colored Map" was published in Lisbon showing a Portuguese "corridor" linking the two colonies. It was not difficult to see that his plans for the interior were calculated to frustrate any that the Portuguese might have, and in consequence that it was not unreasonable for them to be suspicious of him.

Livingstone, of course, would have denied that he had any such thought. His scheme, he would have said, was purely philanthropic, unsullied by any imperialist *arrière-pensée,* and this explanation has always been accepted by his admirers. There is, however, evidence that it was not the whole truth, and it is contained in a letter written to a friend shortly before his departure on the Zambezi Expedition. The letter was to Professor Sedgwick of Cambridge; it is now in the Rhodes-Livingstone Museum in Livingstone, Zambia.

That you may have a clear idea of my objects I may state that they have something more in them than meets the eye. They are not merely exploratory, for I go with the intention of benefiting both the African and my own countrymen.

I take a practical mining geologist to tell of the mineral resources of the country—an economic botanist to give a full report of the vegetable productions—an artist to give the scenery—a naval officer to tell of the capacity of the river communications—and a

---

* Half-caste traders.

moral agent to lay a Christian foundation for anything that may follow.

All this ostensible machinery has for its ostensible object the development of African trade and the promotion of civilization, but I hope it may result in an English colony in the healthy highlands of Central Africa. (I have told it only to the Duke of Argyll) . . .[8]

As pointed out by Seaver, who is the only one of Livingstone's biographers to quote it, the secret plan disclosed in strict confidence in this letter "was to prove nothing less than the seed-thought of future colonial expansion in Central Africa." The seed was to bear fruit in such future developments as the scramble for Africa, Rhodes's dream of an all-British Cape-to-Cairo railway, the conquest and occupation of Southern and Northern Rhodesia, the creation of the Central African Protectorate (afterward Nyasaland and now Malawi), the Jameson Raid, the Second Boer War, and the annexation of the Transvaal and Orange Free State. At the end of it all the whole of South and South Central Africa, including the large part of it claimed by Portugal in the "Rose-colored Map," was firmly in the hands of the British; and this they owed, more than to any other cause, to the pioneering work of Livingstone.

The letter also revealed—or so a foreigner might have thought—the true face of *perfide Albion,* disguising its acquisitive designs with sanctimonious hypocrisy, and using for its agent a subtle operator who masqueraded as a missionary and hid his real intentions behind a smoke screen of high-sounding phrases about "legitimate commerce," civilization and Christianity. Had it by unhappy chance fallen into the hands of the Portuguese their worst suspicions would have been turned to certainty.

In his defense Livingstone could have argued that the ends justified the means. He sincerely desired to rescue the Africans from slavery and "degradation" and believed that he was the only man who could do it. He also believed that the British were the people best fitted to undertake the civilizing task. Although he had no great opinion of traders generally, he thought that English merchants were "more honest and more humane" than most. He had seen the way the Boers treated natives; and although he admired the Portuguese for their freedom from racialism and kinder treatment of Africans, they had been either unwilling or unable to suppress the slave trade through their territories, and this for Livingstone was good enough reason for brushing them aside.

The fact remains that he deliberately deceived both them and his own Government. While inviting the cooperation of the Portuguese (without which the Expedition could not have started), soliciting their help (which was to prove very necessary), and holding out hopes of their benefiting from his initiative, he was all the time plotting something which he must have known they would never willingly sanction: that is to say, the establishment of a British colony on their back doorstep which would forever block the junction of their own two colonies. The concealment of this part of his plan from the British Government also is even more difficult to excuse. He was, after all, taking money from them himself, and persuading them to spend a lot more on the Expedition, and this they would never have done had they had an inkling of his real intentions.

Even as it was, the Foreign Office realized that there was a serious risk of international complications and that the Portuguese needed to be handled carefully. Livingstone's own idea, after friendly discussions with the Portuguese Ambassador, was to proceed to Lisbon himself and, armed with an introduction from the Prince Consort, arrange everything directly with King Pedro. But an outbreak of yellow fever in Portugal prevented his visit, and negotiations were then conducted through the normal diplomatic channels, by the British Minister in Lisbon, Mr. Howard, acting on instructions from the Foreign Secretary; the Portuguese Foreign Minister, the Marquis de Loulé; and the Portuguese Minister of Marine and Colonies, Viscount Sá da Bandeira.*

The overtures started well, with the Foreign Minister immediately offering to render all aid to the Expedition, and the appropriate instructions being sent to the Governor General of the Province of Mozambique (as Portuguese East Africa was officially named) and to the Governors of Quelimane and Tete. A *portaria*,

* For the whole of this correspondence see State Papers in Public Record Office, London, F.O. 63/842 and 63/843.

containing a copy of the orders, was also to be prepared for Livingstone to carry as a sort of passport and to present to the two latter officials.

Soon, however, the first cloud appeared. The Foreign Minister had suggested, by way of being helpful, the attachment to the Expedition of a Portuguese representative. The last thing, of course, that Livingstone wanted was to be spied on, especially in view of what he was keeping to himself; so instructions were sent to Mr. Howard to decline the offer: he could make the excuse that similar requests to accompany the Expedition by private individuals and societies in England had all been turned down on practical grounds, since its personnel was limited by transport facilities. On which King Pedro commented huffily that this was not the same as rejecting the application of a friendly foreign Government.

To give the leader of the Expedition an official status it was proposed to appoint him as Her Britannic Majesty's Consul in Quelimane, Sena and Tete, but the Portuguese would only give their exequatur for Quelimane, the other two places, as they explained, not yet being "open to foreign commerce." This attitude infuriated Livingstone when he was told of it, the free movement of goods on the Zambezi being an essential ingredient of his plan to introduce legitimate commerce to the interior. "In reference to the refusal of the Portuguese Government to recognize the right of free intercourse up the Zambezi," he wrote to the Foreign Office (February 8, 1858), "I beg to suggest it is very undesirable to admit the claim, as it involves the admission of their power over the independent tribes on its banks, which they neither hold nor pretend to possess." It would therefore be better, he suggested, that no town or area should be specified in his commission, and that he should be accredited to Sekeletu, chief of the Makololo, and to other independent tribes beyond the Portuguese possessions, thus making it "clear that native power is supreme on the Zambezi."

A rejection of the Portuguese claim to control commerce on the Zambezi, as recommended by Livingstone, would have been tantamount to challenging Portugal's sovereignty over a colony where her flag, however tattered, had flown for more than three centuries, and was obviously a step that Britain could not contemplate taking against a friendly nation, especially when it happened to be her oldest ally. Clarendon therefore contented himself with expressing "the disappointment of Her Majesty's Government on learning that the Portuguese Government should appear desirous to restrict commerce in regions about to be visited by Dr. Livingstone instead of taking this opportunity to encourage and extend it," and asking when this measure would be adopted. The Foreign Secretary also decided to maintain Livingstone's appointment as Consul at Quelimane, after being advised by Mr. Howard that H.M.G. were not entitled to insist on the exequatur for Sena and Tete, but adopted his proposal to accredit him to Sekeletu and other native rulers in the interior. The letter of accreditation, for which Livingstone wrote the draft, was addressed in the name of the Queen "To Our Esteemed Friend, Sekeletu, Chief of the Makololo, in South Central Africa." After thanking him for his previous assistance to "her servant" and roundly condemning the slave trade, the letter requested his further assistance in opening the Zambezi to the free commerce of all peoples and concluded with the observation that "this is, as all men know, God's pathway." "God's Highway" was the expression more often used by Livingstone, but would have been meaningless to African tribesmen, who knew of paths but not of roads. As Clarendon penciled in the margin of the draft: "Not in the approved F.O. style, but no objection if useful to L." Similar epistles were addressed to Shinte, chief of the Balonda; Cazembe, chief of the Batoka; and six other native rulers.

In his letter of protest against the closure of the Zambezi to foreign commerce, Livingstone had questioned the authority of the Portuguese over the tribes living along its banks. This prompted Clarendon to ask him to clarify his meaning "respecting the limits of the Portuguese territory, in order that we may place something on record about it with the Portuguese Government." Livingstone hastened to comply.

In answer to your inquiry respecting the limits of the Portuguese power in East Africa, I beg leave to say that . . . it resembles our own in China with the important difference that the Portuguese are so few and weak that they can scarcely hold the few fortresses they possess. They have no authority on the south bank of the Zambezi until we come to Sena. . . . The Portuguese inhabitants of Sena, about half-a-dozen in number, have several times paid tribute to the independent tribes adjacent. There is a hiatus again in their authority above Sena until we come to Tete, another village and fort. There is a stockade on the river below Tete which commands the river, and this is possessed by a native chieftain who has at different times waged war with the Portuguese. The north bank is under a chief who has also been at war with the Portuguese. Leaving, however, all the territory to which from previous knowledge or relationship they may feel disposed to claim the sovereignty of, if we ascend the Zambesi to 30° East Longitude, we enter an immense extent of territory of which the Government of Portugal never had any cognizance. . . . The Makololo people possess the chief power therein.[9]

Here again Livingstone, if not deliberately misleading the Government, was distorting the picture. It was a fact that Portuguese authority in the Zambezi valley at that moment was at a low ebb, but this was not the same as to suggest that it had never been exerted or could be in the future. Livingstone had been glad enough to accept the assistance of the Portuguese on his way down the river, and he would soon be accepting it again on his way up. It was showing little gratitude to go out of his way to disparage them. His object of course was to force the Government to "get tough" with Lisbon, and to achieve this he was quite prepared to blacken the colony and its administration.

The Portuguese Ministers did not need to be telepathic to guess what was happening in London, and by this time their fears were thoroughly aroused. Before Clarendon could put "something on record" about the limits of Portuguese territory—and there is no knowing what that "something" would have been—he was forestalled by the promulgation in Lisbon, on February 4, 1858, of a royal decree directing that "the name of Zambezia shall be given in all official documents to all the territories to which the Crown of Portugal has a right in the valley of the Zambezi from the mouths of that river to beyond the fortress of Zumbo, which is situated at the confluence of the said river with the Aruangua (Loangwa)." In the covering letter to a translation of the decree which he dispatched to the Foreign Secretary, the British Minister in Lisbon pointed out that it was intended to show the extent of the territory claimed by Portugal in the valley of the Zambezi, which territory was formerly known as the Rios de Sena.

While it removed any doubts as to Portugal's determination to assert its sovereignty over the colony, the decree was better, from Livingstone's point of view, than it might have been. By fixing the western limit of the territory claimed at Zumbo, whose ruins he had explored on his downward journey, it left free the country beyond, which he had marked out as his stamping ground. "I am glad," he informed the Foreign Office, "that the limits assigned to Zambezia coincide exactly with those I pointed out by a blue line on a map for the information of the Earl of Clarendon. In fixing on longitude 30E. I was guided by a wish to avoid every spot to which they could have the least pretension or claim. 30E. is beyond Zumbo."

Moreover, as if to soften the effect of the decree, the Minister of Marine and Colonies instructed the Governor General to allow "all merchandise of Dr. Livingstone to be carried up the Zambezi free of duty," and a copy of the *portaria* containing this order was enclosed by Mr. Howard in the same dispatch.

There remained the question which Clarendon had put when expressing "the disappointment of Her Majesty's Government on learning that the Portuguese Government should appear desirous to restrict commerce in regions about to be visited by Dr. Livingstone . . ." as to when this policy would change. The answer came in a dispatch from Mr. Howard, sent after Livingstone had already sailed for Africa, reporting an interview with Viscount Sá da Bandeira in which the Portuguese Minister had said that

his wish is to make arrangements for facilitating commerce on the Zambezi and that the idea which has struck him is that the best means of doing so might be to establish one Toll at the mouth of the river, when more ample information shall have enabled him to fix upon the locality, leaving the further course of the river free, organizing, however, at the same time a River Police by means of launches of a light draught of water, to prevent marauding on the part of the natives.

It was perhaps lucky that Livingstone was too far away to be asked to comment. When he did eventually hear of the Portuguese proposal to levy a customs duty at the mouth of the river, he wrote from Sierra Leone to protest on the grounds that "they have no customs house, no village, and they themselves pay tribute to the independent nations on the southern banks."

Three months later—that is, in June 1858—the Portuguese Government followed up their decision by the issue of a "*Portaria* Relating to Trade and Navigation in Zambezia." This made it clearer than ever that the chief, if not the only, effect of Livingstone's original offer of "co-operating" was to arouse them to the need to protect their own interests by putting their house in order. Thus steps were to be taken immediately to raise a military force for the subjection "of the Landeen and other tribes of caffres," and for the colonization of Zambezia with a "military colony near Tete." Security of communications by land and water was to be re-established to Zumbo, with a fortress there and if necessary at intermediate stations. There was to be control of the trade in arms and gunpowder. A customs house must be established on the Luabo, one of the mouths of the Zambezi, and boats would only be allowed to navigate the river "under the Portuguese flag and with a permit."

All this sounded fine but did not necessarily mean that anything would be done—at least for a long time. So many other *portarias* had remained dead letters that this one did not need to be taken too seriously. In one respect, however, it was of the greatest significance for Livingstone, since it killed stone-dead his plan for opening up the Zambezi to free trade. No English merchants would be interested in a region where they had to pay Portuguese customs duty and send their goods in Portuguese bottoms, nor would any other nation. And since the opening up of the river was the whole point of the Zambezi Expedition, the Expedition was doomed to failure even before its members landed in East Africa.

On receipt of the *portaria* the British Government again registered their "disappointment" that Sena and Tete were not to be opened to "foreign flags," to which the Portuguese Ministers replied that Portugal "was merely doing what England does in India and other colonies." The argument continued for some weeks, but Livingstone was no longer at hand to goad the Foreign Secretary and after some further desultory exchanges the subject was dropped.

This concluded the negotiations. On the whole, as Coupland points out, the Portuguese had come off best. They did not like Livingstone's scheme, which they feared would show them up, and they suspected (as we have seen rightly) that he had ulterior motives. But they could not refuse facilities to a man of his reputation and had therefore been forced to maneuver skillfully.

They had shown all the interest in the Expedition and all the sympathy with its objects and had offered almost all the official facilities that could reasonably be expected of them. But they had given nothing important away. They had been firm on the vital points. They had definitely strengthened and safeguarded their position on the Zambezi.[10]

It is easy with hindsight to see that this was inevitable and to blame Livingstone for failing to appreciate it. Had he done so he would probably never have set out, and by the time he got an inkling it was too late to turn back.

4

Voyage of the "Pearl"

March 1858–July 1858

If Livingstone's plan, depending as it did upon two conditions—the navigability of the Zambezi River and the agreement of the Portuguese—neither of which would be fulfilled, was ill-conceived and doomed from the start, no such criticism could be made of his detailed preparations, where he thought of everything and left nothing to chance. This meticulous care and foresight come out in the letters[1] he wrote to Kirk between the appointment of the latter as the Expedition's botanist and medical officer and its departure from England. They start with a warning that

I shall not be answerable for luxuries of any kind whatever. Expeditions of this kind cannot be successful unless all members are willing to 'rough it', and it will be well if we all thoroughly understand this before setting out. The salary is £350 per annum.

Among the duties of the botanist would be a study of plants and woods suitable for dyestuffs, and Kirk is enjoined to make himself familiar with this subject, if necessary by consulting a Mr. Napier of Glasgow. He is also authorized to spend £15, later increased to £50, on the purchase of medicines.

Allow me to suggest a good stock of Resin of Jalap. I found a pill composed of that with calomel and quinine an excellent remedy in fever. Also Fowler's Solution of Arsenic—a large quantity of soda as it is very useful in allaying obstinate vomiting—a decided increase in Epsom Salts for the natives. . . . It will be desirable to give Quinine wine to all the Europeans before entering and while in the Delta.

As a qualified doctor Livingstone took a professional interest in tropical diseases and he had discovered the value of quinine as a remedy for malaria during his early journeys in Bechuanaland. His insistence on its regular use, both as a preventive and a cure, probably saved the lives of the members of the Expedition. On the only previous British exploration of the Zambezi, that of Captain Owen in 1824, all of the three naval officers taking part had died of the fever; and on other African expeditions the mortality had never been less than thirty per cent and in one instance, that of Lander and Laird to the Niger in 1832, more than eighty per cent.[2] Livingstone was also one of the first travelers to notice that where there was malaria there were also mosquitoes, although he failed to draw the right conclusion and thought that the fever was caused by miasma from stagnant water.

From the other illness most common among Europeans, namely dysentery, Livingstone himself was a sufferer; he never found an effective remedy, and it was probably what killed him on his last journey, his condition being aggravated by chronic colitis, brought on by years of deprivation and living on an inadequate native diet. An alternative theory advanced by Gelfand is that the bleeding of which he complained just before his death came not from dysentery but from severe hemorrhoids. He was for years a martyr to this complaint, but refused to be operated on on the grounds that the bleeding relieved his headaches. However, the illness which was his constant companion in later years only attacked him occasionally during the Zambezi Expedition, when he was still a relatively young man and his constitution had not yet been undermined.

By the end of February 1858 all was ready and the members of the Expedition, seven in number, were instructed to proceed to Birkenhead, there to embark in the S.S. *Pearl.* This was a combined screw steamer and sailing ship bought by the Colonial Office for the Government of Ceylon, which had agreed to transport the Expedition and its equipment as far as Tete, 300 miles up the Zambezi River, for the modest sum of £300. On its deck were to be carried the sections of the steam launch *Ma Robert,* and also of the iron hut which was to be erected somewhere in Central Africa to serve as depot for the Expedition. The party was completed by Mrs. Livingstone and her three-year-old son, Oswell, named after her husband's friend and former traveling companion, William Cotton Oswell. We do not know why Livingstone took with him his wife and their youngest child on what was obviously a hazardous enterprise, but it may well have been that she refused to be left behind. They had already been separated once for nearly six years, while he was carving immortality in Africa and she was living in penury and misery in England, without friends, cut off from her own parents in South Africa and not on speaking terms with his. To such an existence even the malarial Zambezi might have appeared preferable. But the swelling of the Expedition, which was already on the large size either for safety or comfort, particularly by the addition of a woman and a small child, was not a happy augury for its success and was viewed with concern by Captain Washington, who in a letter to the Foreign Office of February 8 expressed the opinion that the party was much too large "to make a good exploring journey in Africa in addition to increased risk of loss of life."[3]

Owing to delay in the arrival of the *Pearl* from Greenock and to other causes, the departure from Liverpool was delayed till March 10. As the ship steamed down the Mersey the weather was fine and bright, but she was soon rolling heavily in a stiff breeze, and most of the party, including the naval officer, were seasick. Four days later they had sufficiently recovered to attend a Sunday-morning service conducted by Livingstone, and from then on, as Kirk noted in his diary, they were to have "morning reading and prayer daily."[4]

On the same day, Livingstone assembled the whole party and in the presence of Captain Duncan, master of the *Pearl,* read out the Foreign Office Instructions to the Expedition. "They seem sensible," Kirk wrote, "but the most sensible part is that we are left much to our own discretion. The sum of them is, live at peace with the natives, obtain all the information we can, and try to begin civilization among them by introducing arts and commerce as far as may seem proper."[5]

For the next two days Livingstone was busy writing out separate instructions[6] for every member of the Expedition. To each of them he began by repeating the main objects of the Expedition: "to extend the knowledge already attained of the geography and mineral and agricultural resources of Eastern and Central Africa, to improve our acquaintance with the inhabitants, and engage them to apply their energies to industrial pursuits, and to the cultivation of their lands with a view to the production of the raw material to be exported to England in return for British manufactures," all in the hope that "by encouraging the natives to occupy themselves in the development of the resources of their country, a considerable advance may be made towards the extinction of the slave trade, as the natives will not be long in discovering that the former will eventually become a more certain source of profit than the latter."

In another paragraph which was included in each set of instructions Livingstone set the tone of the enterprise.

Although these explorations . . . are very desirable, you will understand that Her Majesty's Government attach more importance to the moral influence which may be exerted on the minds of the natives by a well regulated and orderly household of Europeans setting an example of consistent moral conduct to all who may congregate round the settlement, treating the people with kindness and relieving their wants, teaching them to make experiments in agriculture, explaining to them the more simple arts, imparting to them religious instruction as far as they are capable of receiving it, and inculcating peace and good will to each other.

The instructions conclude with a strict injunction "to take the greatest care of your health," and in those to Kirk, who as its medical officer had responsibility for the health of the Expedition as a whole, some typical words of advice are added.

My own experience teaches the necessity of more than ordinary attention to the state of the Alimentary canal. Constipation is almost sure to bring on fever and it would be well if you kindly explain to the different members [of the Expedition] the necessity of timely remedial aid to overcome any tendency to it, especially if accompanied by drowsiness, want of appetite, dreaming, unpleasant mouth in the mornings. And if Quinine, combined with a mild aperient, be administered, this precautionary measure will often ward off an attack of this formidable disease.

In Livingstone's eyes constipation ranked almost with original sin as the root of all evil, and whether it was to his own family, his ailing sisters in Scotland, or members of his staff in Africa, he never lost an opportunity of urging the value of aperients. It is possible that excessive use of them by himself may have contributed to his death.

The instructions also laid down that in the event of anything happening to Livingstone, leadership of the Expedition would devolve on Commander Bedingfield, the second-in-command; after him on Kirk, and then on Charles Livingstone, the explorer's parson brother. Bedingfield's main duty was to take charge of the *Ma Robert* and her crew, and pilot the *Pearl* on her journey up the Zambezi and return to the sea. He was also to survey the river, take soundings of the channel, and make a report on its "capabilities for navigation" for transmission to the Foreign Office. In a significant passage which was to play a part in his subsequent quarrel with Bedingfield, Livingstone emphasized that

it is absolutely necessary that no risk or damage to the Colonial vessel should be incurred and the utmost precaution must be used in our course above Senna so as not to take her higher than where it will be safe for her to come down before a strong stream.

The ultimate destination of the *Pearl* was Ceylon and it had been impressed by the Government on both Livingstone and Bedingfield that she must not be delayed more than was necessary to take the Expedition as far up the Zambezi as was practicable, and that in no circumstances must any risk be taken of her stranding in falling water and being stuck there until the river filled again.

After a quick passage of just over a fortnight the *Pearl* reached Sierra Leone and anchored off Freetown on March 25. Here she coaled and watered and took on board the twelve native Kroomen who were to man the *Ma Robert*, while the members of the Expedition, four of whom had never seen Africa before, took a welcome opportunity to stretch their legs ashore. Freetown had been given its name as the place where slaves were dumped after being removed from captured slave ships by British cruisers.

When we compare the state of the people of Sierra Leone with that of the population of the Congo [Livingstone noted], we see the greatness of the change which has been effected. Posterity will look upon this establishment as a great fact.[7]

Nine days out from Freetown, during which the *Pearl*, with her light draught, rolled as badly as ever in the southeast trade wind, "making nearly all unfitted for mental work in consequence," Livingstone made the disconcerting discovery that his wife, who had been prostrated with seasickness ever since leaving England, was also pregnant. He therefore decided to leave her at Cape Town, where she could accompany her brother John to Kuruman, home of their parents, the Moffats, rejoining her husband after her confinement, "in 1860."

This is a great trial to me [he wrote in his journal], for had she come on with us she might have proved of essential service to the Expedition in cases of sickness and otherwise; but it may all turn out for the best.

To the other members of the Expedition it was a relief to know that it was not to be burdened with a woman, and a sick one at that. "I cannot but think that this is a lucky move," wrote Kirk, "although I regret extremely Mrs. L's indisposition. However, we may expect her to turn up after a year, perhaps with an additional member of society* and in company with her brother who will leave England this month for the Cape."[8]

The brother in question was the Reverend John Moffat, whom Livingstone had agreed to support on condition that he and his wife went as missionaries to the Matabele or Makololo. John's father, Robert Moffat, had recently returned from a visit to

---

* He was presumably referring to her unborn child.

Mosilikatse, the Matabele chief, which was intended to pave the way for the new mission, and on hearing that the *Pearl* was shortly due at Cape Town, he hurried down from Kuruman to meet his daughter and her husband. The meeting with his revered father-in-law, whom he had not seen for six years, was a happy surprise for Livingstone and took a weight off his mind, since it meant that his wife could travel back with her parents.

From Moffat, who had learned it at Mosilikatse's, Livingstone heard the news that his faithful Makololo were still waiting for him at Tete, where he had left them two years before on his descent of the Zambezi. "They will be most important aids," he wrote in his diary, "in conveying to the people on the Zambezi a correct idea of the views of H.M. Government in sending the Expedition."[9]

The encounter with Moffat also afforded an opportunity to discuss the two new missions, to the Matabele and Makololo respectively, which, as we have seen in a previous chapter, had been recruited at Livingstone's instigation. There is no record of what passed between the two men on this subject, but it is known that Moffat was strongly opposed to the project, especially the part of it concerned with the Makololo. It was notorious that their capital, Linyanti, was unfit for white people, and that the mission was only feasible if the tribe could be persuaded to move to healthier ground. But supposing they refused, the consequences could be disastrous, as Moffat pointed out in a letter to Tidman written after the departure of Livingstone from the Cape.

> Without there be a considerable degree of certainty of their removal to a more healthy situation, the inhabitants of Linyanti will not feel willing to leave their swamps and rivers, especially until they have been assured that they shall not be molested by the Matabele. This they will require to know from a source on which they can place the fullest reliance, i.e. from Livingstone or myself. That they will break up their town and remove some hundreds of miles immediately on the arrival of the missionaries without some assurance we can hardly expect. Now all this makes it rather a serious matter to recommend three missionaries and their wives to proceed at once to Linyanti. In summer this might prove fatal to some, if not all.[10]

In other words, in Moffat's opinion, not only the success but the safety of the mission to the Makololo depended on Livingstone's ascending the Zambezi and reaching Linyanti before its arrival, in order to prepare the tribe for its reception and give them the necessary assurances without which they would not be prepared to move to a healthier spot.

As that of the most senior, the most experienced and the most distinguished of the L.M.S. missionaries in South Africa, Moffat's warning, which was to prove only too prophetic, should have been heeded by the Directors. But by the time it reached them, the missionaries, who had arrived in South Africa soon after Livingstone, were already preparing to set out and it was almost too late to reverse the decision. In any case such was the prestige and character of Livingstone that the Directors would have needed to be brave men to go back on their undertaking to him. Perhaps they would have been more ready to do so had they realized that he meanwhile had more or less washed his hands of the whole affair and, with his attention fixed exclusively on his own Expedition, felt no particular responsibility for the mission to the Makololo, even though he was the man who had proposed and pressed for it.

Livingstone had not been liked at the Cape, where missionaries generally were unpopular and he in particular was considered too friendly to the "Kaffirs," as blacks were called. When fitting out there for his first journey he had met with nothing but obstruction from the authorities, who resented his attacks on the Government's conduct of the latest Kaffir War. But now that he was famous and the leader of an important Government expedition, the colony was eager to make amends; and when he landed from the *Pearl* he was treated as a great man, presented by the Governor, Sir George Grey, with a silver box containing 800 guineas raised by public subscription, and entertained at a public banquet. "The first two-thirds of it passed off very well," young Thornton wrote to his sister, "and then Mr. Moffat made a 40-minute speech, a deal of which was very good but far too long for an after-dinner speech, and consequently a lot of persons at the bottom of the table had time to get elevated a little, and became rather noisy, but they were kept pretty quiet."[11]

While the members of the Expedition were being wined and dined in Cape Town, the *Pearl* steamed round to Simonstown to take in stores and coal at the naval base. The Admiralty had given instructions to the Navy to afford every assistance to the Expedition, and in the absence of the Admiral, the senior naval officer, Captain Lyster, "entered with great cordiality into the task of supplying our wants."[12] H.M.S. *Hermes,* Captain Gordon, was detailed to accompany the *Pearl* to the Zambezi, and Lieutenant Skead, R.N., the Admiralty surveyor, was seconded to the Expedition to help in charting the delta. "The Cape people look with much favour on our object," Livingstone recorded, "and will vote money for the postal arrangements."[13] These were intended to provide a postal service between Cape Town and the Zambezi by means of donkeys, which were chosen as transport for their supposed immunity to the tsetse fly.

On May 1, 1858, the *Pearl* sailed from Simonstown on the last stage of her voyage. The passage was slow because of adverse currents and heavy seas, and was further delayed by the *Hermes,* whose captain liked to anchor at night. This led Livingstone, ever suspicious of other people's motives, to deduce that "Captain Gordon seems unwilling to perform the service imposed on him."[14] On their side the Navy were perhaps a little suspicious of Livingstone. Two years earlier a boat's crew of H.M.S. *Dart* and three officers had been drowned in an attempt to keep a rendezvous with him at Quelimane, and during the next five years risks would be repeatedly taken and more lives would be lost by the Navy on his account.

On May 13 the *Pearl* came in sight of land and on the following day stood in for the shore opposite the mouth of a river wrongly believed to be the West Luabo, a branch of the Zambezi. After a consultation with Captain Gordon, Captain Duncan decided to risk the bar, steered the *Pearl* safely across it and anchored inside. The Expedition had arrived.

Captain Duncan could be forgiven his mistake. There was no proper chart of the coast, and the mouths of the Zambezi, of which according to Livingstone there were four, had never been fully surveyed. It took nearly a fortnight to discover the error, while the *Ma Robert* explored creeks, followed by the *Pearl,* which frequently stuck on the mud and on one occasion was only got off after two hours. In a first reference to differences which were already arising between Commander Bedingfield, in charge of the launch, and Captain Duncan, on board the steamer, Livingstone noted that there was "a disposition shown to blame each other rather than assist in getting her out of the scrape. I ordered the *Ma Robert,* when she saw us in any difficulty, to come at once and help us."[15] Every channel tried ended in a swamp and finally a canoe appeared with "seven niggers, one of them a half-caste Portuguese," who informed them that the river they were in was the Luawe and did "not lead to the Zambezi at all, which we had now found out for ourselves."[16] They therefore returned to the mouth and anchored again.

Here they were met by the *Hermes,* which meanwhile had put in at Quelimane and was returning with the important intelligence, communicated to Livingstone by signal, that "natives have beaten off Portuguese at every station."

"It is well," Livingstone commented, "this took place before we entered the river, as the blame would have been laid to our account."[17] The next day, May 30, leaving the *Ma Robert* in harbor, Livingstone went out in the *Pearl* to where the *Hermes* was waiting beyond the bar. Her captain came on board and delivered letters from Quelimane which gave further news of the fighting. From this it appeared that a half-caste called Mariano, a slave dealer notorious for his cruelty, with a fortified stockade at the confluence of the Shire and Zambezi rivers, had been resisting the Portuguese for the last six months. Hoping to buy off the Governor, he had recently gone to Quelimane, but had been arrested and the rebellion was now being carried on by his brother, one Bonga. However, there was no question of the Portuguese being driven from their stations, as the *Hermes'* signal had implied; they were collecting their forces and preparing for a new offensive against the rebels. Among the letters was one from Livingstone's old friend and former host, Major Sicard, offering the use of his house at Tete for the Expedition.

That the Portuguese were in trouble was not unwelcome news to Livingstone; it confirmed what he had told the British Government about the decline of their authority, and in the event of things going badly for them opened up interesting prospects of a British takeover on the lines mooted by Murchison in the letter to Clarendon already cited.[18] His policy he now declared was to remain strictly neutral in the war, and when later he received a letter from the Portuguese commander at Mazaro, the place where the fighting was taking place, offering assistance and protection to the Expedition, he was inclined to reject it. "The Doctor," Kirk recorded in his diary, "rather turns up his nose at protection from the Portuguese as he seems to take the side of the rebels."[19]

But the immediate problem was to find an entrance to the Zambezi. One of the two eastern branches, known as the East Luabo, was found to be barred by a "double line of breakers right across the entrance," through which it was impossible to enter; and when Livingstone insisted on exploring it in the *Hermes*' cutter, thus endangering not only his own life and that of his companion, Lieutenant Skead, but also those of the boat's crew, it became necessary for the ship's captain to recall him by firing a gun. The incident was reported by Gordon in a dispatch dated July 19 to Rear Admiral the Honorable Sir F. W. Grey, K.C.B., naval commander at the Cape.

Dr. Livingstone made a further exploration of the bar of the Luabo, but only ran a useless risk of getting entangled in the breakers towards dark, and so far from the ship, that I was obliged to get under way and enforce the cutter's return on board.[20]

It is not necessary to read between the lines of this report to sense the tension building up between the Navy and the Expedition. Obstinate and ruthless in pursuit of his goal, Livingstone on occasion could be as reckless of other peoples' lives as of his own. It was also his boast that he never allowed himself to be influenced by advice but always followed his own judgment. This was fair enough as regards the territorial exploration of Africa, on which there was no greater living authority, but in matters nautical he had no qualification and had he been a less arrogant man he would have heeded the professionals. The naval officers for their part were responsible for the safety of their men and it was exasperating for them to see their greater experience overruled by one whom they regarded as an irresponsible landsman.

Gordon had already recommended another entrance, the Kongone, seven miles to the west, and on the following day this was tried and successfully negotiated by the *Pearl.* "Here there is an excellent bar," Livingstone recorded, "and we ran in and found a large harbour sheltered by a low sandy island."[21] While Livingstone and Skead explored the river in the cutter, the *Hermes* steamed round to the Luawe, took the *Ma Robert* in tow after providing her with "beer and eatables," and brought her to the new entrance. Here she crossed the bar in heavy breakers which threatened to smash her, but got safely into the harbor, much to the relief of Kirk, who had remained on board her for a week with Bedingfield, Baines and Rae.

The discovery of the Kongone ended a period of great anxiety and the assistance given by the Navy was at last appreciated at its worth.

"Gordon now became quite attentive and kind," Kirk noted, "so that we must excuse him from any personal ill-feeling to us as an expedition, but it seems he is a very restless impatient individual and that accounts in part for his former queer conduct."[22]

Having ascertained that the Kongone was indeed a branch of the Zambezi and joined the main stream about twenty miles inland, Livingstone decided to take the *Pearl* up it. Before leaving, however, he wrote to Gordon requesting the assistance of the Navy to carry the *Pearl* safely through the district disturbed by the rebellion.

It will be our duty to remain properly neutral and I have no doubt but that it will be in our power to be friendly with both parties, as soon as the natives are assured that we are English. Yet as some time may elapse before we get into communication with them, should you favour us with a boat's crew and enable the *Pearl* to avoid being placed in a helpless position, you will render an invaluable service to the Expedition.[23]

Gordon promptly offered the *Hermes*' pinnace and her boat's crew, and in addition volunteered his own services up the river. On both sides it seemed the previous misunderstandings were now forgiven and forgotten. "He has done everything required of him," wrote Livingstone, "in the most cordial and handsome manner and shewed the greatest interest in the success of the Expedition." New difficulties, however, were soon to arise.

On June 10 the whole Expedition left harbor and started the ascent of the Kongone, with the *Ma Robert* going ahead to show the way and the *Pearl* following. For the first twenty miles it was plain sailing, but they then entered the channel which led into the Zambezi and which in places was only thirty yards wide. All went well until just as she was turning to enter the main river the *Pearl* ran aground on a mudbank and remained firmly stuck. As the tide was ebbing there was no chance of getting her off that night, and when it rose again in the early morning she still would not come off. The day was spent putting out hawsers, taking an anchor ashore for hauling on with the windlass, and constructing a raft of spars and casks to be placed under the bows. With the aid of these devices she was finally floated on the afternoon tide and moved to deeper water where she anchored. Since the level of the river was falling every day, there was a risk of her stranding indefinitely, and had this happened, the naval officers, and especially Gordon, who was on board the *Pearl* at the time, would have been blamed. This helps to explain Kirk's comment that "Capt. Gordon is a very excitable man. He was in a dreadful fuss all the time we were stuck."[24] He had reason to be.

The incident also brought to a head the quarrel which had been simmering for some time past between Bedingfield and Duncan. As a fairly senior officer of the Royal Navy—he had the rank of commander—the former thought himself entitled to teach the merchant seaman his business, which the latter quite properly was not prepared to accept. Livingstone supported Duncan, both on the principle that its captain must be master in his own ship and because he liked him and admired his professional capacity, while having a poor opinion of Bedingfield.

The flare-up came after the *Pearl* had anchored in the main stream. Bedingfield then brought the *Ma Robert* alongside, climbed on board the steamer and in Livingstone's words

immediately commenced in an overbearing bullying way another of those altercations with which he has disturbed the harmony of the ship three times already. As he directed his observations to me I said, 'Captain Bedingfield I must have no more of these altercations and I wont have them.' He replied, 'Then I shall give it to you on paper.' 'Very well' replied I, 'you must do it in a civil way, even on paper.' In the evening I received the following letter, although Mr. Skead tried to dissuade him from sending it.[25]

The row with Bedingfield was the first crisis of the Expedition and also the first and most crucial test of Livingstone's leadership. For several weeks it occupied his mind to the exclusion of almost everything else, as is shown by the care with which he entered every detail of it in his journal; the laborious copying out of all the correspondence—each copy being duly attested as true by a witness; the pains he went to to obtain evidence favorable to himself; and the lengthy dispatches on the subject which he wrote to the Foreign Secretary. He was acutely aware that in quarreling with his second-in-command at such an early stage of the proceedings he could be exposing himself to criticism. Bedingfield was by far the most senior and most experienced of his companions, with a professional standing that none of the others possessed, and a salary, including his half pay, higher than Livingstone's. He also came from the "officer class," as did Kirk and Thornton, but not Baines, Rae or either of the Livingstones. Qualified to command a man-of-war, he was put in charge of a small vessel which would normally be entrusted to a petty officer. This was no grounds for complaint: he had volunteered for the service; but in compensation he should have been treated with rather more deference than the others and taken much more into Livingstone's confidence, which as second-in-command he was entitled to be. His real complaint was that he was never told of his leader's plans, and as he wrote in his final letter of resignation, "most of the misunderstandings would have been avoided and the Expedition benefited, had you treated me as your second-in-command and allowed me to know your plans and see your wishes carried out, at least as far as getting to our destination, which I think concerns me more than any other member of the Expedition."[26]

Livingstone, unfortunately, was incapable of the kind of communication needed to ensure the loyalty and enthusiasm of subordinates in a difficult enterprise, the sort of "thinking aloud" and uninhibited exchange of views which enables everyone to make some contribution, and which is all the more necessary when a group of people are living cheek by jowl in uncomfortable or dangerous conditions. Although he would expand to those he trusted, he was secretive by nature and was always on his guard with strangers or with people he suspected might not be in sympathy with his views. Moreover, never having exercised command he lacked the assurance and easy manner which comes partly from social confidence and partly from the practice of giving orders, and thought the way to assert authority was to remain aloof and brook no questioning.

All this having been said, there remains no doubt that Bedingfield was unfitted both by background and temperament for the post of second-in-command, and that his eventual departure was in the best interests of the Expedition. This was also the view of all the other members. For example, Kirk, who never took sides and had a very balanced judgment, when officially asked by Livingstone to state his opinion wrote: "I consider the acceptance of Captain Bedingfield's resignation as necessary, under the circumstances, to prevent further disorganization of the Expedition."

In his first letter of resignation, written immediately after the altercation on the deck of the *Pearl,* Bedingfield complained of the want of confidence shown in him by Livingstone, alleged that unnecessary delay had occurred and the *Pearl* had been endangered by not following the precautions he had advised, and requested to be allowed to return to England "as soon as it can be done without inconvenience to the Public Service." "You can hardly suppose, Sir," the letter continued, "that an officer of any standing can be spoken to Publicly in the way you thought it necessary to speak to me this evening without remonstrance." After expressing regret "should I in the warmth of my temper at seeing the public service trifled with have said anything you may have thought disrespectful," the letter concluded with the statement that "if the duty onboard the *Pearl* had been carried out as it ought to have been we should ere this have been at Senna."[27]

The scarcely veiled criticism of both himself and Captain Duncan was not calculated to appease Livingstone, and in his reply, dated "Screw Steamer *Pearl,* 12th June 1858," he rejected all Bedingfield's imputations, agreed to relieve him of his command and send him home in the *Hermes,* and concluded with the statement that

I am sorry to part with you thus, as our personal intercourse has uniformly been of the most amicable kind, but as you kick at the very first instance your overbearance has been curbed, and the success of the Expedition depends on the good tempered obedience of all its members, I feel compelled to that of which I sincerely lament the necessity.[28]

Having written the letter Livingstone decided that it would be "prudent to wait a few days before delivering it"; and on the next day he set off in the *Ma Robert,* with Bedingfield still in charge, and accompanied by Gordon, some seamen from the *Hermes,* and Thornton, to explore the river as far as Mazaro, where the rebels were ensconced, "before taking the *Pearl* into what might be hostile country." After a short time the river broadened from about one to two miles or more, but the channels, which zigzagged diagonally across the stream, became shallower and were seldom more than twelve feet deep. Having passed Maruro, where the house of Mr. Azevedo, a Portuguese trader, was found plundered and all the outhouses burned, they came in sight of Mazaro. Here some 200 natives, well armed with guns and bows and arrows, were waiting to receive the party as enemies, supposing them to be Portuguese; but on Livingstone calling out that they were English and pointing to the Union Jack flying from the stern of the *Ma Robert,* some of them gave a shout and came running toward the shore carrying bananas and chickens for sale. They were allowed on board and treated to rum by Bedingfield. The result was as might have been expected.

One of them got his mouth to the can in which the Liquor was, and could scarcely be separated until he had taken enough to make him quite drunk. I resolved never to allow anything of the kind again. The English shall not appear by this Expedition to be a set of drunkards making other people drunk.[29]

Others remained suspicious and would "neither lay aside their arms nor sit down to talk." After leaving a message for the rebel leader announcing that he had arrived and would be coming up the river, Livingstone went to inspect a creek called the Mutu just below Mazaro. This was shown in a Portuguese map as a main branch of the Zambezi, by which its waters reached the sea at Quelimane. To his great satisfaction Livingstone found the bed of the creek dry and three feet above the level of the main river, thus proving the Portuguese to be either liars or ignorant. In fact the Mutu *was* used as the principal channel of communication between the upper Zambezi and the sea, but only during the months when the river was high. However, by the time Livingstone came to write the book[30] in which he recorded this incident any stick was good enough to beat the Portuguese, whom he was then blaming for the failure of the Expedition.

This book, which had a considerable success though not as great as its predecessor, is more interesting today for what it conceals than what it reveals, and as a masterly exercise in "covering up." It makes the whole desperate enterprise, which only a man of iron determination could have carried through, sound like a nice walk through pretty country full of interesting flora and fauna. It also enables instructive comparisons to be made between what its author wrote for public consumption after his return from the Expedition with what he entered at the time in his private journal. For example, the rebels who would "neither lay aside their arms nor sit down to talk" had become, six years later, friendly people who "warmly approved our objects, and knew well the distinctive character of our nation on the slave question."[31] Did they really?

On the return journey Gordon spoke to Livingstone about Bedingfield's letter of resignation, expressed his regret over the incident, and offered to act as mediator in getting the letter withdrawn. After considering this carefully Livingstone decided that "it would not be doing as I would wish to be done by if I did not give him the option," and that evening, at Bedingfield's request, returned the letter.

On arriving back at the *Pearl* a council of the whole party was held to plan the next move, and the momentous decision was then taken to send the steamer away and leave the Expedition to its own devices.

Seeing that the river was falling at the rate of nearly ten inches a day, that time would be required for the survey [of the channel] which would be necessary, the *Pearl* drawing 9 feet 7 in., very long, 160 ft., does not back readily nor obey her helm except at full speed, and moreover her provisions were expended and we were under stringent orders to see that she ran no risk of detention in the river, we all came to the conclusion that it was best to land the iron house and goods on an island and allow the *Pearl* to go on her way to Ceylon.[32]

Neither the laconic entry in Livingstone's journal, nor the brief reference to it in his book, give any idea of the gravity of this, the first setback to the Expedition, which the decision represented. The plan proposed by Livingstone and accepted by the Government assumed that the *Pearl* would carry its passengers and their many tons of goods rapidly through the unhealthy delta and up the river to Tete, 300 miles from the coast, where the *Ma Robert* would be launched and proceed without delay to explore the Kebrabasa Rapids. But all this had now gone by the board. The Expedition was to be dumped among the swamps a bare fifty miles from the sea and left to shift for itself.

It was typical of Livingstone that to himself and again in his dispatch[33] to Lord Malmesbury he blamed the *Pearl* for the setback. If she had not drawn so much water, he implied, or been so long or so difficult to maneuver, all would have been well. But no ocean-going vessel of the size required to transport the Expedition, its launch, its iron hut and all its baggage could have safely navigated the Zambezi, at any rate at that time of year, any farther than did the *Pearl,* let alone as far as Tete; and the truth was that Livingstone had greatly overestimated the capacity of the river for carrying traffic. He virtually admitted this in the same dispatch when he asked the Government to send him another boat—"a small paddle-wheel vessel of from four to five feet draught to survey this river as far as the rapid of Kebrabasa above Tete." The trouble was that when the season was healthy the river was too low, and when it had enough water the climate became deadly, so that there was no moment when it was both practicable and safe for any but the shallowest-draught boats to navigate; and this Livingstone could have discovered in advance had he consulted the Portuguese and taken them into his confidence. But to do so would have gone against the grain. He had made patronizing offers to work with them in developing the Zambezi; but this was done chiefly to reassure the British Government, and his real sentiments were probably reflected more truly in Murchison's suggestion that Portugal might cede her colony to Britain. He was now paying the price of his duplicity and had only himself to blame, but this of course was the last thing he would ever do.

Having selected an island in the middle of the river as being safe from surprise attack, all hands were put to disembarking the iron hut, erecting it on the island, and landing the baggage. With the help of the engineer and carpenter of the *Hermes* and some seamen, the hut was put together, not quite as intended—"an ugly unworkmanlike job but did after all not so badly as it gave us two long projecting eaves"—and the goods stored pending removal to Tete. "The Doctor is for anything done in an afternoon," comments Kirk, "so we have orders to get a cargo in and be off this afternoon."[34]

By the last week in June all was ready and the *Pearl* was preparing to take her departure when a fresh quarrel broke out between her master, Captain Duncan, and his old enemy Bedingfield. Livingstone had promised Duncan that when the *Pearl* descended the river the *Ma Robert* would be available to pilot her. Bedingfield objected to this on the grounds that it would cause unnecessary wear and tear to the launch, which had been in constant service for more than a month and was already showing signs of strain—the result of heavy towing for which she was not designed—and that unless time was to be given to paint her rivet heads, which were beginning to rust, she would "hardly last to tow the luggage of the Expedition up to Tete." He also pointed out that there was no need for the *Ma Robert* to act as pilot, since there was a boat from the *Hermes* which could see the *Pearl* over the bar and both Gordon and Skead, the Admiralty surveyor who had been charting the channel, would be on board.

These were reasonable arguments and had they been put to Livingstone quietly there would have been no reason for Duncan to object. Instead Bedingfield announced publicly that the *Ma Robert* was not going down the river again, to which Duncan, with Livingstone's promise in mind, replied, "I can assure you that whether you like it or not the launch shall come down." Bedingfield then saw Livingstone, who told him he had not the right to dictate and that his duty was "to do as you were bidden." A little later, however, he changed his mind and asked Duncan to release him from his promise, to which the latter immediately agreed.

There the matter might have ended but for a letter written by Bedingfield, before he knew that Livingstone had given in, setting out the case for not sending the *Ma Robert* and concluding as follows:

I regret exceedingly that I should be obliged thus officially to remonstrate, but the discourteous way in which you received my advice today would make me more anxious that my conduct may be understood and I beg most respectfully but pointedly to deny the imputations you were pleased to make on another occasion that private resentment against the Master of the *Pearl* influenced my public conduct.[35]

Livingstone was in half a mind to ignore this altogether, but after hesitating for several days he decided to reply. With the *Pearl* soon departing he evidently hoped that the incident could be closed and a new chapter could begin, and he ended his letter with what was no doubt intended as friendly advice.

Now that Captain Duncan is gone I hope that you will be disposed to give that consideration to the rest of your companions which you will wish to be awarded to yourself. A pretty extensive acquaintance with African Expeditions enables me to offer a hint which, if you take it in the same frank and friendly spirit in which it is offered, you will on some future day thank me and smile at the puerilities which now afflict you. With the change of climate there is often a peculiar condition of the bowels which makes the individual imagine all manner of things in others. Now I earnestly and most respectfully recommend you to try a little aperient medicine occasionally and you will find it much more soothing than writing official letters. I shall strive to treat you with the same respect as heretofore, but at the same time other thoughts and duties are more in our line than long rigmarole letters to show our friends at home.[36]

Livingstone wanted to be conciliatory, but he could not resist having a last dig at Bedingfield, and the mixture of implied criticism and fatherly counsel was calcuated to infuriate rather than appease, while the advice to "try a little aperient medicine" had the same effect on the recipient as Mr. Neville Chamberlain's historic admonition to Anthony Eden, his Foreign Secretary, to "go home and take an aspirin." "The latter part of your letter, I need scarcely remark," Bedingfield wrote in reply, "had been better addressed to a child"; and he went on to express the hope "that for the great cause we both have at heart, that of spreading civilization and the gospel far into the interior, we may pull together until an opportunity offers of your getting a better man, or one that you like better, when I will gladly return to England."[37]

It was not a letter of resignation, merely one expressing willingness to resign if a successor could be found, and Livingstone did not immediately act upon it. Perhaps he still hoped to patch up the quarrel. But things had gone too far; after biding his time for a month he wrote to inform Bedingfield that his resignation was accepted. Arrangements would be made for his return to England and meanwhile he was "required to deliver into the care of Dr. Kirk all public property, including the chart of the river for further use and all the scientific observations you may have made." Bedingfield objected strongly to what amounted to dismissal, denied having ever disobeyed an order, but finally resigned himself to depart for Quelimane, where he was picked up by a warship and taken to the Cape for passage to England. There he wrote a number of letters to the Foreign Secretary protesting his innocence and the injustice of his treatment. These were referred to Washington, who after considering all the facts pronounced that Bedingfield had "failed to clear himself," a verdict that was accepted by the Foreign Secretary. Washington also made the point that, even if there was something to be said for Bedingfield, it was essential to the safety of the Expedition that the leader's authority, including his power to dismiss, should be upheld.

In the ten-page dispatch[38] (of July 31, 1858) which he wrote to Malmesbury justifying his action, Livingstone left nothing unsaid that could damage his opponent: in addition to insubordination and quarrelsome behavior, Bedingfield was accused of hanging back in the face of danger, of inciting the Kroomen to refuse to work on Sunday, of thwarting "the progress of the Expedition while ostensibly anxious to promote it," of failing to keep the launch clean, and of "dancing and singing" in front of the Kroomen when his resignation was accepted.

All this may have been true, although if so it is curious that in his immediately previous dispatch, that of June 22, written only a few weeks earlier, Livingstone had several times gone out of his way to praise the work of his second-in-command. One can only conclude that however serious were the naval officer's failings, the faults were not only on his side, and that Livingstone's treatment of him was ham-handed and tactless.

The opinion of the Navy on the affair was probably expressed by Gordon in the final paragraph of the letter he wrote eighteen months later in support of Bedingfield's attempt to have the case reopened.

In conclusion I must observe that considering the numbers of officers and seamen who have been drowned whilst forwarding Dr. Livingstone's undertakings, and also the great assistance he has received from the naval service and the risks to which H.M. vessels have been exposed to on his account—the feelings of gratitude which every right thinking person possesses should have prevented his extraordinary and unjustifiable conduct towards you.

It was not a very logical argument, but the sentiment was perhaps understandable. Dedicated as he himself was to a Higher Purpose, Livingstone considered that, while those who opposed him could only be inspired by evil motives, those who helped him were merely doing their duty and that he was under no obligation toward them. There is none so self-centered as the man who sees himself as the chosen instrument of God.

5

The White Elephant

July 1858–November 1858

WHEN, ON JUNE 26, 1858, after a farewell dinner given by Captain Duncan, the *Pearl* weighed anchor and headed down the river, carrying the naval officers with her, those left behind may have felt a momentary qualm. They were losing their last link with civilization. Henceforth they would be on their own, their home a mud flat covered with mangroves, their only company alligators and hippopotami, the unhealthy season setting in, and still 250 miles from their destination, with a mountain of baggage and only a small paddle boat and the *Hermes*' pinnace, lent to the Expedition by Captain Gordon, for transport.

To make matters worse there was the demoralizing influence of Livingstone's quarrel with Bedingfield. Although the second-in-command was no longer officially a member of the Expedition, he must remain with it until means were found of sending him to Quelimane and thence back to England. Meanwhile the altercations which its leader found so distasteful continued, and crowded as they were on the little refuge, which they had named Expedition Island, there was no way for the others to escape the effects.

Livingstone was now more than ever in a hurry to get away from the malarial delta, but since his transport was insufficient to move the Expedition and its impedimenta in one journey, there would have to be several trips up and down the river, with the

Ma Robert towing the pinnace. On July 1 the launch set out on the first of these, with Livingstone, Bedingfield, Thornton and the engineer, Rae, on board, leaving Charles Livingstone, Kirk and Baines to look after the island.

Meanwhile, fighting had broken out again between the Portuguese and the rebels, and when the launch came in sight of Mazaro, the site of Livingstone's previous encounter with the insurgents, the battle was still raging. When Livingstone landed to greet the Portuguese, among whom he recognized some of his old friends, he was sickened by the smell and the sight of the "mutilated bodies of the slain." The Portuguese commander, Colonel José da Silva, Governor of Quelimane, was down with fever and Livingstone was requested to take him in the launch across the river to Shupanga, which he immediately agreed to do. On entering the hut where the sick man was lying, Livingstone saw that he was too ill to walk and asked for men to be sent to get him down to the water. As none appeared and the firing was getting very close, he requested Bedingfield, who had just arrived at the hut, to go back to the launch and send some of the Kroomen to carry the Governor. After waiting some time in vain, with the "balls whistling overhead," he then lifted the Governor himself and with the help of a sergeant got him down to the beach. "He was a very tall man," Livingstone wrote when describing the incident, "and as he swayed hither and thither from weakness, weighing down Dr. Livingstone, it must have appeared like one drunken man helping another."[1]

The battle ended in the repulse of the rebels, and the Portuguese, having exhausted their ammunition, then withdrew to an island off Shupanga to await fresh supplies. Shupanga was a small trading station on the right bank of the Zambezi consisting of a one-storied stone house from which a sloping grass lawn led down to the river. From here one looked across the water to fields and tropical forests, with the majestic mountain of Morambala towering above them, and beyond a view of distant hills. A hundred yards east of the house there stood, and still stands, a magnificent baobab tree, now casting its shade over two graves, each marked with a simple cross. One of them is that of Lieutenant Kirkpatrick, R.N., a member of the Owen Expedition, who died of malaria in 1826; in the other is buried Livingstone's wife,

Mary, who was to succumb to the same disease in a few years' time.

On arrival at the station the Governor was put to bed, and in spite of his protests was treated by Livingstone with strong doses of quinine, as a result of which he quickly recovered. All the Portuguese were very friendly and expressed their willingness to assist the Expedition in every way. Two of them, Major Tito Sicard of Tete and Colonel Nunes of Quelimane, were old acquaintances with whom he had struck up a friendship on his journey down the Zambezi two years previously, and gave practical effect to their offers of help by sending men to cut wood for the launch and to help in unloading. Although he only gave a hint of it in his joking account of the incident, Livingstone had risked his life to rescue the Governor and probably saved him again by his knowledge of medicine. This was something the Portuguese could appreciate and they were genuinely anxious to show their gratitude.

The following weeks were employed in moving the bulk of the Expedition another stage up the river, from Expedition Island to Shupanga. This necessitated several journeys both ways by the launch, a day going down if all went well and two coming up, but liable to be much longer if she was delayed by groundings. Knowing that two of the men left on the island were already sick, his brother Charles and the artist, Baines, Livingstone was in a desperate hurry to get them off it and showed increasing exasperation with the shortcomings of the launch, which he contemptuously dubbed the "Asthmatic."

Our steamer's badly constructed furnaces consumed a frightful amount of wood. Fires were lighted at two in the morning, but steam was seldom up before six. A great deal of time was lost in wood-cutting. The large heavy-laden canoes could nearly keep up with us, and the small ones shot ahead, while the paddlers looked back in wonder and pity at the slow puffing 'Asthmatic'. For us steam was no labour-saving power; boats or canoes even, would have done for the expedition all that *it* did, with half the toil and expense.[2]

It may have been true that the launch's furnaces were badly designed, but it is also possible that this was unavoidable because of her necessarily shallow draught. There is also no doubt that owing to the collapse of the plan to take the *Pearl* up to Tete she was constantly overloaded, and in addition was expected to tow a heavily laden pinnace, and possibly a couple of canoes as well, for which she had not been designed.

When the launch went aground, as frequently happened in the constantly shifting shoals, the whole crew had to jump into the water to push her free, and sometimes an anchor had to be put out to winch her off. To add to his troubles, after the departure of Bedingfield Livingstone himself would have to do the navigation and spend long hours standing precariously on the paddle box, the only place from which he had a clear view ahead, shouting orders to the helmsman which he sometimes got wrong. He would rather, he said, have driven a cab through the London fog; moreover, it prevented him from attending to other duties, such as taking observations and paying visits ashore. But in compensation it was satisfactory to show Bedingfield that the Expedition could do without him. As he was to write later in his Introduction to the *Narrative:*

> The office of 'skipper', which rather than let the Expedition come to a stand I undertook, required no great ability in one 'not too old to learn': it saved a salary, and what was much more valuable than gold, saved the Expedition from the drawback of anyone thinking that he was indispensable to its further progress. The office required attention to the vessel both at rest and in motion. It also involved considerable exposure to the sun; and to my regret kept me from much anticipated intercourse with the natives, and the formation of full vocabularies of their dialects.

While Livingstone was chugging laboriously up and down the river with the baggage, Kirk's hands were full nursing the two companions who had been left in his charge on Expedition Island. Baines, who never spared himself and was always the first to volunteer for any heavy work, was down with fever, brought on partly by painting in the sun without a hat—he had, according to Kirk, "queer notions about hardening himself"—and lay in his hammock for several days, vomiting all medicine given him and part of the time delirious. Charles Livingstone, the laziest of the party, who occupied his time in unsuccessful experiments with photography, was in not much better shape. The iron hut had been thatched with grass, but at the first shower the water poured in and could only be stopped by covering the roof with sails and tarpaulins. After a week the two invalids were sufficiently recovered to be sent off to hunt game, but got nothing.

It was a relief when the launch returned, but the peace of the island was soon disturbed by another row between Livingstone and Bedingfield, this time about working on Sunday. With the meticulous objectivity which makes his record so valuable, Kirk described the incident in his diary.

This morning when in the cabin, I was called out to speak to the Doctor who was on shore with Bedingfield. All the Krumen were in the launch. When I stood on the gunwhale, the Doctor told me that he wished me to hear him ask Jumbo [the head Kruman] whether he had complained of working on Sunday. Bedingfield stated that Jumbo had asked him to speak to the Doctor to give them the Sunday free of work. Jumbo stated that he had asked whether they could have it but said now that they understood how matters were, and that the only thing that made the Doctor work on Sunday was to get out of the unhealthy district rapidly and to get all the party together again, he did not think it unreasonable to work on Sundays. The Doctor then broke out on Bedingfield [still before the hands] stating that he had deceived him regarding the steaming of the launch at Liverpool when fed with wood. Bedingfield stated that he had been at the trial and took Mr. Laird's word that she had been steaming with wood.[3]

Bedingfield was a stickler for observance of the Sabbath, and also thought that one of the objects of the Expedition was to discover the Ten Lost Tribes: on which Livingstone dryly commented, "As if of all things in the world we had not plenty of Jews already!" All this was undoubtedly very tiresome, but it was also highly improper of Livingstone to abuse the commander of the launch in front of the crew and the incident showed up the deficiency in his own leadership. It would, for instance, have been much better to explain in advance why it was necessary to work on Sunday, and everybody would then have accepted it without a murmur.

By the first week of August all was ready for another move.

The iron hut was taken down and the launch, pinnace and a large canoe were loaded with it and some more baggage. Baines, who as usual had done most of the work, was taken ill again but was sufficiently well to sail with the rest of the party when they set off on August 9. Two days later they landed at Shupanga, where the iron hut and goods were stored in the stone house. While Kirk and Baines took up their quarters in the house, sharing a mess with Colonel Nunes and another Portuguese officer, Livingstone returned with the launch to load the last of the baggage and leave a message in a bottle at Expedition Island to say where he had gone and that he would be back at the harbor of Kongone by Christmas. Then for the last time he turned his back on the pestiferous mud flat and on August 16 was back at Shupanga once again. Here Bedingfield was landed to await passage home, after delivering a final protest to Livingstone against the latter's "harsh treatment" of him.

He protests against my using his first resignation. This after he had told me he was sorry it had been withdrawn, and telling both Dr. Kirk and myself that he had given in a second resignation and also written in his log that he had resigned twice. I never met an individual who seemed to trust more in the power of lying than Commander Bedingfield.[4]

That night must have been almost the first that Livingstone slept soundly since his arrival at the mouth of the Zambezi three months before. During all this anxious time he had been preoccupied by the pressing need to get the Expedition away from the coastal region, which could so easily have become another "white man's grave," but his mind had also been constantly distracted and irritated by the nerve-wearing war with Bedingfield. Now the immediate danger was past without loss of life or serious illness, and he had seen the last of his enemy. His relief can be sensed in the more cheerful note which now broke into his journal.

However, he was not the one to ease up as soon as difficulties are over; and on the very next day, August 17, leaving Kirk and Thornton at Shupanga, he set off again in the *Ma Robert,* with his brother, Baines and Rae on board, heading for Tete, 200 miles up the river. This was to be the base for the critical exploration of the Kebrabasa Rapids, which would decide the fate of the Expedition, and Livingstone was impatient to get there while the water was still low, enabling the bed of the narrows to be examined. In any case he could never brook the slightest unnecessary delay in carrying out a plan.

Livingstone's description of this journey in his published *Narrative* gives little idea of the hardships and frustrations endured on it. When not being lyrical about the surroundings, as in this passage:

The sky was cloudy, the air cool and pleasant, and the little birds, in the gladness of their hearts, poured forth strange songs, which, though equal to those of the singing birds at home on a spring morning, yet seemed somehow, as if in a foreign tongue . . .

he would understate the frustrations by making a humorous anecdote of them:

The navigation was difficult—our black pilot John Scissors, a serf, sometimes took the wrong channel and ran us aground. Nothing abashed he would exclaim in an aggrieved tone, 'This is not the path, it is back yonder.' 'Then why don't you go yonder at first?' growled out our Kroomen who had the work of getting the vessel off. When they spoke roughly to poor Scissors, the weak cringing slave spirit came forth in, 'Those men scold me, so I am ready to run away.'[5]

In fact the journey took more than three weeks, with progress averaging less than ten miles a day, which was less than would have been made in fast canoes or on foot with porters. Even with a favorable wind and the sails up, the launch made only a few knots against the current, and on most days she grounded several times and was often got off only with difficulty. Since her speed was further reduced by the heavily laden pinnace towed astern, after a week the devoted Baines volunteered to remain behind with the pinnace while the launch, relieved of this burden, went on by itself. There was more delay while Rae, the engineer, who had only just recovered from a bout of malaria, repaired the engine pump.

It ought to have been a ball valve instead of an India rubber one [Livingstone complained in his journal]. Mr. Laird has served us very ill and now we feel the effects of his greediness in saving a hundred pounds or so by giving us an old cylinder and bad boiler.[6]

A few days later, unable to find the right channel, he fell back on prayer.

We shall succeed but I feel much concerned about our companions down the river. The Lord look in mercy on us all. It is his work we are engaged in. The high position I have been raised to is not of my seeking nor was the eclat which greeted me at home a matter of my choice. I therefore commit all to the care and help of him who has said Commit thy ways unto the Lord: trust also in him and he shall bring it to pass.[7]

To reach Tete it was necessary to pass through the Lupata Gorge, a narrow defile in which the current flowed strongly round rocky promontories. Native paddlers held it in such respect that they placed "meal on the rocks as an offering to the turbulent deities which they believe preside over spots fatal to many a large canoe." With a strong stern wind, however, the *Ma Robert* got through the pass in six hours, and two days later, on September 8, 1858, anchored safely off Tete.

When Livingstone went ashore, a crowd of natives, attracted by the strange spectacle of a steam paddle boat, were waiting on the beach. As he landed, a number of them rushed forward to grasp his hand, and even to clasp him round the body, until one of them called out, "Don't do that, you'll soil his clothes." "It is not often I have shed a tear," he wrote that night in his journal, "but they came in spite of me, and I said, 'I am glad to meet you, but there is no Sekwebu.'" He then told them that Sekwebu, one of their fellow tribesmen, had committed suicide at Mauritius when on his way to England with Livingstone two years earlier.[8]

The enthusiastic tribesmen were the faithful Makololo who had accompanied Livingstone as porters on his journey down the Zambezi between November 1855 and March 1856, and who had been waiting at Tete ever since for him to fulfill his promise to return and lead them back to their home in Barotseland. They had waited for two and a half years, during which time the local people, as they told him, had often taunted them by saying that the Englishman would never return; but they had always believed in his promise and now their hearts rejoiced to see that he had not failed them.

As we have seen, the need to keep his promise was one of the reasons why Livingstone, while in England, had been in such a hurry to return to Africa; and he had only decided to postpone his return after being told that the Portuguese Government had given orders for the Makololo to be maintained at public expense. In fact, no such order was ever received at Tete, and they owed their survival to the generosity of its commandant, Major Sicard, who assisted them out of his own pocket and also gave them land and implements to raise food for themselves. Thirty of them had died of smallpox and another six had been murdered by a half-caste ruffian called Bonga, who, like his namesake living farther down the river, was in a more or less permanent state of rebellion against the Portuguese. The men had been cut to pieces with axes and iron stakes had been knocked into their heads. Livingstone had heard of the incident on his way up the river but took it philosophically. His sympathies were always with the rebels, however atrociously they behaved, and in conversation he would refer to them as "the people called by the Portuguese rebels"—on which Kirk, always a realist, commented: "I should class them, were I a Portuguese, exactly as we do the rebel Indians. The atrocities here have been of the same sort, even impaling children . . ."[9]

The incident helps to explain why the Makololo were so anxious for Livingstone's return. Under the protection of his prestige and personality they had been prepared to march nearly 1,000 miles from their country on the upper Zambezi to Tete, and to take the risk of being attacked in hostile territory on the way. They were willing to follow him anywhere else, but they would never have attempted the return journey without him.

There was, however, no question of his being able to escort them home immediately; nor, since they were all in good health and happy now that he had kept his promise, was there any urgency about it. Moreover, a number of them had settled down, found wives and would not be returning to Barotseland anyhow. He had thus no need to worry about the Makololo and could give his mind to the main objective of the Expedition, which was the exploration of the Kebrabasa Rapids.

First, however, he had to set up a permanent base at Tete and then go back and collect the other members of the Expedition and the rest of the baggage, which had been left behind at Shupanga. The ever-helpful Major Sicard had offered half of his own house, known as the *Residencia,* rent free for the Expedition, and it was here that Livingstone and his companions with their stores now installed themselves in a fair degree of comfort, after being conducted to it by a band of Makololo carrying the goods, with a minstrel at their head "jingling his native bells and chanting an energetic song extemporised for the occasion."[10]

Here too we may leave them for a time while we describe the adventures of the rest of the party.

It will be remembered that when the launch with Livingstone and the others on board set out for Tete, Kirk and Thornton had remained at Shupanga to guard the stores for which there had not been room in the launch, and to await its return. Meanwhile the Portuguese, having received fresh supplies of ammunition, were preparing to renew the offensive against the rebels.

The camp is taking on quite a warlike aspect [Kirk wrote]. The slaves are cleaning their guns and making preparations for the march in the direction of Morambala where the rebels have their stronghold.[11]

Morambala was the name of a high mountain which stood near the confluence of the Zambezi and Shire rivers.

On August 18 the commander gave the order to move, leaving the two Englishmen alone in the house. He had provided a cook and a servant to look after the guests and left instructions that they were to be supplied with food. Thornton was confined to the house with sores on his foot, while Kirk busied himself with botany. He also made the acquaintance of some friendly Portuguese traders, who told him that in the dry season there was only a three-foot channel in the river and "nothing like a direct passage above this as far as Tete." Kirk, although unswerving in his loyalty to Livingstone, was privately skeptical of his leader's optimism and frequently scoffed at the exaggerated claims made by the latter for the Zambezi—"it was certainly aggravating," he wrote once with hardly disguised satisfaction, "to see his pet river go and dry up to a two foot stream."[12] Soon, however, Kirk's hands were full again nursing the wounded returning from the war. The Portuguese had no doctor of their own, and for his services to their men Kirk was later to receive the official thanks of the Portuguese Government.

After a month had passed of this relatively pleasant existence, the leisurely routine of Shupanga was enlivened by the arrival of a slave announcing the approach of an English boat. They walked down to the landing place and found two naval officers, Mr. Medlicott, mate, and Mr. Cooke, second master, of the gunboat H.M.S. *Lynx*, who had just arrived in the ship's whaler with a crew of two British sailors and three native Kroomen. The officers carried a letter from the commanding officer, Captain Berkeley, informing Livingstone that he had on board provisions and stores from the Cape and requesting him to come down to the mouth of the river to collect them. They also brought mail for members of the Expedition.

Since there was no means of reaching Livingstone or of knowing when he would appear again, Kirk borrowed canoes from the Portuguese, who had just won a bloodless victory over the rebels, and set off with native crews for the coast. On reaching the bar of the river they met two more of the *Lynx*'s boats, the cutter and the galley, which had been sent to look for the other armed with "12 lb. Congreve rockets" and to exact revenge in case it was found to have been molested. From their crews Kirk learned the sad news that a week previously the cutter had been capsized on the bar and six out of her crew of ten drowned. They could see the ship herself some miles out to sea, her captain being reluctant after this experience to risk coming nearer, and were rowed out to her.

After many weeks spent with the same companions, often in great discomfort, Kirk could appreciate the relative luxury of the

Lynx's wardroom and the society of her officers. One of them, the ship's doctor, had been at Edinburgh Medical College with him.

Over dinner with Captain Berkeley there was a discussion of what to do next. The *Lynx* had anchored off the mouth of the East Luabo, which was considered the more dangerous of the two possible entrances to the Zambezi, and Kirk advised that she should try the Kongone, where the *Pearl* had crossed the bar without difficulty. Eventually it was decided to send Medlicott in the galley to meet Livingstone, while the whaler, under Mr. Cooke, would go under Kirk's guidance to get the canoes round to the next mouth by the canal and then join the ship and see about landing stores.[13]

For the next week Kirk was constantly out in the open boat, trying to find another channel over the bar and losing his way in a labyrinth of creeks while looking for the canal that was supposed to connect the two mouths of the river. Sometimes sleeping on board and at others on a mudbank ashore, frequently soaked by the sea, cold and hungry, he was also more than once in danger of his life. One evening, having failed to find a passage through the surf, the boat was forced to return to the ship but was carried away by the current and had to battle for hours in a gale before reaching safety. On another occasion the terrifying experience of crossing a bar in a high sea is best described in Kirk's own words.

On getting close to the entrance to the channel we find the breaking right across the whole way, so as to make it very dangerous for us to attempt. The gunner and I looked at each other, as much as to say let us go back as soon as possible, when up got a roller behind us. There was no other way for it but to let her go with our oars up in the air, the boat on the steep inclined surface, the broken water on top behind us. The speed of the boat only keeping her from being overtaken, we went a good 14 miles [per hour] over the ground, the water flying from the stern as though we were in tow of a whale. Now all chance of turning was gone. We had passed the worst. I should think we had a dozen broken surfs. The whaler took them all splendidly. The gunner, Mr. Hart, and crew did their duty well for one instant's hesitation with anyone and we should have been upset. Several times the boat swerved from the wave and tried to get broadside on.[14]

On gaining smooth water the occupants of the boat were rewarded by the sight of the *Ma Robert* at anchor with Livingstone aboard.

While on his way down the river he had been met by Medlicott at Shupanga and had decided to take the opportunity of the *Lynx*'s presence to send off his dispatches. These were mainly concerned with his dismissal of Bedingfield and he was anxious they should reach England before the latter arrived there with his own version of the affair.

When Kirk rejoined the *Ma Robert* after his perilous passage across the bar of the Kongone, the *Lynx* was still outside, and when attempting to enter the harbor, on September 30, she went aground on the bar and remained stuck. Early the next day, after throwing overboard all her shot and moving the guns forward so as to place her on an even keel, she was floated off at high water and then came in and anchored safely beside the *Ma Robert*. As she steamed past, Livingstone recorded, Mr. Medlicott, standing at the masthead, called out, " 'Three cheers for Dr. Livingtsone and his Expedition,' and they were given in all heartiness by the crew."[15]

However, the happiness of this new encounter with the Navy was somewhat overshadowed by the loss of the six bluejackets a short time before. "It is unfortunate that this serious accident happened," commented Livingstone, "as people are prejudiced against the river by such things. She had no officer on board and the Captain is very much blamed." No word of sympathy, be it noted, for the victims. This is a different Livingstone from the man who two years before had been filled with deep compassion and bitter remorse on hearing that a boat's crew of H.M.S. *Dart*, sent to meet him at Quelimane, had been drowned on the bar. Some iron, it seemed, had entered into his soul and left no room for pity. Perhaps it was the rancor left by his quarrel with Bedingfield, perhaps the consciousness already dawning that in accepting the leadership of the Expedition he had taken on a burden too heavy to carry.

Although he was the cause of their losing six good men, the Navy did not grudge their help. Captain Berkeley sent the *Lynx*'s carpenter and calker to repair the deckhouse of the *Ma Robert,* which was "so leaky that Mr. Rae got a fresh cold by the rain pouring down on him," and himself volunteered to take the place of Bedingfield, as did also Mr. Medlicott and Lieutenant Mandeville. But Livingstone, now chary of engaging naval officers, declined the offer, and instead asked for the loan of a quartermaster, John Walker, and a leading stoker, William Rowe, which was willingly granted. These two men, who were paid double their normal full pay, were to give excellent service. Walker in particular had already distinguished himself by his handling of boats in the river and through the surf. "So I hope we shall manage him properly," Kirk commented, doubtless thinking of Bedingfield, "as no one who knows him will put the blame on him."

Another unfortunate incident, caused by Livingstone's thriftiness and lack of *savoir-faire,* was only averted by the tact of Kirk, showing the difference in their breeding. The *Lynx* had brought from the Cape a quantity of provisions ordered by Livingstone, but when he learned the price of them he was "horrified" and wanted to send them back.

As this would seem to me ungracious, to say the least [wrote Kirk], we propose taking them as mess stores and paying our proportion. While I can with all justice claim a few luxuries as medical stores, still the Doctor does not take all and thinks that he cannot transport them. I feel this is very awkward as he has asked the mess of the *Lynx* to take what we don't need and I know they need them as little as we do, for they took in abundance before leaving England.[16]

From his following remarks, however, the matter seems to have been settled amicably.

Dined with the Doctor and Capt: in the Wardroom, had a good jollification until lights were ordered out, which was done unusually early for this ship. I presume the Captain wished to seem very strict before the Doctor.[17]

From these two entries we get a picture of Livingstone sketched by the man who for four years lived closest to him, and it is not very attractive, revealing the subject as stingy, ill-mannered and puritanical.

By October 6 Livingstone had completed his interminable dispatches, the stores brought from the Cape had been transferred to the *Ma Robert,* and the Expedition was ready to make another start. But Captain Berkeley had asked the Doctor to "see him over the bar," and it was only the next day, when the *Lynx* steamed out, passed safely through the channel and hoisted the agreed signal that all was well, that the launch weighed anchor and headed up the river.

After a stop at Shupanga to hire canoes to carry the baggage which had been stored there, and which included the cotton presses and sugar mills, the launch left the Zambezi and proceeded up the Shire River. Here Livingstone had a meeting with the other Bonga, the defeated rebel leader, and invited him to dinner on board. The chief had sent his uncle to Sena to negotiate peace with the Portuguese and wanted to go there himself in the launch but was apparently dissuaded from doing so by Livingstone, who suggested instead "that he should send a messenger and not trust in the officials until he had got the promise of safety from the Governor of Quilimane." Livingstone had accepted help and hospitality from the Portuguese, but behind their backs he was making overtures to a man who was in revolt against their authority, and who was also a brother of the infamous Mariano, the most notorious and barbarous of the half-caste slave dealers. The Portuguese were bound to discover this double-dealing sooner or later, if they did not already suspect it. Although he did not overtly criticize his leader, various entries in Kirk's diary make it clear that he privately disapproved of this sort of behavior.

Livingstone's policy, as we have seen, was to remain neutral as between the Portuguese and the rebels. This was sound in principle, but for Livingstone more than principle was at stake. Already plans which he had conceived before leaving England for planting a British colony in the interior of Central Africa were beginning to mature in his head.

It is the mission of England [he wrote in his journal] to colonise and plant her Christianity with her sons on the broad earth which the Lord has given to the children of men. I am now working out the problem of a way into the Interior healthy highlands.[18]

If such a way were found it would be essential to cultivate the friendship of native tribes living along it, and this is why Livingstone did not want to compromise the future by taking sides against them.

After noting that it was quite safe to enter the Zambezi between May and August, provided certain precautions were taken —and he rated bodily exercise "to produce perspiration every day" more important than dosing with quinine—and that the river could be navigated the whole year round by "a vessel drawing three feet and of sufficient engine power," he returns to the theme of colonization.

The idea has been deeply impressed on my mind for some time past that emigration—colonisation of Christian families—ought to form a feature of this age. A great deal of the good done in Foreign missions is effected by the lives of the missionaries and those of converts. This good might be done by Christian families sent out by their richer friends. They would be a double blessing, a blessing to our overcrowded population at home and a blessing abroad. . . . How many millions might flourish in this Africa, where but hundreds dwell.[19]

It is an ironical reflection that barely a century later the only Christian nation that would have agreed with Livingstone about the virtues of colonization were the descendants of the same Portuguese whom he would have liked to supplant in East Africa.

After returning to the main river the launch stopped next at Sena, a few miles up on the right bank, which Livingstone found "wonderfully altered" since his visit two years before. It then only contained "a few miserable huts and dilapidated ruins of Portuguese houses." Now there were several stone houses, the largest of which, with a fine veranda in front, belonged to a trader, Senhor Ferrão; a new stockade had been built, "a mile long and a quarter broad," giving security to a population of 4,000 natives; and the fort had been repaired. It was evident that if it had done nothing else the presence of the Expedition had had the effect of stirring the Portuguese into unwonted activity. They were not having it said that their colony was being neglected.

From Sena the journey to Tete was rendered excessively tedious by the repeated groundings of the launch, usually several times a day, when she had to be pushed off by her long-suffering Kroomen working up to their waists in water, or dragged off by laying out her anchor and heaving on it with the winch, procedures which prompted the sardonic Kirk to observe dryly that he didn't "admire the land transport principle in a steam boat." Livingstone insisted on directing the operations himself, although "nothing more than a landsman out of his element"; as a result he had "too much exposure to the sun and was out of sorts."

This he has imposed on himself from liking it. Seemingly Walker the Quartermaster, who is an experienced seaman, is ready to take it and would have more power over the men if he went in that position.[20]

At last on November 5, just a month after leaving the coast, the launch arrived at Tete, where Charles Livingstone and Baines, who had found his way there in the pinnace, were waiting for it. For the first time almost since their landing in Africa all the members of the Expedition were assembled in one place, and even now some of their baggage was still missing. Tete was intended to be the starting point of the Expedition and it had taken eight months to get there from England. For Livingstone they had been months of unceasing labor and constant anxiety, and all he had to show for them were a few boxes of botanical specimens, most of which never reached England, some unsuccessful attempts at photography by his brother Charles and a portfolio of charming artist's sketches by Baines. In a tenth of the time and at a tenth of the cost he would have achieved more by himself. Through no fault of theirs his companions had added nothing; they were simply another burden on him, having to be cared for and given things to do; and transporting them and the impedimenta for so large an Expedition had had the effect of reducing it to a snail's pace. How bitterly Livingstone must have regretted the enthusiasm of his admirers who had wished on him such a cumbrous and unwieldy white elephant!

6

Kebrabasa Rapids

November 1858–December 1858

"Our curiosity had been so much excited by the reports we had heard of the Kebrabasa rapids, that we resolved to make a short examination of them, and seized the opportunity of the Zambezi being unusually low to endeavour to ascertain their character while uncovered by the water."

It was thus casually that Livingstone, writing six years later in his *Narrative of an Expedition to the Zambesi,* referred to the most crucial event of the whole enterprise. To read him one would imagine that he was describing a pleasant sight-seeing trip undertaken by a party of tourists to view some interesting scenery. There is no hint that on the result of the examination depended the success or failure of the Expedition and the whole future of Livingstone, who had staked his reputation on finding the rapids navigable. Having found them unnavigable he had to play their importance down so as not to disillusion his readers. This is a typical example of the dishonesty of the book.

From his companions, however, he could not conceal his anxiety. "The Doctor," wrote Kirk, "speaks of remaining only two days at Tete and going on then to Kebrabasa to see the rapids, which he talks of blasting!! to clear a channel if possible. This, he said, he would spend six months over to say there was water communication all the way to the Makololo country."[1]

Since Thornton and Baines were both sick, and Charles Livingstone was busy with photography—"he has made a mess of it," commented Kirk—it was decided to leave them behind at Tete in the comfortable house provided by Major Sicard for the use of the Expedition. Baines, who had found his own way to Tete in the pinnace after it had been cast adrift to lighten the load on the *Ma Robert*, was already coming under suspicion from Livingstone for certifying that Bedingfield had been willing to retain the command of the *Ma Robert* until a suitable successor was appointed. This went counter to Livingstone's thesis that the naval officer had resigned and that he had merely accepted his resignation.

He had an attack of intermittent [fever], which as usual went to his head [Livingstone noted]. He is to be watched, as it is known he formerly had brain fever.[2]

In fact, according to the editor of Livingstone's *Journals* who also wrote Baines's biography,[3] Baines had never suffered from brain fever. But to suggest that Baines was subject to brain fever was to discredit him as a witness and to call in doubt his recollection of what had been said by Bedingfield, and this, perhaps unconsciously, was what Livingstone wanted to do.

On November 8, 1858, the launch set out from Tete with Livingstone, Kirk and Rae on board. A day and a half's steaming brought them to the entrance of the gorge, where the river narrowed to from sixty to eighty yards in a fissure about ten fathoms deep. The launch proceeded for another four miles until it came to the first rapid, which it passed safely, and then to a second, which was only about twenty yards wide. Here the current swung her round and to save her from being swept away Livingstone steered for the side and hit a rock, punching a hole in the port bow, fortunately above the water line. Having secured the vessel he and Kirk then went ashore on the right bank to explore. What they saw is best described in Livingstone's own words.

The scenery presented to our view is quite remarkable and totally unlike anything that has ever been said of the Kebrabasa rapids. A series of lofty hills, among which those of a conical shape prevail most, encloses a dell resembling a river bed. This dell is the bed of the river at high water, and it is a strange mass of huge rocks containing a deep chasm winding from side to side along it. This fissure or cleft is at first, on entering it from below, not more than twenty feet deep, but it soon becomes eighty or even one hundred and twenty feet deep. The presence of islands or huge masses of perpendicular rock makes the water branch off at some spots and there the main channel is as little as 20 or 25 yards broad; but generally it is forty or fifty yards wide. . . . We saw abundant evidence that the water in flood rises more than a hundred feet perpendicularly and as the rise at the opening is not more than thirty the rush of waters must be terrific.[4]

When they had gone about a mile Livingstone was for returning to the launch immediately and making another attempt to get her past the rapids, but he was persuaded by Kirk to make a land reconnaissance first. After clambering all day among the rocks, which were baked so hot by the sun that they burned the hand and blistered the bare feet of the Makololo porters, they camped for the night on some sand. The next morning they continued the exploration until shortage of provisions forced them to turn back. By the evening, although only three miles from the launch, they were all too tired to go on and decided to sleep where they were and sup off a goose shot by Kirk.

We had him roasted but when he came on one of our men, the native pilot, came in with a jolly good dinner. He had gone ahead and told the men at the launch all that we needed, so instead of dividing the goose among all of us, we had more than we could eat.

During the arduous journey they had discovered several more rapids, at one of which the water was divided by a large rock, leaving two channels of which the larger was only fourteen yards. This was enough to convince Kirk that it would be impossible to take the launch through, but Livingstone was still optimistic and wrote in his journal:

I believe that when the river rises about six feet, the cascades may be safely passed. If not then at flood when the water is spread over all the dell.[5]

Returning to Tete on November 13, Livingstone immediately started to prepare for a second assault on Kebrabasa. But a few days later he was attacked by a skin disease (herpes) and under its depressing influence his mood changed to pessimism.

Things look dark for our enterprise. This Kebrabasa is what I never expected. No hint of its nature ever reached my ears. The only person who ever saw the river was José St. Anna,* and he describes it as fearful when in flood. This I can very well believe from what I saw. A Governor sent down two negroes in a canoe and neither they nor canoe was ever seen again. Then a canoe alone and that was smashed to pieces! What we shall do if this is to be the end of the navigation I cannot now divine, but here I am, and I am trusting Him who never made ashamed those who did so.

As always when things went wrong, he searched his conscience to see how, if at all, he was to blame.

I look back to all that has happened to me. The honours heaped on me were not of my seeking. They came unbidden. I could not even answer the letters I got from the great and noble, and I never expected the fame which followed me.

And as always it was his Christian faith, and his belief that in all he did he was as but the humble instrument of God, that consoled him.

It was thy hand that gave it all, O thou blessed and Holy One, and it was given for thy dear Son's sake. It will promote thy glory if Africa is made a land producing the articles now raised only or chiefly by slave labour.[6]

The gloom of their leader was not lost on the other members of the Expedition, but probably the only one to appreciate the reason for it was Kirk.

It being all up, the commerce all the way by the river to the interior, is a serious thought with the Doctor. Indeed the further

* A Portuguese half-caste trader.

progress of the Expedition becomes only a flying visit into a new country, and as matters look now, if it is impossible to get the launch up, which I believe it to be, I think the Doctor will as soon see us all back again and go on alone with his brother.[7]

Livingstone, however, was not the man to rely on hearsay. Although he must have feared already that the Kebrabasa was impassable, he had to see it for himself and so far he had seen only a part. Accordingly on November 24 the *Ma Robert* again left Tete, this time with the whole party on board, since Livingstone thought it was better for them all to be active. Also in the company were Senhor José St. Anna, who knew the country above Tete; five of his servants, including a pilot; and ten Makololo as porters. While Baines sketched the scenery, Charles Livingstone took photographs, few of which, however, came out.

After anchoring the launch near the entrance of the gorge, the whole party landed on the left bank and proceeded up it on foot. It quickly became apparent that it was a mistake to include the less fit members. Baines and Thornton had only just recovered from malaria and soon found the going in the grueling heat much too hard for them, although they struggled on. The weakest link in the chain, however, was Livingstone's brother Charles.

Mr. L. gets up his photographic apparatus and might have had several splendid views, but having accustomed himself to lounging indoors and never exposing himself without an umbrella and felt hat, with all the appurtenances of an English gentleman of a well regulated family, he cannot stand the fatigue of standing in the sun and after taking one, which he subsequently made a mess of, he knocked off and had a cup of tea under a stone. He being too tired to continue the march, we are to remain until tomorrow in situ . . .[8]

Seen from the other side of the river, for they were now on the left bank, the gorge appeared even more forbidding than before. From the foot of the mountains which enclosed it, perpendicular cliffs from eighty to 100 feet high, which would be covered at high water and were worn smooth by the force of it, fell to a deep and narrow ravine, where the stream wound its way through a jumble of enormous rocks, sometimes pouring down in falls of twenty feet or more, at others flowing smoothly but with dangerous eddies and whirlpools. It might well be that at high water the falls would disappear, but then the current, contained between the cliffs, could be expected to flow at a terrifying pace. All this was depressing enough for Livingstone, and the presence of passengers in the party was the last straw. His frustration boiled over in an outburst of wrath against the unoffending Baines for failing to issue rations to the Makololo, although he had received no orders to do so and it would have meant that the Kroomen of the launch went short.

"Baines too is scarcely off the sick list," commented Kirk, "and has been, I should say, the hardest worked member of the Expedition."[9]

Although the length of the gorge was only about twenty-five miles, such was the terrain that only a few miles' progress was made each day, with frequent halts to allow Charles Livingstone to rest. After wading up to the chest across a tributary of the river, Thornton fell sick and had to be left behind. The rest of the party continued for another two days, alternately scaling some mountain to obtain a better view of the river and descending to the bank to inspect some rapid.

Having covered most of the distance in a week's painful tramping, Livingstone was informed by some natives living in the neighborhood that he had seen the worst and that there were no serious obstacles farther ahead. He therefore decided to turn back. That evening, however, one of the Makololo, by name Masakasa, told him that he had heard from the same natives that there was another waterfall "as high as a tree and so difficult of access that, though perishing with thirst, a man would retire in fear from it." After a night spent in considering this statement, Livingstone decided that there must be some truth in it and the next morning announced his intention of returning by himself on his tracks to investigate, while the rest of the party carried on to the launch.

That he should prefer to be alone was natural. His companions, through no fault of their own, had been of little help so far in furthering the aims of the Expedition, and by their number, the amount of their baggage and their frequent sickness had merely retarded its progress. Now that things were going badly their presence was unendurable. Moreover, only one man was needed to prove or disprove the existence of the reported waterfall, and Livingstone could do that much more quickly if he traveled alone.

However, the implication that the others were simply a drag on him was strongly resented, especially by Kirk, who had never shirked hardship and was as capable of enduring it as his leader was. He pointed out that if Livingstone went off alone it would be considered an insult to the members of the Expedition and "that there were some who had not been sick nor been behindhand with any work, and had kept up with anyone there, as far as we had gone." The force of this reasoning eventually prevailed.

Dr. L., on reflecting a little, said if I chose to volunteer I might go, so of course I was only too glad of the chance, not only of seeing new country but also of avoiding the slur offered us by the Doctor. In fact, too, one felt their honour rather touched by the insult which after all, I believe, was not meant for anything more than that he would do it himself and was doubtful if any other could. However, as turned out I stood the work, which he said was the hardest he ever had in his whole lifetime, quite as well as he.[10]

With four Makololo and some guides lent by a village chief, Livingstone and Kirk then started westward again. The ground was now worse than ever, and on the third day both the Makololo and the guides struck, declaring that there was no path ahead and refusing to go on. Showing him the broken blisters on the bare soles of their feet the Makololo told Livingstone that they had always thought he had a heart but were now convinced he was mad. They next attempted to persuade Kirk to give up, but since he did not speak their language had no better luck.

The two white men then went forward alone and spent several hours in getting about a mile farther on.

Such climbing I have never seen [Kirk wrote]. We had to find our way among these gigantic stones, every step as if we should slip and go down some great crack, out of which it would be no easy thing to extricate oneself, even with all his bones entire.[11]

Forced by failing daylight to retrace their steps, they met the men struggling on and camped for the night by the river. The next morning there were more arguments, to which Livingstone listened patiently but without budging. He had met this sort of situation on his previous travels and was prepared to wait indefinitely until the men either abandoned him, in which case he would probably have gone on alone, or obeyed his wish. It was this passionate curiosity, combined with an iron will to satisfy it, that distinguished Livingstone as an explorer. Once a question had been raised in his mind nothing short of death or disablement would prevent him seeking the answer. Eventually the guides got up and set off, as Livingstone at first thought to return to their village. However, they took the direction of the river and the Makololo, still protesting, followed.

Starting onwards we came to a fisherman mending his net. He gave the guide who was forward with us a fish and pointed out a way by which we might get on far enough to see the fall. We were very soon worsted by a perpendicular rock which required to be climbed for 300 ft. The heat was excessive probably 130, for the hands could not hold on the points we in our ascent were fain to grasp. There we were, clambering up the face of the slippery promontory, certain that if one of the foremost lost his hold he would knock all the others down who came behind him.[12]

At last their efforts were rewarded by the sight of the waterfall. It was called by the natives Morumbua, had a drop of thirty feet at an angle of thirty degrees, was approached by steep inaccessible boulders and was flanked by perpendicular walls of rock, between which it was impossible for a craft to pass. Livingstone, however, estimated that the rise of water when the river was in flood would be at least eighty feet and that the waterfall would then be obliterated. With his habitually excessive optimism he reckoned that a suitable vessel would be able to stem the current, but noted in his journal that to make it permanently available for commerce the assistance of a powerful Government was necessary and a "company of sappers" to clear out the channel.

This [he added] is perhaps the most favourable circumstance connected with the affair, for it would be difficult to induce the Portuguese to give up their pretensions if they could take all the trade into their own hands without.

To get back to their base the explorers had to cut their way through thick bush to the top of a hill, then descend the other side to a village, where they slept. After two more days, mostly clambering over rocks, their provisions were running low, when they were met by Baines bringing fresh supplies and "sketching, as he always does, indefatigably." To Baines they "looked lean and haggard as if from long illness" and the new soles of their boots were worn through. The next day they rejoined the steamer and twenty-four hours later were back at Tete.

The two journeys to Kebrabasa had taken exactly four weeks, of which the last was the most grueling in Livingstone's experience as an explorer. If the result was disappointing at least he had the satisfaction of having traveled the gorge from end to end and seen for himself the worst of its obstacles. Moreover, he still clung to the hope, not shared by anyone else, that at high water the narrows would be navigable, and in his dispatch of December 17 to the Foreign Secretary he wrote:

Though there is an impediment to canoe navigation it would prove none to a steamer capable of going 12 or 14 knots an hour. . . . We are all of the opinion that a steamer of light draught would pass the rapids without difficulty when the river is in full flood in January or February.[13]

The statement that "we are all of the opinion" that the gorge could be navigated at high water was, to say the least, misleading. The only other member of the Expedition who had seen the Morumbua Rapids was Kirk, and he remained skeptical. After reading Livingstone's dispatch he wrote in his diary:

The Doctor writes for a new boat and gives a very favourable account of the rapids, much more than I could do.[14]

Baines, who with Charles Livingstone returned to Kebrabasa in January, when the river had risen thirteen feet, and made an exhausting journey by himself as far as Morumbua, reported that although many of the rocks were now submerged "the eddies were unsafe for anything larger than a boat to enter" and that "in the small space of still water between it would be in danger of running on concealed rocks."[15] Livingstone, of course, had not seen this report when he wrote his dispatch in December, but even after receiving it he ignored Baines's warning and made no mention of it in his own report to the Foreign Office (of February 14, 1859), although Baines's experience in the handling of boats was much greater than his own.

In any case, it was asking a good deal of the British Government, which had already spent a considerable sum on fitting out the expedition, to supply another vessel so soon. Livingstone justified his request by another vicious attack on his old scapegoat, the *Ma Robert.* Such an unworkmanlike engine, he told Lord Malmesbury, was never turned out of any shop, and though he had always heard the yards of the Lairds at Birkenhead highly spoken of he fervently hoped that "no other African expedition will ever be sent out trusting to their engineering workmanship." He would therefore await with much anxiety His Lordship's decision (about his request for a new boat), as on it would depend a march to the Makololo country on foot, "a mode of travelling which my former experience in Africa does not make me much in love with."

This dispatch, sent off at the end of 1858, did not reach London until the following summer, and it was only in October that Lord John Russell, who had succeeded Malmesbury at the Foreign Office, sent a copy of it to the Admiralty with a request to supply a new paddle boat for the Expedition. Captain Washington, the naval hydrographer, who replied for the Admiralty, took the opportunity to defend the builders of the *Ma Robert* against Livingstone's aspersions. She had been built, he pointed out, to Livingstone's own specifications, and so designed that she could be carried on the deck of a steamer in parts, or be portable by land past rapids, with no section, including the boiler, weighing more than forty hundredweight. With a length of seventy-five feet, a draught of eighteen inches and a speed of eight knots, it was necessary to use only the lightest metal—one of the points of which Livingstone had complained; and if she had proved unsatisfactory it was, in Washington's opinion, because she had not been used with "sufficient care by Dr. L."

As for the new boat, Washington advised, it should be 100 feet in length, with fourteen-foot beam and three-foot draught, and be driven by a pair of "Penn's oscillating engines" each of sixteen horsepower, giving a guaranteed speed of ten knots. This was less than the "12 or 14 knots" proposed by Livingstone, which was quite impracticable given the other conditions, but was evidently considered by the experts as sufficient. The cost of the vessel would be £4,000, plus another £1,000 for boats, stores, etc. She could be completed in four months, sail to Africa under her own steam, and be at the mouth of the Zambezi by July 1, 1860, "in good time for any expedition Dr. L. might like to take as soon as the water rose."[16]

At the end of November the Treasury gave their consent, but in a letter to the Foreign Office issued a warning that "sums of this magnitude"—£31,325 for the Niger Expedition and £7,949 for the Zambezi Expedition plus a further £5,000 for the new vessel—"should not continue to be expended without some clear and settled plan of future policy."[17]

In any event, as will appear, Livingstone was to abandon his plans for it long before the new boat appeared on the scene; and when it arrived he had no better opinion of it than of the much maligned *Ma Robert,* which in spite of its deficiencies carried the Expedition over a total distance, as computed by Livingstone,[18] of 2,690 miles, before its bottom fell out and it subsided once and for all into the sandy bed of the Zambezi. This, however, is to anticipate our story. Meanwhile such was his influence with the Government, and their trust in his judgment, that there was no hesitation, if some nervousness at the Treasury, in granting his demand.

In his heart Livingstone must have known that at the Kebrabasa Rapids he had met an insuperable obstacle to all his schemes. But he was not prepared to admit it, even to himself, until he had some balancing success to set off against it, and it was to achieve this that he now turned his thoughts in a new direction.

7

The Shire and Lake Shirwa

December 1858–June 1859

AFTER THE RETURN from Kebrabasa morale was very low. With the exception of Kirk, who was too busy treating the others to become sick himself, all the members of the Expedition had been down with malaria at some time or other and now Livingstone himself succumbed. As usual he kept a careful record of his symptoms.

Had a slight touch of cold which, as most diseases in this country do, assumed the form of a partial fever. The malaria seems the link that binds them together in a family tie . . . Quinine has a good and prompt effect in all cases if used with other remedies and in sufficient quantities. I took about 30 grains in 6 hours and it made me deaf soon after. I remained so till this morning and am now well. When bowels are constipated these must be cleared out while it is given.[1]

A week later the fever returned, accompanied with "unusual languor" which made it difficult to write his dispatches. It was perhaps of this period he was thinking when in his *Narrative* some years later he described the effect of malaria on the mind.

Cheerfulness vanishes and the whole mental horizon is overcast with black clouds of gloom and sadness. The liveliest joke cannot provoke even the semblance of a smile. The countenance is grave, the eyes suffused, and the few utterances are made in the piping voice of a wailing infant. An irritable temper is often the first symptom of approaching fever. . . . Nothing is right, nothing pleases the fever-stricken victim. He is peevish, prone to find fault and to contradict, and thinks himself insulted . . . If a party were all soaked full of malaria at once, the life of the leader of the expedition would be made a burden to him.[2]

Although quinine was effective as a cure, it was no good as a prophylactic, and Livingstone was probably right in believing that the "best preventive against fever is plenty of interesting work to do and abundance of wholesome food to eat." He found, moreover, that for himself bodily activity with plenty of perspiration was better than mental activity, and that he kept fitter traveling in the noonday heat than sitting in the shade writing his dispatches. Accordingly, after recuperating at Tete, he was soon anxious to be off somewhere else and decided next to explore the Shire River.

This, the principal tributary of the Zambezi, joins its northern bank about 100 miles from the coast, after flowing for 300 miles in a southerly direction from Lake Malawi (formerly Lake Nyassa), whose waters it drains. The Portuguese had never explored the river, and because of the hostility of the native population their traders never ventured far up it. It was known, however, that somewhere to the north there was a very large lake and this now became Livingstone's new objective. He also thought that the Shire might provide an alternative route of access to Central Africa easier than the Zambezi and with the additional advantage of being outside Portuguese control. It was therefore with high hopes that on December 20, 1858, he set off again in the launch, accompanied by Kirk and Rae, and leaving his brother and Baines behind with instructions to make another trip to the Kebrabasa as soon as the water rose.

After stopping one night in the Revubue River, a few miles from Tete, where Thornton had been sent to prospect for coal, the *Ma Robert* proceeded to Sena and thence to the Shire, where she anchored off Mount Morambala. The next day Livingstone and Kirk climbed the mountain, which rose to about 4,000 feet and was topped by an undulating plateau, extensively cultivated.

They passed several villages and made friends with a headman, who gave them a hut to sleep in and "a plate of oranges plucked from trees planted long ago"—presumably by the Portuguese, since they were not indigenous.

In the morning they descended to the river, stopping on the way to visit a hot sulfurous spring, where Livingstone

> had a good bath 100 yds. below the eye. Muddy bottom but it does not stick. What a boon this would be to persons afflicted by skin disease, but the Portuguese durst not go near it.[3]

Continuing the journey up the Shire they found plenty of water, with no shoals, and the mass of floating duckweed, against which Livingstone had been warned by the Portuguese, proved no impediment. The river widened as they ascended, from eighty to 150 or 200 yards, and ran between banks not more than ten or twelve feet high. On either side stretched a flat valley, thickly populated, abounding in game, and with a soil that Kirk, in the report which Livingstone asked him to prepare for the Foreign Secretary, judged "capable of growing not only cereals but also cotton and sugar-cane of excellent quality and in almost unlimited amount."[4]

Villages were frequent, but the people, although not overtly unfriendly, were evidently suspicious. They belonged to a tribe called the Manganja, which had the reputation with the Portuguese of being hostile and ferocious. All the men were armed with bows and poisoned arrows, and although they were willing to trade and did not molest the wooding party, which landed daily to cut fuel for the launch, they "had about as little faith in us," Kirk wrote, "as I had in them." Their custom was to stop all travelers and make them either go back or pay for the privilege of passing through their territory. This Livingstone was determined not to do, and he therefore instructed his native interpreter to inform them that he and his companions were Englishmen and did not require "leave to pass." The interpreter, a slave, being scared out of his wits, took no notice of the order, but instead began to entreat for permission to pass. Livingstone, furious, then put the launch to "ahead."

About 300 yds further on another large party stood and as the headman spoke civilly I stopped to talk; but this fool of an interpreter would do as his fears dictated. I told him to ask where the chief was; this he would not do, though I repeated my request again and again. Having anchored I called on the chief man, who had now come from the other place, to come on board. He refused but, telling him myself if he did not come I would go on, he at last came with five or six in a canoe and would not step on board until a hostage went into the canoe. I gave him a present for his chief and two yards of calicoe for himself, showing him at the same time our arms [which Kirk had prepared and loaded] and telling him if he wanted to fight we had the means of doing so but were not anxious to quarrel. He went off satisfied, but I was very much dissatisfied, as it appeared to him he had forced us to ask his leave to pass, and he showed it by calling out to us, Go, go, go, when he reached the shore.[5]

A rather different version of this incident is given by Livingstone in the *Narrative,* written several years later:

At the village of a Chief named Tingane, at least five hundred natives collected and ordered us to stop. Dr. Livingstone went ashore; and on explaining that we were English and had come neither to take slaves nor to fight, but only to open a path by which our countrymen might follow to purchase cotton, or whatever else they might have to sell, except slaves, Tingane became at once quite friendly.[6]

It is curious, if he *did* go ashore on this occasion, that neither he nor Kirk mentioned the fact in their respective journals. Indeed, both of them make it clear that they did not leave the launch, did not meet Tingane and were unable to make themselves understood except when threatening force; if a totally different version was given by Livingstone to the public, it was presumably so as not to upset those of his admirers in England, including the Quakers and other pacifists, who believed it was quite wrong for a missionary to be accompanied by armed men, let alone carry arms himself, whereas Livingstone thought that a show of strength was the best way to avoid fighting.

The next day they were in danger again, this time of being

charged by a wounded elephant, and after putting it to flight with a volley, they almost stepped on top of a lion concealed in long grass. To complete the day's adventures, it only remained for Livingstone to stumble over one of the numerous elephant traps set by the natives, an eight-foot hole, covered with grass, into which he was prevented from falling by Rowe, the naval stoker from the *Lynx*.

Wood was now running short and there was none in sight for cutting, but the discovery of a deserted hut, and a cache of elephants' bones, which Livingstone had the bright idea of burning as fuel, enabled the launch to limp forward until it reached a group of palmyra trees, which saved the situation.

On January 8, 1859, they arrived at the first of a series of cataracts, which stopped any further progress, and which Livingstone decided to name the Murchison Falls after his friend and patron, the President of the Royal Geographical Society.

The advantage of having an English name [he wrote to Lord Malmesbury] is to perpetuate the nationality of the discovery and the point when the native name has changed.

The falls were not steep—about twelve feet in 150 yards—but large rocks stuck up in the water, which was "far too shallow to allow of anything like a ship being drawn through and I fear anything much smaller would be too weak."[7] Moreover, it was only the first and the least formidable of half a dozen rapids extending over thirty miles of the river.

If Livingstone felt any disappointment at finding his way barred again, he did not reveal it. Perhaps the idea which he later adopted was already revolving in his head, of having his own boat built which could be taken to pieces and carried overland past the falls.

From the local natives they learned the existence of two lakes, the smaller of them a day-and-a-half journey off and the larger a ten-day journey. From this Livingstone concluded rightly that the Shire ran out of Lake Nyassa, but in view of the attitude of the natives it was deemed unsafe to leave the launch and attempt a land journey until the confidence of the population had been won in another visit. Therefore, after waiting a few days to fix the position by sun sight, Livingstone turned the launch around—hitting a rock and narrowly escaping shipwreck in the process—and headed down the river.

With the current helping her the *Ma Robert* made good speed back and in five days reached Shupanga. Here the ever-observant and indefatigable Kirk made one of the many entries in his diary which are so revealing of the day-to-day life of the Expedition.

JAN. 17TH. The men off cutting wood. When ashore Galdini has a long talk with me. It is clear that there is some undercurrent of opinion among the Portuguese which has no love to the Doctor and still less the brother. This comes from being Missionaries I believed, although no one can accuse either of them doing much in that line. On coming aboard at night Walker [the naval quartermaster borrowed from H.M.S. *Lynx*] reported the Kroomen were disobedient and personally insolent to him. For long he had been leading a poor life and I had spoken to him to seize the first case and report it. The Doctor took it up in a serious light and gave them such a palaver that Walker's position is like to be established at last. Having been left in the wrong position, or rather in no position at first, it was not to be expected that the Kroomen would give in easily, and a succession of attempts to get rid of his authority was a consequence of not making it publicly known to them that Walker was an officer to be obeyed.[8]

It was not surprising that the Portuguese were suspicious of Livingstone. He had gone out of his way to be friendly with the people who had lately been at war with them and was now planning to plant an English colony on their doorstep. He had been playing with this idea even before leaving England but had kept quiet about it, fearing no doubt to alarm the Government. But now he felt confident enough to put it forward for the consideration of the Foreign Secretary. In a dispatch from Tete dated March 4, 1859, reporting a shipment of slaves, nominally as "free emigrants," from Massangane, south of Quelimane, to the French island of Réunion, he explained his reasons.

Viewing the indifference of the Portuguese, whose presence at widely separated points in this vast country prevents other nations from entering it . . . to the cotton, sugar cane, coal, etc. etc., and their eagerness to engage in slave-trading as soon as our squadron allows it, I cannot help calling to mind how thousands of our countrymen are anxious to develop lawful commerce, were their presence here admitted. While enriching themselves they would crown with success the efforts of England to abolish the slave trade—this French scheme threatening to render all our past efforts fruitless. The conviction is thus forced upon the mind that a small colony of our own nation on the healthy highlands, beyond the Portuguese influence and pretensions, would eventually be of immense value both to Africa and England. There are hundreds of square miles of all but unoccupied though fertile country. Large districts have been depopulated by war and we have now the near prospect of the scourge being again set in motion by the demand for slaves at Massangane. One of these districts situated near the Kafue* could be purchased at a cheap rate: thousands of natives would flock to it as they have to Natal: they have a general longing for the presence of a superior power, and the English, so far from being considered intruders, would increase the high moral influence which the French scheme is damaging.[9]

Malmesbury considered this dispatch of sufficient importance to be shown to the Prime Minister. Palmerston had no hesitation in rejecting Livingstone's plan out of hand. "I am very unwilling," he noted in the margin, "to embark on new schemes of British possessions. Dr. L's information is valuable, but he must not be allowed to tempt us to form colonies only to be reached by forcing steamers up cataracts."

This was the voice of liberal England, which almost to the end of the nineteenth century—usually considered the golden age of British imperialism—and whatever Government was in power, remained stubbornly "anti-colonialist," as it would be called today. It was not only the idea of spending money on "forcing steamers up cataracts" that put off Palmerston and successive Chancellors of the Exchequer; it was also dislike of assuming re-

* The Kafue River is a tributary of the Zambezi which flows into it from the north, near Lusaka, capital of the former British colony of Northern Rhodesia and of the present independent state of Zambia.

sponsibility for new countries, of burdening Government with new problems, of facing possible foreign complications. Nor were the businessmen any keener to take the risk of entering "unknown and perilous fields." For example, when Stanley, coming twenty years after Livingstone, tried to interest the City of London in the Congo, which he had just explored, he found no interest at all. He then took himself off to Belgium, where he was immediately engaged by King Leopold II to develop a colony in Central Africa. In fact, the only conscious British imperialists before Rhodes were idealists like Livingstone, who believed that colonization was the best means of raising Africa from slavery and degradation, and it was through their influence, and not through that of financiers and flag-wavers, that public opinion came reluctantly to accept the notion of "the white man's burden."

On the day after the *Ma Robert* returned to Tete, Baines and Charles Livingstone got back from the trip they had made to Kebrabasa to inspect the rapids at high water. "Report favourably on the possibility of passing," Livingstone wrote in his journal. Did they really, or was he indulging in wishful thinking? Baines's report, afterward published in the R.G.S. *Journal*, to which reference has already been made, made it clear that in his opinion navigation would be dangerous for anything larger than a rowing boat. Livingstone, however, in his dispatch to the Foreign Office of December 17, had committed himself to the statement that "a steamer of light draught would pass the rapids without difficulty when the river is in full flood," and he was perhaps not prepared to listen to any evidence to the contrary, especially from Baines, against whom he was already prejudiced following a quarrel between the latter and his brother.

Since the quarrel was the source of much future trouble, it is worth quoting the account of it given by Baines's biographer.

Both Charles and Baines submitted reports, the former's scanty and little to the purpose, the other's careful and detailed. Naturally neither included any reference to an unpleasant clash between them when they first took to the land, but Mrs. Baines gives a sufficient account in a letter to her married daughter.

Baines was busy upon a drawing of the turbulent rapids, while Charles reclined under a tree beneath the shade of his green umbrella. 'He never hurt himself with work,' writes the indignant widow, 'but expected to be waited upon, till your brother told him he was not there as his servant but as an officer that had duties of his own to attend to.' It was a trivial affair, but not insignificant.[10]

From this and everything else we know of the two men it is not difficult to visualize the scene: Baines, always the hardest worker, intensely conscientious, going off alone to obtain a sketch of the Morumbua Rapids after his Makololo porter had refused to walk farther, while Charles, abandoning the attempt at the first difficulty, lolled in the shade and, with an inflated idea of his own importance as third-in-command, took umbrage because Baines was not there to take orders. The significance of the incident was that Charles considered that insufficient respect had been paid to his authority, never forgave Baines, and from that day plotted against him, with the results we shall see.

After a month in Tete Livingstone succumbed to one of his periodical bouts of gloom and introspection.

I have been more than usually drawn out in earnest prayer of late—the Expedition, the cares for my family, the fear lest B's [Bedingfield's] representations of my conduct may injure the cause of Christ. The hopes that I may be permitted to open this dark to the blessed Gospel. I have cast all before my God. Good Lord, have mercy upon me.[11]

And so on for another half page. As always his mood was made worse by the irritating presence of his unwanted companions.

Thornton evidently disinclined to geologize and has done next to nothing for the last three months. Gorges himself with the best of everything he can lay hands on. Baines sent for four bottles of brandy to the launch. I was obliged to speak sharply to him about it. He receives £1 a day and does next to nothing.[12]

This was probably true, since there was nothing for him to do. He had sketched everything in sight and was reduced to doing portraits of his Portuguese friends. That he should have made such friends was his real crime in Livingstone's eyes.

The cure for depression was activity; so on March 15, accompanied again only by Kirk, Livingstone left Tete on a second visit to the Shire. As before, Charles Livingstone was left behind in charge, this time with instructions to organize an expedition to the Manica gold field. For some reason the ship's engineer, Rae, was also left behind, his place being taken by Rowe, the naval stoker, somewhat to Kirk's consternation.

To be away for four months without an engineer in a boat which he has officially pronounced as unsafe is a thing that may work but is more likely to come to grief. Then this is the unhealthy season. Mere bad health and a touch of fever is nothing, were it not for the bad humour it puts everyone in and sickness is a thing which the Doctor has no patience with either in himself or any one else . . . He knows to come it round niggers very well, but if his digestive system don't go all right, he loses his diplomatic power wonderfully.[13]

On entering the Shire again they found the natives much more friendly, thus justifying Livingstone's belief that if treated properly, that is, fairly but firmly, their confidence could be won. On March 26 they reached the village where there had been trouble before, and this time landed and were received hospitably by the chief, Tingane. It was no doubt of this visit rather than of the former that Livingstone was thinking when he wrote his account of the meeting with Tingane in the *Narrative,* and the confusion of the two may well have been a fault of memory rather than deliberate misrepresentation.

Arriving once again at the foot of the rapids which Livingstone had named the Murchison Falls, they made friends with another chief, called Chibisa, who promised guides to lead them to the smaller and nearer of the two lakes which they had heard about on their previous visit. This was Lake Shirwa, distant only about forty miles from Chibisa's, but owing to ignorance, misunderstanding or duplicity on the part of the guides—it being the policy of African chiefs to discourage their visitors from going farther for fear of losing any trade they might bring—they marched in circles for nearly a fortnight without getting much nearer their goal. Livingstone's account of these wanderings in the *Narrative* is in the vein which shows him at his best: making light of danger or hardship and extracting humor from misfortune.

The party pushed on at last without guides, or only with crazy ones; for, oddly enough, they were often under great obligations to the madmen of the different villages: one of these honoured them, as they slept in the open air, by dancing and singing at their feet the whole night. These poor fellows sympathised with the explorers, probably in the belief that they belonged to their own class; and uninfluenced by the general opinion of their countrymen, they really pitied and took kindly to the strangers, and often guided them faithfully from place to place, when no sane man could be hired for love or money.[14]

They were now approaching the territory of the Ajawa, a slave-trading tribe who, knowing the views of Livingstone on slavery, had persuaded the people not to help him. The presence of the trade was indicated when in one village they were shown a "taming fork," the implement used by the slavers to discipline any recently bought slave who was troublesome.

It is a piece of wood four or five inches thick 6 or 7 ft. long, forked at one end. The neck is inserted in the fork and another slave carries the free end. At night, when tied by the other end to a tree, the slave is helpless. Kavumo [the local chief] justified the chiefs selling people by saying only criminals and thieves or persons committing adultery are sold.[15]

At last, on April 18, they reached the shores of the lake and gazed admiringly over its blue surface, which stretched beyond the horizon, before wading into the water, only to be attacked by myriads of leeches and driven back.

The discovery of Lake Shirwa, sixty or seventy miles long and twenty-five to thirty wide, and also of Mount Zomba, 6,000 feet, was a considerable feat of exploration which Livingstone made the best of in his next dispatch to the Foreign Office (May 12, 1859).

The Portuguese do not even pretend to know Shirwa, it is necessary to state this because after the first European had crossed the continent the Portuguese claimed the honour for two black men . . . and these blacks, in the memory of a lady now living at Tete, came thither dressed and armed as the people of Londa, but proceeded no further. They thus failed by about 400 miles of what was claimed by them. . . . We made frequent enquiries among the people if they had ever been visited by white people before and we were invariably answered in the negative. . . . It is claimed for Dr. Kirk and myself as *Europeans* who accomplished it, entirely ignorant of any information that may or may not be locked up in archives.[16]

The discovery of the lake, however, was less important than that of the fact, learned from natives living on its shores, that it was separated from the much larger lake they had been told about—i.e., Lake Nyassa—by only a narrow strip of land; and it was reasonable to conclude, therefore, that the latter, which was known to "map-makers and believed to extend pretty well up to the Equator," was equally accessible. Indeed Livingstone's only fear was lest it should have already been discovered by the East African Expedition of Burton and Speke. However, his present object being "rather to gain the confidence of the people by degrees than to explore," he considered "that they had advanced far enough into the country for one trip" and decided to return to the launch.

This was just as well since Walker, the English quartermaster who had been left in charge, had been down with malaria and they found him seriously ill. A large dose of calomel soon put him on the road to recovery and the *Ma Robert* then proceeded down the river, bound for the coast, where it was hoped to meet a British man-of-war with fresh provisions. While waiting in the Kongone harbor for it to appear, Livingstone employed his time adding a sheet to his last dispatch.

Our movements seem to have awakened the jealousy of the Portuguese and they seem afraid that England may set up a claim to the countries first explored by us. A settlement is about to be made at the confluence of the River Shire, the first they have on the north bank of the Zambesi, by way of laying a claim to all the Lake territory with which we are engaged. . . . A customs house is to be erected at the Luabo and Kongone mouths of the Zambesi, whose navigability we alone discovered. We have explained the uses of the cotton gin and offered to lend them two or three other machines for experiment, but they seem to imagine that we have some other objects in view than the promotion of trade. They are exactly like the negroes and fancy that our motives are identical with their own.[17]

Here for the first time Livingstone recognized the snag on which the Zambezi Expedition was finally to be wrecked. As the British Government realized long before he did, it was inevitable, since he was operating in their territory, that any discoveries made by Livingstone would be exploited by the Portuguese, and that ultimately they would become the main beneficiaries. Could he really imagine they would remain indifferent while he stamped about their colony, fraternizing with their enemies, making plans for the introduction of British trade and generally for the expansion of British influence at their expense? And were there not grounds for their suspicion, which he dismisses so contemptuously, that "we have some other objects in view"? What about the plans for a British colony which he had just proposed to the British Government in this very same dispatch? If he imagined this would be seen by other countries as a move of disinterested idealism offering no threat to themselves he was singularly naïve. But he was no such fool, and what he undoubtedly hoped was to persuade the British Government to use the immense power of Britain to coerce the Portuguese; and in this case he should not have been surprised if they saw in all his transactions the hand of *perfide Albion*. Perhaps the explanation was that "to the pure all things are pure," but it was asking too much of the rest of the world to see the Zambezi Expedition in that light, and Kirk, as so often, put his finger on it when he wrote in his diary:

The Portuguese don't like us as an expedition and some have a personal dislike also. With several of our members the feeling is mutual. All I can say is they are fools to let us in at all and it is what we would never have done to foreigners in Australia or the like.[18]

However, jealousy of the Expedition and distrust of its motives were not the only reasons for the Portuguese attitude, as a further entry shows.

There is no doubt we demoralize, as they term it, their slaves. We can't help it. . . . We must and ought to treat the Makololo as men. We don't make fools of them by supposing they are equal with ourselves. We would not call a Frenchman a brother and it is not likely we shall begin with niggers; but they are decent fellows for savages and will do some work well and for that we pay them. But the Portuguese slaves see that we take care of these men and see them comfortable and having looked on them before our arrival as something far under themselves, of course they are demoralized, but we can't help it. If our niggers wear trousers, why we can't take them off.[19]

When at the end of a week no ship was yet in sight, it was decided to wait no longer and to return to Tete. The trip was uneventful except for a misadventure to Rowe, which Kirk describes with a medical man's special sense of humor.

Rowe, the second engineer, got into a disagreeable mess from what he calls Botanizing, which he swears he will never do again. He had been unsuccessful in shooting a buffalo and before returning sat down in the bush on a call of nature. In a dreamy state he began amusing himself slicing up the branches of a *Euphorbia* tree, and when the Mosquitoes began to trouble him he rubbed them off, his hands being covered with the milky juice. Soon after returning he found himself burning like fire and the next 48 hours he spent bathing with cold water a certain part which now had left all human form and was covered with a multitude of small blisters. On the third day things got better, but a considerable loss of leather ensued and he had to display himself in Highland costume, sailor's trousers not being well adapted for the interesting state he was in.[20]

On June 23, 1859, the launch with its party arrived back at Tete after an absence of more than three months. The journey had opened a new vista to Livingstone, and in his mind he already saw in the Shire River and Lake Nyassa a possible means of redeeming his defeat at Kebrabasa. But at this moment of renewed hope he was once again distracted by further quarrels with his staff.

8

Lake Nyassa

June 1859–December 1859

On the day that Livingstone returned to Tete he wrote in his journal:

Baines has been heady for three weeks and made away with Expedition goods to a large amount while so affected. Asked them to put him in confinement. Thornton doing nothing: is inveterately lazy and wants good sense.[1]

Two days later he wrote to Thornton to inform him that he was dismissed from the Expedition for laziness and his pay stopped from May 3, that is, from seven weeks previously. A few weeks later Baines, falsely accused of theft, was similarly dismissed and ordered to return home. Both men were the victims of Livingstone's prejudice and his brother's spite. The injustice of his treatment of Baines, particularly, is the biggest blot on his reputation and can only be excused by the extreme mental and physical strain under which he was suffering. Even so it suggests that he was quite unfit to be the leader of such an Expedition.

In the case of Thornton, Livingstone's fault was to leave an able and willing but totally inexperienced young man to his own devices in a savage country, without proper instructions, supervision or any provision for medical care. While Livingstone and Kirk, the two doctors, were away on the Shire, Thornton, with

Baines and Charles Livingstone, had been left at Tete, and as geologist of the Expedition he had been ordered to examine coal seams in the neighborhood. He was provided with guides and workers, but could not speak either Portuguese or the native language and had no authority over the men, who led him where they wished, refused to obey his orders and absconded with his provisions. He managed, nevertheless, and in spite of frequent bouts of prickly heat and malaria, to find a suitable seam and get a tunnel driven into it for the extraction of coal, which was used in the *Ma Robert.* He tells the sequel in a letter to his sister Helen, written shortly after his dismissal. Where he speaks of a "cold" he is probably describing malarial fever.

I chose a seam of coal on the river Morongoge as being the most suitable, and removed my traps to it and pitched my tent near to it. The next day I was unwell, but determined to go to Tete for tools, etc. I took 2 men with me, leaving the rest to build a shed for themselves by my return—but instead of doing so they packed up all the traps and followed me to Tete. At Tete I found that the Dr. was preparing for a long journey up the Shire river to the great lake. Dr. Kirk alone was going with him; they would be away for 4 months leaving the rest of the members at Tete all that time—the most unhealthy part of the year—without a doctor. I returned on 10th March to the coal and commenced work . . . I taught the men how to use the pick and blasting tools, and then had only to overlook them and the first of the blasting. At the latter end of March I took a severe cold and on 3rd April I returned to Tete to recruit. In about 8 days I was better and returned to the coal. At the latter end of April I was again taken ill. I kept at the coal until 3rd May, when I was again taken ill. Cld. eat nothing and was very weak. My legs were nearly covered with large festered sores resulting from mosquito bites, which I had irritated with scratching. I sent to Tete for a *machela* [a kind of palanquin carried by two men] and returned to Tete. The first few days my legs were worse and I determined to lay them up and not stir off my bed more than necessary. It was three weeks before I could wear a shoe; during this time I had another very bad cold and at the end of it a slight attack of fever.[2]

This and other letters, as well as the diaries he kept for four years, crammed with geological and topographical information, are sufficient refutation of the charge that Thornton was lazy. After his dismissal by Livingstone he made a pioneering journey with some Portuguese traders to Zumbo, 250 miles above Tete, and up the valley of the Loangwa River. He then found his way to East Africa and accompanied the German explorer Baron von der Decken on the first ascent of Mount Kilimanjaro. He subsequently rejoined the Zambezi Expedition at the invitation of Livingstone, who needed his maps and geological studies to include in the results of the Expedition, but on his own terms, which left him free to do what he liked. He died on April 21, 1863, as a result of hardships endured on a heroic journey to bring food to his companions. Livingstone virtually admitted his mistake by approving the payment of arrears of salary (but not of expenses) to Thornton's heirs, but never publicly acknowledged it.[3] He could not forgive him, any more than he could Baines, for being friendly with the Portuguese.

Thornton had all the qualities necessary to success in the career he had chosen—"guts," intelligence, industry, independence of spirit—and but for his tragic death he might well have achieved eminence in the geological exploration of Africa. It was a defect of Livingstone's leadership that he failed to bring out these qualities, although Thornton had already shown them in his excellent survey of the Zambezi River, and that they only emerged after he had escaped from the Expedition and the baneful influence of Livingstone's brother.

The case of Baines is more complicated, but here again the sinister role of Charles Livingstone was decisive. It will be recalled that the latter and Baines had made a trip in January to inspect the Kebrabasa Rapids at high water. Charles as usual collapsed as soon as he became tired, and Baines then went on alone, and after several days of very difficult travel succeeded in reaching the highest of the rapids and making a sketch of it. On his return two days later to the place where he had left Charles, he found that the latter had got tired of waiting and had gone off in the boat, leaving only a note. Baines, already exhausted, ill with fever and without provisions, had then to struggle on for another two and a half days before he reached the boat and found food and rest. "The last half day he was so weak and ill," Thornton wrote to his sister, "that he could not keep his legs; he fell down continually. When he got to Tete his knees and shins were a mass of bruises, and himself in high fever."[4]

After this the two young men could only have contempt for Charles Livingstone, and doubtless he was well aware of it. The upshot was related by Thornton in the same letter to his sister.

I must go back a little way now to tell you that ever since I arrived at Tete, the Dr. and I have not agreed at all, and his brother, who commonly goes by the name of 'the long one', had an old grudge against me because I would not let him have all his own way in the *Pearl,* and have not since shown him quite as much respect as he liked. Since Christmas he has (except when the Dr. was at Tete) been commanding officer at Tete: he has lived in state at one end of the house while Baines and myself have lived in one room at the other end. We only saw each other at meal times. Well, neither the Doctor nor his brother are liked by the Portuguese, so that he got no visitors, while lots came to our end; also presents of fruit, etc., were generally sent to our end, so he got spiteful, and set the Makololo to spy after all our doings indoors and out. Now the Makololo get lots of cloth, etc., from Mr. L., whilst if they came to our end of the house I always turned them out, so they wildly exaggerate any of our doings and 'the long one,' who keeps the public journal, added his own exaggerations and writes all off to Senna for the Dr. and by the time the Dr. arrived in June had a long bitter account against Baines and myself.[5]

Among the "doings" of the two reported to Livingstone was "skylarking" with the Portuguese, and this was their real offense in his eyes. Skylarking was bad enough in any circumstances to a man who, except possibly with his wife, had never had any fun in his whole life; but with the Portuguese—those decadent, corrupt, slaveowners—it was something quite beyond excuse, meriting the sternest punishment.

However, it was necessary to find some solider ground for convicting Baines, who at least could not be accused of laziness. He was therefore charged, on Charles Livingstone's evidence, with "having given away considerable quantities of public property (by your own confession) to Generoso and others"; with "skylarking with the Portuguese . . . taking the whaler without authority and very materially damaging the boat"; and with spending "Expedition's time and materials in painting Portuguese Portraits."

It is right that I should inform you [Livingstone continued in his letter of accusation] that Cdr. Bedingfield complained twice of your incompetency saying 'Old Baines knows nothing of storekeeping.' I never altered my conduct in the least to you in consequence, but now having seen the stores left to whoever chose to steal them, and Mr. Thornton even allowed to take what he liked in your presence, I hereby caution you that if what I have taken the trouble to arrange myself, so that you can easily examine them every day—and Sr. Sicard has engaged to take charge of them when you are ill—be not properly attended to, I must perform the painful duty of separating you from the Expedition.[6]

It is evident from this letter, written on July 11, 1859, that Livingstone himself did not feel there were sufficient grounds for anything more than a warning of dismissal if Baines's storekeeping did not improve. But shortly after this he left Tete in the *Ma Robert*, bound once again for the Shire, with his brother, Kirk and Rae on board. During the journey down the river he was got at again by his brother plying him with further details of Baines's alleged misdemeanors, in which Rae, a mischief-maker who to curry favor with Livingstone would tell stories against the others, probably joined. From an entry in his journal on July 28 it would appear that Livingstone accepted these additional accusations without question.

Found that a piece of serge belonging to Mr. Rae had disappeared and was in Baines' box. He gave away the mess wine to the Portuguese whenever they called on him. I saw him open one myself and then when he had finished it declared it had been fairly drunk at the mess table. He uniformly took precious care of his own things while secretly giving away the goods of the Expedition. . . . On reflecting on the matter I resolved to send the following and did so by Augustus, requesting Sr. Sicard to take charge.[7]

The "following" was another letter to Baines, dated "Senna, 21st July, 1859," informing him that "on further examination of your conduct in my absence: . . . it appears that while making away with large quantities of public property, you took very good care of your own private property." In consequence he was to consider his salary stopped and himself as separated from the Expedition from July 30. He was to hand over to the charge of Major Sicard, the obliging Portuguese commandant at Tete who had lent his house to the Expedition and was now asked to act as its honorary storekeeper, all public property and all his paintings and drawings, "properly secured." He might continue to use the artist's materials and draw his rations, but the earliest opportunity would be taken of sending him home. In Livingstone's best official style it was the sort of letter one might have written to a dishonest butler found drinking the vintage port.

It will be noted that Livingstone proffered no new charge against Baines, unless taking good care of his own private property was a crime. Nothing was said about the "piece of serge" allegedly stolen from Rae, while the "large quantities of public property" made away with were apparently the "mess wine" given to the Portuguese "whenever they called," as would be normal hospitality in the circumstances. Naturally Livingstone, who did not drink himself, was thrifty to the point of meanness and was ignorant of many social customs, could not see it in that light.

Having written the letter he was evidently conscious that he had not made out much of a case and added a postscript specifying his charges more precisely.

In a dispatch to the Foreign Secretary dated July 26, 1859, Livingstone reported briefly on the dismissal of the two men and promised fuller particulars later. "Their state of health," he added, "or rather weakness, prevented them being kept under my own eye. They could not rough it in the field and would not obey the officer left in charge of them."[8] This was a travesty of the truth: the facts were that Livingstone could not be bothered with the other members of the Expedition and was only too glad to find an excuse to reduce their number; that Baines was as willing to rough it as anybody else and much more so than Charles

Livingstone; and that the latter was quite unfit to be left in charge of anybody or anything. Livingstone, however, never scrupled to twist facts to his purpose when it was necessary to justify his own conduct.

By some unfortunate chance the letter of dismissal did not reach Baines at Tete till the beginning of September, long after Livingstone's damning report was on its way to England. On receiving it he immediately replied (in a letter to Livingstone dated September 10), rebutting all the charges. The most serious allegation was that *by his own confession* he had given away the Expedition's stores. Baines's answer to this was that the confession had been simply a repetition by himself, while lying in a state of delirium brought on by malaria, of the words of accusation spoken by Charles Livingstone. He admitted giving a few things to Sicard as a slight return for the latter's help to the Expedition in bringing the pinnace up to Tete after Livingstone had set him adrift in it on his way up the Zambezi. To do less would have been ungracious, to say the least. He had also made presents to other Portuguese, either under orders or on his own responsibility when he believed Livingstone would have approved. Of the five portraits complained of, two had been on the leader's instructions, while another had been reported and not objected to. In any case he never willingly undertook portrait painting, which was "not in his line." As for the damage to the whaler, it had capsized at its moorings in a storm and he had gone out, although ill, to help in righting it. In conclusion Baines wrote:

If you intend to send me home for prosecution, of course I do not object to it: but I protest against being sent home for any other purpose, being perfectly willing, as I have mentioned to you before, to serve without any further remuneration than that of being allowed to sketch whatever may be of interest in the countries we pass through.[9]

Baines's willingness to remain on without pay, and also to pay for any goods that had been lost, which he had already expressed to Livingstone on first being accused, was afterward taken as an admission of guilt; it was, however, perfectly in accord with

Baines's character. As storekeeper he was responsible for the goods and it was the gesture of an honest man to make good any loss, even if he was not to blame for it. As for working without pay, he was never interested in money, but was an enthusiastic traveler and artist, and asked for nothing better than to be allowed to work his way through Africa, earning his living by the sale of his pictures. This request, however, was refused.

Having got rid of Bedingfield, Baines and Thornton, the diminished Expedition steamed down the Zambezi en route for the coast, where another ship was expected. It was not a happy journey. There was fighting between the Sierra Leone Kroomen and the Makololo and a near mutiny was only quelled by Livingstone's intervention.

The head ones would not work and gave a look of defiance at the Doctor when he ordered them into the water to shove the ship off a bank. In a minute he was after them with the cook's ladle. They were too much for him, however, in the water. He fortunately came across the fellow who peeled my hand in the morning and gave him a thrashing. This was following the advice he gave me in the morning, to break their heads if they did not do as I told them, which plan of proceeding I objected to, as being rather out of place under such circumstances, I meant for my own dignity, not a bit for theirs.[10]

The entry in Livingstone's own journal is reticent about this incident. "Men much in the water shoving her off when aground" is all it says.[11]

By dint of being dragged so often over shoals the hull of the launch, only one-sixteenth inch thick to start with, was worn paper thin, and the vessel leaked like a sieve. In spite of frequent pumping the compartments were continually flooded and everything inside was permanently wet. The effect of such conditions, and of the unhealthy climate as they approached the delta, was demoralizing: Rae, the engineer, Walker, the quartermaster, and Rowe, the stoker, were all "sick and tired" of the Expedition and wanted to quit. Even the long-suffering Kirk was beginning to grumble inwardly, although he kept his thoughts in a private diary and wished "ten times the curses of Tristram Shandy" on anybody (like the present author) who subsequently used it "to prove anything."[12]

On July 30 they reached the mouth of the river and found a warship, H.M.S. *Persian,* anchored outside the bar. After supplying the Expedition with "salt provisions and slops," she took on board Walker, who was being invalided home, and the twelve Kroomen, who were being sent back to Sierra Leone, before sailing for the Cape with Livingstone's dispatches.

The next day the launch was beached for repairs to its bottom. It was found impossible to replace the plates and the best that could be done was to plug the numerous holes with clay in canvas bags. A week later, while on the way up the river, the launch touched a rock and began to take water again, necessitating another overhaul. To make matters worse, the funnel was in holes, the bridge of the boiler broke for the fourth time, and the Makololo crew, with no experience as sailors, were unskilled and rebellious. When one of them, acting as stoker, "seemed inclined to promote a general mutiny," Livingstone "gave him a beating with a flat piece of wood about 2 inches broad and thin," but afterward "felt it was degrading to be obliged to punish Matengo."[13]

Livingstone did not believe in beating Negroes, and that twice in six weeks he should have been constrained to do so against all his principles and to his own disgust is a measure of the difficulties he was faced with and the strain they imposed on him. But dismissals, disaffection, mutinies and dependence on a crazy boat which might founder at any moment did not stop him from dreaming his dreams and weaving his schemes.

Private. Have a strong desire to commence a system of colonization of the honest poor: I would give £2000 or £3000 for the purpose. Intend to write to my friend Young about it and authorise him to draw if the project seems feasible. The Lord remember my desire, sanctify my motives and purify all my desires.[14]

While steaming up the Shire at night the launch ran on a bank and was then carried by the current out to midstream. Two boats towing astern were brought broadside on and the first one was swamped. All its occupants were rescued except two, who were carried downstream. One of these, who could not swim, was picked up by a canoe a mile farther down, but the canoe overturned and the man was saved just in time by the arrival in a boat of Rowe and a seaman called Hutchins, who had replaced Walker, the quartermaster, when the latter was invalided home. The other man sank at once and was never seen again. "This puts a damper on all our spirits," Livingstone wrote. The boats were overloaded with the Makololo, for whom there was no room in the launch, and the cause of the accident, according to Kirk, was a sudden turn which placed the towing rope at right angles to the leading boat. Considering the utter confusion which followed, that the launch, with one boat under its stern and another tied to it, was disabled, and that its "decks were so full of men that we could do nothing without capsizing the ship," it was a miracle that no more lives were lost.

Livingstone's objective now was the other and larger lake of which he had received definite information on his second visit to the Shire, and he was spurred on by news, brought by the *Persian,* of the spectacular success of Burton and Speke in discovering Lakes Tanganyika and Victoria Nyanza. Livingstone had feared that the two explorers might be making for *his* lake, but that prize was still unclaimed and he was in a hurry to reach it before anyone else.

In the last week of August 1859 the leaking vessel and its tenders arrived at Chibisa's, the last village before the Murchison Falls. From here Livingstone, his brother, Kirk and Rae, with thirty-six Makololo attendants and two guides, set off on foot for the north, leaving the launch once again in charge of Rowe and another sailor.

Livingstone's account of this overland journey, which resulted in the discovery of Lake Nyassa, takes nearly thirty pages of his published *Narrative* and is filled with descriptions of the country and its people, which he evidently remembered with pleasure. It was a relief to them all to get away from the cramped quarters and everlasting damp of the *Ma Robert,* and in the cool, dry air of the highlands which they were now crossing, the spirits of the party revived. Livingstone was out of his element on water, but once on dry land, meeting new people at every stop, with a constantly changing scene and a worthwhile goal ahead, his zest for travel returned.

Moreover, his policy of peaceful penetration was paying off. His two previous visits to the Shire had allayed the fears of the Manganja tribesmen living along the river. They had seen that the Englishmen, although prepared to defend themselves, had no aggressive intention; that they wanted to trade but disapproved of slave dealing; that they had a book which they claimed to contain the Word of God, and that this might well be a form of witchcraft superior to their own which it would be wise to treat with respect; and that the book said they were to grow cotton which the English would come and buy. As a result, on this third visit, there had been no trouble with the river people on the way up.

What reception they would meet in future from those who would be seeing white men for the first time was less certain, and Livingstone was taking no risks. The four white men carried revolvers and the thirty-six Makololo were armed with muskets, which, although probably more dangerous to themselves than any enemy, made a good show of force. In any event there was no need to use force, the only person who tried to stop the party being a drunken tribesman who stood in its path and was removed with a push and a slap in the face.

Although the distance to be covered in a straight line was barely 100 miles, the journey, through strange country, took nearly three weeks. The chiefs of the villages were suspicious and often refused to supply guides or even give any information as to the route. At one point the whole party became ill and suspected they had been poisoned, until it was discovered that the cook had put a whole can of "paste" in the mulligatawny soup. Charles Livingstone, always the weakest link in the chain, was unable to move and the rest had to wait several days while he recovered.

On September 17, 1859, Livingstone made a one-line entry in his journal: "Reached Lake Nyassa from which the Shire emerges." As far as exploration was concerned, this was the highlight of the Zambezi Expedition and one of the outstanding feats which establish Livingstone as the greatest discoverer of his age. At the time, however, though pleased to have beaten his rival,* he was more interested in the possibilities of developing the country he had come through for cotton growing and putting a stop to the slave trade.

While in the vicinity of the lake they had run into a party of Arab slavers, with their chained and yoked captives, and discovered that the main slave route from the interior forded the Shire River just south of the lake, whence it continued due east to the coast. This suggested to Livingstone an easy means for putting an end to the trade.

> It is highly probable [he wrote to the Foreign Secretary on October 15] that a small steamer on the Shire and Lake Nyassa would, through the influence of the English name, prevent slave parties from passing the fords and should our merchants not be obliged to pay dues for entering upon English discoveries for trade by a part of the Zambezi unused by the Portuguese, goods could be furnished to the native traders at Lake Nyassa as cheap as they can get them on the East coast which involved a month's journey farther.[15]

The point, of course, being that if the native traders could obtain these goods, and pay for them with agricultural products, they would not need to deal in slaves and the human traffic would wither away for want of incentive. Or so Livingstone believed.

This plan now took complete possession of him. The Kebrabasa obstacle no longer mattered. In the Nyassa highlands he thought he had found a healthier and more fertile region than the one on the Batoka Plateau, north of the Victoria Falls, which had been the original objective of the Expedition. Here also he saw the chance of realizing his cherished scheme to plant a British colony in Central Africa.

---

* Dr. Albrecht Roscher, the German explorer, reached Lake Nyassa from the Rovuma River two months after Livingstone and was murdered on his way back.

Presuming that H.M.Govt. has acceded to our application for a proper steamer for the Zambezi, this steamer might . . . do good service by affording free passages from England or from the Cape of a few volunteer settlers of good character who might render essential service to the cause of African civilization and the production of the raw materials of our manufactures, by giving an example of lawful trading and improved agriculture. There is no doubt but that the chief hope is in the Africans themselves, yet the presence of a small body of colonists with their religious and mercantile institutions, industriously developing the resources of the country, would materially accelerate the movement . . . It may seem premature to advert to this when so much remains to be done before the way is fairly open for settlement, but it seems right to mention the impressions made on the mind by the magnificent healthy region we have discovered and remembering the sore evils which press on our overcrowded population at home while the great Father of all has provided room enough to spare for all his offspring. It is to be borne in mind that the tract of country which so delighted my companions by its beauty and numbers of running rills at the driest season of the year is but a small corner of hundreds of miles which I passed through to the West almost unoccupied by Man and which, from its fertility and abundance of water, is quite capable of becoming a counterpoise to the American Slave states.[16]

There is a confidence, an eloquence, a controlled excitement in this passage which suggests that Livingstone at that moment felt that he had arrived at a point where vast new vistas were opening up. It was as if the goal to which he had been groping his way through so many years of toil and struggle, of hardship and danger, had suddenly appeared in all its shining glory and the promised land was at last within reach. For all the pieces with which he had been juggling now seemed to be coming together, forming a blueprint for the rescue and civilization of Africa: ousting of the slave trade by "lawful commerce," education of the African by the example of white settlers, production of raw materials, especially cotton, which would make the English manufacturers independent of the American slave labor they so much disapproved of, and finally another outlet for British emigrants.

The last was a new element in Livingstone's thinking and the more he thought of it the more important it became for him. Nobody knew better the miserable conditions of the British working class of his time. Had he himself not been sent, at the age of eight, to work for fourteen hours a day in a Lanarkshire cotton mill? He had seen, and for a time lived in, the slums of Glasgow and London and had been a daily witness of their appalling poverty, fetid squalor, drunkenness, vices and crime. In the matter of human degradation, indeed, there was not much to choose between the condition of the poor in England and that of the African in his primitive hut. How much better they would be cultivating the fertile soil of the healthy highlands of Nyassa!

The only snag was the obstructive presence of the Portuguese, but Livingstone now saw a way to get round this. In another dispatch[17] he had contested their right to impede the free navigation of the Zambezi as far as its confluence with the Shire, arguing that they never used the lower Zambezi, had never discovered where it could be entered from the sea, and did not control the right bank, which was at the mercy of the Landeens, or Zulus. As for the Shire itself they had never explored it for more than a few miles and dared not go up it. Why therefore should English merchants pay dues to Portuguese officials who could not even protect them?

All this might be true, but it was equally clear that the Portuguese were not going to accept Livingstone's proposition that "whatever may have been the position of the Portuguese establishments in former times, they cannot now be considered Colonies," or surrender their control, however theoretical it might be, of the Zambezi. As we have seen, Lisbon had already given orders for a customs house to be set up at the Kongone mouth of the river, discovered by Livingstone, and he had obligingly supplied local officials with information how to get there. Nor could he really hope, in spite of all his urgings, that the British Government would be prepared to put pressure on Portugal to make the Zambezi free.

It was therefore necessary to find an alternative access route to the interior entirely outside Portuguese control, and the one that suggested itself to Livingstone was the Rovuma River. Forming what at present is the northern frontier of Mozambique, this river runs into the Indian Ocean at about the same latitude as the northern end of Lake Nyassa. If by any chance it connected with the lake, then Livingstone's problem was solved.

It has been visited several times by H.M. Cruisers [he wrote to the Foreign Office], and found to possess a deep and safe entrance without any bar. It is reported by the inhabitants to be navigable for fifty leagues inland and, as put down in the Admiralty chart, coincides exactly with what we suppose to be the upper end of Lake Nyassa. It agrees too with the statement of the natives that 'the Lake went a long way to the North and then turned round to the sea.' An intelligent woman stated that she had gone from the Lake to the sea by going along its banks while her master pursued the same course in a canoe.[18]

He thought it possible, therefore, that the Rovuma would prove a better way to the lake than the Shire, besides having the advantage of being beyond the claims of the Portuguese, should they "obstinately refuse free entrance by the Zambezi."

But whether by the Rovuma or the Shire there would be cataracts in the way, which would obstruct the passage of the Expedition's steamer. To get round this obstacle Livingstone asked the Government to supply another and smaller vessel, "capable of being unscrewed into pieces of 300 lbs. or 400 lbs. each." The pieces could be carried overland on "two strong Scotch carts drawn by mules." Four "volunteer sappers" could undertake the work and if they were "privates of good character on double full pay" would be preferable to any other Europeans, "especially," Livingstone added, perhaps thinking of his brother, "of that class that readily engages in what seems romantic and instantly collapse on coming to hard matter-of-fact toil." The sappers could also help in building a road past the cataracts and erecting blockhouses to be used as trading stations.

Thus Livingstone set out his new master plan, different both in scope and direction from the one he had proposed just two years before and to which the Government had given their approval. None of the original objectives had been achieved, and he no longer seemed interested in them. He had discovered a much more promising field for his activity and all his thoughts now ran on colonization. This was a radical departure from anything he had suggested before, and if approved would commit the Government much further than they had contemplated. He could therefore scarcely expect a quick decision, and knew that in any case it would be many months before he could receive any reply. Meanwhile, the conviction that he had hit on the only solution, not only for the problem of underpopulated Africa, but also for that of overpopulated Britain, continued to crystallize in his mind.

The plan which rises up before my mind in desiring to act for the benefit of my fellow men during the portion of my life that may still be allotted to me on earth, is to make Africa north of Lat. 15° South a blessing to Africans and to Englishmen. The sons of the soil need not be torn from their homes in order to contribute to the wealth of the world. There is room for them where they are, and they may be led to produce their quota, and a large one, to the circulating wealth of the world. There is room and to spare for English emigrants to settle on and work the virgin soil of the still untilled land of Ham. As the African need not be torn from his country and enslaved, no more need the English poor be crowded together in unwholesome dens, debarred from breathing the pure air of Heaven. There is room for all in the wide and glorious domains of the Lord, king of all the Earth.[19]

Worried about the state of the launch, which he had left in a sinking condition, Livingstone did not dally by the lake and after two days the party started on the return journey. After a detour to ascend Mount Zomba, which Charles Livingstone was too weak to climb, they returned to the *Ma Robert* on October 8, after an absence of forty days during which they had marched 250 miles. All of them, including Livingstone, were in bad shape, as Kirk recorded.

Dr. L. is passing a great amount of blood and is quite sick. Mr. C. L. is all done up with the late fatigue, and Mr. Rae no better than he ought to be. In fact 250 miles at this season and in this country on foot and on strange food is enough for the strongest and to have no better fare, not even flour or biscuit or decent sugar when on the return, is more than anyone can stand between the wet and dry. Mr. C. L. . . . horribly disagreeable company.[20]

Weather excessively hot [noted Livingstone], renders me for the first time in Africa useless. . . . Very ill with bleeding from bowels and purging. Bled all night. Got up at 1 A.M. to take Latitude.[21]

While the party were recuperating below the Murchison Falls, they received news that H.M.S. *Lynx* was off the coast and waiting to rendezvous with the Expedition. This seemed to Livingstone a good opportunity for disposing of Baines and Thornton, whom he was anxious to see out of the country as soon as possible. He therefore gave orders to Kirk and Rae to proceed overland to Tete and bring Thornton and Baines down to the harbor of Kongone together with materials to mend the bottom of the launch. Seemingly as an afterthought he also instructed Kirk to "examine Baines's boxes and take over all public property in his charge." This may have been suggested by Charles Livingstone, or Livingstone himself may have thought that he needed more evidence to justify his dismissal of Baines.

After a grueling journey, racked with fever and suffering from thirst and hunger, the two men arrived at Tete. Thornton had left on an expedition upcountry and Baines was away at the coal field, but he returned the same evening. Kirk carried out his distasteful task of searching Baines's luggage with tact and consideration. With the possible exception of a piece of naval canvas, which Baines could have brought back from his Australian venture, he found no Expedition property. As to the stores, there was one cask of sugar unaccounted for, but this could have been stolen when there was nowhere to lock up the goods, or could have been consumed without proper entry. It was certainly not sold or eaten by Baines. He had given "two boxes of sardine to Rapozo and several things to Tito (Major Sicard) when he was on his way up in the pinnace," but these, he claimed, were in return for services rendered to the Expedition. In short, Kirk found no evidence that Baines had been dishonest.

That Baines had been so accused naturally aroused the sympathies of the Portuguese he had made friends with, and they showed their indignation at the injustice of the charge by refusing to provide men and canoes to take the Englishmen down the river. It was only with great difficulty that Kirk succeeded in getting a crew. For this Baines was later accused by Livingstone of "stirring up" the Portuguese against the Expedition.

Arriving at the mouth of the river on November 20, they found the *Ma Robert* beached "in a horrible state" and Livingstone and Rae waiting for the arrival of the warship. Here Baines was summoned to the presence of Livingstone and subjected to cross-examination in inquisitorial style. All the old charges, which he had already answered, were repeated, and new ones added, such as owing Livingstone some money and drawing a bill on the Expedition for his expenses at Tete after his salary was stopped. When it came to the missing cask of sugar, Baines demanded to know where the evidence was that he had taken it. But his answers were sometimes confused, as well they might be after all he had gone through, and according to Kirk he had "no presence of mind in making replies." He asked to be taken back to Tete, where he had left his boxes, so that the matter could be properly investigated at the scene of the alleged offense, but this was refused. He then demanded to be given a fair trial in the nearest British town; this too was refused. Finally he was judged by Livingstone to be guilty, placed under what amounted to open arrest and, pending his shipment out of the country, condemned to live apart—"like a moral leper," as his biographer puts it—in one of the whaleboats, with a sail as an awning.[22]

I do not allow Baines to come to our table [wrote Livingstone], but send him a good share of all we eat ourselves.[23]

How generous! Some of the other members of the Expedition showed more humanity. They helped Baines with money and any clothes they could spare, since he had left his own at Tete, apparently expecting to return there, together with his notes, sketches and pictures. Most of these he never saw again.

On December 7 he was told by Livingstone to prepare himself to board H.M.S. *Lynx,* which had arrived a few days previously.

He made a final plea to be given a chance to clear himself by proper trial, but once again Livingstone refused on the grounds that it would hold up the work of the Expedition. When Baines complained that unless he was duly prosecuted the imputation of dishonesty would stick to him for life, Livingstone replied that he had been given an opportunity of explaining and it had been unsatisfactory. In other words, he had constituted himself prosecutor, judge and jury, and allowed no appeal.

Two of the *Lynx*'s boats had capsized while crossing the bar, fortunately with no loss of life, but with the loss of mail for the Expedition. Her departure was further delayed while her crew transferred stores and helped in repairing the *Ma Robert*. She sailed eventually, with Baines on board, on December 20 and a week later landed him at Cape Town. From there he wrote a letter to the Foreign Secretary, setting out the whole affair and again demanding a fair trial.[24] Lord John Russell was for submitting the matter to referees at the Cape, but he was talked out of this by Washington, who was then asked to examine the case himself. Inevitably he came down on the side of Livingstone. "Where there is an absence of military or naval command and discipline," he had written in the case of Bedingfield, "some powerful stimulus must be applied to keep a selfish or bad-tempered or troublesome man under control and I know of none more sure than the power in the hands of the leader to stop the pay, in case of non-compliance with reasonable orders, or of obstructive behaviour." As for Baines, "the best point in his favour," Washington wrote, "was that he remitted half his pay to an aged mother in Norfolk. However, the leader's word must be law where there is no other law." So Baines's plea was rejected.

Baines was not without friends at the Cape who had heard of his treatment by Livingstone, and one of them persuaded the Attorney General to look into his case. The result was as to be expected from a member of the Government. While admitting that "Dr. Livingstone's procedure in regard to Mr. Baines was neither well considered nor well conducted," he was also satisfied that "having done all he could to obtain a full investigation into his conduct Mr. Baines was wasting his time by pursuing the notion of a trial."

Refusing to be discouraged, Baines strove for the next seven years, "with a persistence," as his biographer writes, "which in itself is strongest proof of innocence," to induce Livingstone to do him justice, but without success. Meanwhile he continued his career as artist and traveler, made a number of notable journeys and acquired the reputation of an explorer of courage, resource, enterprise and integrity. He led several expeditions from the Cape into the interior, and when he died at the age of fifty-five was one of the colony's most respected pioneers.

Nobody who knew Baines well believed for an instant that he was capable of a dishonest act. Kirk, Rae and Sicard, who investigated the question of the missing stores at Livingstone's request, all testified in his favor, and nobody who has studied the episode since has come to any other conclusion. The worst he could be accused of was carelessness, as is admitted even by Dean Seaver, the latest biographer of Livingstone and one of his most fervent admirers.

As to his defects as store-keeper [Seaver writes], (a task for which he was totally unfitted) the remark of Kirk, 'Baines is a good-natured soul,' says much and probably explains everything.[25]

It was typical of Livingstone that having done his best to destroy Baines's character he refused ever to admit that he might have been wrong and felt only resentment at Baines's attempts to establish his innocence, which he took as a personal injury. In a letter to Murchison[26] written several years later, after his return to England, he sought to justify his action on the grounds that the diminution of the stores had made the Expedition short of provisions and but for the unexpected arrival of fresh supplies would have exposed its members to "a course of low diet" which might have had "fatal results." If this was true it is curious that no mention of it was made at the time by either Livingstone or Kirk in their respective journals, or by Livingstone when making his full report (of December 17, 1859) to the Foreign Office.[27] It seems more likely, in fact, that it was something Livingstone thought up afterward, like the story that Baines and Thornton indulged in "orgies" with the Portuguese. This was a ridiculous description of the mild little parties in which on occasion they took part, but of course any drinking was an "orgy" to Livingstone. It was true that left to their own devices the two young men were on friendly terms with the local Portuguese (which it behooved them as foreign visitors to be), and may well have preferred such company to that of their egregious compatriot Charles Livingstone, and it was this really that Livingstone could not forgive, rather than the fact that a few stores were missing.

As to the manner of getting rid of Baines, Livingstone wrote sanctimoniously in the same letter to Murchison, "in sending him away I did it in the mode least calculated to injure his future prospects. I *published nothing*, and had Mr. Baines been advised by some of those whom he quotes as friends to follow the same course the whole affair would long ago have been forgotten."

As if it were any better for a man to be falsely accused of stealing in front of three other persons than in front of a hundred or a million; and as if a man so accused would ever want the affair to be forgotten until he had been given a chance to clear his name! The person in whose interest it was that the affair should be forgotten was Livingstone, and because Baines would not allow this he carried his spite against him for years, even recurring to it on his last and fatal journey.[28]

9

The Long March

January 1860–November 1860

THE LOSS of the mailbag depressed them all. It was more than a year since any letters had been received from home, and since they were about to start for another expedition to the interior, it might be eight or nine months more before they got any. As Livingstone was to observe in the *Narrative*, "twenty months is a weary time to be without news of family or friends."

More serious for the leader of the Expedition was to have had no official reply to the dozen or so dispatches he had sent off over the preceding six months. He did not know, for example, whether his request for another vessel had been approved, or his exploration of the Shire, or the dismissal of Baines and Thornton six months previously. Until he had the reaction of the Foreign Office to his various proposals he could make no further plans.

Enforced inactivity was always bad for Livingstone, and he vented his spleen by railing in his journal at those whom he considered as having by their conduct betrayed the Expedition: Bedingfield, Baines, Thornton and that archvillain Laird, the shipbuilder.

The botanist and my own assistant have fully answered my expectations, but the scientific staff has entailed a very large amount of drudgery on me of a nature which would have suited a street porter better than a regenerator of Africa. Instead of doing good service to the cause of African civilization I have been forced to drive a steamer, carry luggage, attend to commissariat as it were, instead of exploring and, by intercourse with the natives, gaining their confidence. All the exploration effected would have been better done alone, or with my brother alone . . . a defect in my plan was not foreseeing the contingency of dishonesty.[1]

A man who had endured so much as Livingstone—from sickness, discomfort, inadequate diet, mosquitoes, heat, damp, isolation, frustration—all in the cause of humanity, cannot but command our sympathy. And yet for most of what he complained of he was himself most to blame: he had made the plan, chosen the team, and if some of them had failed him it was not for want of good will or honesty, but because they were either unsuitable, like Bedingfield, or mishandled, like Baines and Thornton.

Nor were the results so far achieved negligible, although disappointing in comparison with what had been hoped for. One of the objects of the Expedition—indeed the first object—was to survey the Zambezi, and this had been done as far as the Kebrabasa Rapids. That they constituted an impassable obstacle to further navigation was not Livingstone's fault. He had also surveyed the Shire River to its source, discovered one of the largest lakes in Africa and found a fertile, healthy country, fit for white settlers, whose presence he believed would put an end to the slave trade. Considering all the difficulties these were no mean feats, which another explorer would have felt as sufficient justification for returning home to rest and recuperate. But Livingstone was not like any other explorer and was always impatient to be doing more. Moreover, his reputation was such that the impossible was expected of him and he could not afford to fail.

Since, however, the two-year term of the Expedition would soon be up, and its extension required the sanction of the British Government, no new project could be embarked on for the time being. Livingstone, therefore, decided that it was a good moment to fulfill his promise to conduct his Makololo followers back to their homeland. This would involve a march of more than 600 miles each way, from Tete to beyond the Victoria Falls and back, and was likely to take at least six months. The Makololo had been provided by their chief, Sekeletu, to accompany Livingstone as porters and escort on his journey down the Zambezi four years before. He had left them at Tete after promising to return the following year and lead them home. Originally there had been more than 100, but a number had died of disease or been killed, while others had taken wives and settled down, or been engaged by Livingstone for the Expedition. None of them were in a hurry to leave. He had proposed sending his brother instead, but the men, who had no liking for Charles Livingstone, had declined, making the excuse that they had been told by their chief to wait for Livingstone and would be disobeying orders if they returned without him.

For the other members of the Expedition this was Livingstone's affair and had little interest for themselves.

A party with the Doctor go to Sekeletu's [wrote Kirk]. Rae returns at his request to England. Baines goes off now with the *Lynx*. What I do, I know not yet. It seems I can do very little on a tramping excursion of such duration.[2]

Rae was going home to supervise the construction of the new steamer which Livingstone had asked for: the one that could be "unscrewed" and carried overland for launching on Lake Nyassa. The Foreign Office had not yet received his request for this additional vessel, and it seemed rather unlikely that they would be willing to pay for a third boat. But in the event of their refusal he was prepared to foot the bill himself.

If Government furnishes the means, all right [he wrote to Murchison]; if not I shall spend my book-money on it. I don't need to touch the children's fund, and mine could not be better spent. People who are born rich sometimes become miserable from fear of becoming poor; but I have the advantage, you see, of not being afraid to die poor. If I live I must succeed in what I have undertaken; death alone will put a stop to my efforts.[3]

His first book had already earned him £12,000 in royalties, about half of which he had set aside for the education of his family, leaving him at least £6,000, which was a considerable sum in those days.

In a letter (February 17, 1860) to the Foreign Secretary announcing the return of Rae he strongly recommended the engineer, while also taking the opportunity of having another dig at Laird.

He has behaved exceedingly well all the time he has been with us and, as he feels so much interest in the undertaking as to offer to invest his savings (£200) in the vessel, his superintendence would secure everything being done in the most workmanlike manner. This to us, who have undergone so much vexation, delay and toil from a dishonestly constructed vessel and engine, appears of the utmost importance.[4]

Kirk described Rae as "too timid and lazy" to go hunting, and as "a thorough canny, somewhat two-faced Scotchman, a fine fellow, however, especially for an engineer at sea." He seems to have been a gossip and, to ingratiate himself with Livingstone, may well have told tales against Baines. But everyone agreed that he was a good engineer and he must have been to keep the *Ma Robert* going for so long.

After the departure of Rae the membership of the Expedition, originally seven, was reduced to three: Livingstone, his brother Charles and Kirk. Two other white men who acted in a subordinate capacity were the naval stoker, Rowe, and the seaman Hutchins. The reduction in numbers of the personnel was undoubtedly a relief to Livingstone, and he would probably have got rid of Kirk had the latter not made himself so useful. Kirk could get on with all the others, even Charles, although it is clear from his private diary that he detested the "moral agent." He kept his own counsel and, as doctors usually do, always managed to keep going when everyone else was sick. However, he had really had enough of the Expedition by now and was not looking forward to the trip with the Makololo, especially if it was to be done "on the cheap Missionary Society plan." Nevertheless he "should not think of leaving the Doctor alone at this time, that is if he wishes me."[5]

Livingstone planned to start for the interior early in the new year (1860), but on arriving at Tete at the beginning of February he found that the harvest had failed and that there would be difficulty in obtaining food for the party on the way. He therefore decided to defer the departure and in the meantime to go down to the coast again in the hope of finding another warship with letters and dispatches. Thornton, who had just returned from his trip to Zumbo, was offered a passage down the river to enable him to take ship for England, but refused it; although no longer a member of the Expedition he wished to remain in Africa to work on his own and was keen to look for a silver mine reputedly existing at Chicova, above the Kebrabasa Rapids.

While it took from a month to six weeks to ascend the river, the descent could be made in ten days, so by the third week in February they were back at the coast, having learned on the way that the missing mailbag had been recovered from the sea and passed them on its way up to Tete. Three weeks were now spent looking in vain for a ship, while Rae occupied himself once again patching the holes in the launch and the others hunted for fresh food or defended themselves against the mosquitoes, which were "fearful." When, tired of waiting, they eventually headed upstream again, it was to find that the launch, now literally on its last legs—since it was sliding or being dragged across the bed of the Zambezi as often as floating freely—could scarcely stem the current. Its consumption of wood was enormous, and there were stops every hour to enable the boiler to get up a sufficient head of steam. An advance of six miles, helped by the breeze, was considered a good day's run.

When off the entrance to the Shire Livingstone received a letter which "rejoiced his heart." It was from the Bishop of Cape Town, had taken a year to arrive and informed him of the plan to send out to him a Universities Mission headed by Bishop Mackenzie. The Mission had been recruited from Oxford and Cambridge and was the direct result of the wild enthusiasm aroused by an address Livingstone had given at Cambridge, during his last stay in England, in which he had predicted his own death in Africa and appealed to the audience to carry on his work. In a letter to the Bishop of Oxford expressing his gratitude he described the news as "the best . . . we have ever had in Africa." He recommended the Manganja country on the banks of the Shire as a suitable site for the Mission, and a "steamer to serve as home until they have a better." He particularly approved of the appointment of a bishop in command, commenting "we should have been the better of one in the Bechuana country."[6]

Returning to Tete at the end of April 1860, Livingstone immediately started preparations for the overland journey to Barotseland. The *Ma Robert* was berthed at an island, where the two sailors left in charge of her were to occupy their time in growing food for themselves. The cloth, beads and brass wire needed for barter on the journey were packd in canvas bags and each package printed with the name of its bearer. Five oxen were purchased to provide meat. At the last moment a number of Makololo, who had made a new home for themselves in the neighborhood, decided they would be better off by remaining where they were. In the end the party was reduced to about eighty, of whom nearly a third deserted and returned to Tete within a few days after their departure from it, a defection which Livingstone attributed to the bad influence of the Portuguese.

It was during this period of preparation that Livingstone's eyes were opened to the unpleasant character of his brother and that the two engaged in the first of many public quarrels. It all started, according to Kirk, when David accused Charles of allowing one of his pillows to be ruined. This provoked Charles into criticizing David's leadership, not without some justification. To criticize Livingstone, however, was to make an enemy of him, even when the critic was his own brother, and thereafter he had little use for Charles. He gives his version of their first quarrel in his journal. It suggests, perhaps, that his leadership suffered from a double fault, first in putting too much trust in subordinates and then in going to the other extreme by withdrawing his trust completely.

My brother informs me that the members of the Expedition did not get orders what to do, and were always at a loss how to act. . . . All were willing and anxious to help if only I would have told them. He never told me this before. I have given written orders to all and when Bedingfield failed, took his part upon me so far as I was able in order to allow each to follow his own department untrammelled by other duties. On principle I abstained

> from multiplying orders, believing it is more agreeable to men to do their duty in their own way. It is irksome to most men to be in any degree driven as soldiers and sailors are.

Sound enough in theory, but when it was patently clear that the younger members did need more direction it would have been better to give it.

As for Charles:

> Since he seems to let out in a moment of irritation a long pent-up feeling I am at a loss to know how to treat him. As an assistant he has been of no value. Photography very unsatisfactory. Magnetism still more so. Meteorological observations not creditable, and writing the journal in arrears. In going up with us now he is useless, as he knows nothing of Portuguese or native language. He often expected me to be his assistant instead of acting as mine. This ebullition happened because I found fault with his destroying my pillow. It was, he said, all my fault. . . . He allowed £100 of Magnetical Instruments to be completely destroyed by damp, but must not be blamed.[7]

Livingstone's account of the return journey to the interior, between the middle of May and the end of November 1860, is the longest and most entertaining section of the *Narrative*, occupying about a quarter of the book. It is also among the best travel stories ever written, and displays to the full the explorer's extraordinary gifts of observation and description, which have contributed as much to his reputation as his actual achievement. His curiosity was insatiable, and whether it was animal, vegetable or mineral, nothing worth recording escaped his notice. A scientific training had taught him to look for the causes of things, while his range of interests was increased by wide reading. What engaged his attention above all were the native peoples and their customs. Speaking and understanding their language he was able not only to converse with Africans, but also to grasp—what was often more significant and important to him—what they were saying among themselves. Some of his most amusing anecdotes are derived from overhearing conversation between his Makololo attendants or between them and other tribesmen met on the way. It was his eye and ear for detail, however, which made him such a brilliant reporter. Consider, for example, this description of an elephant feast.

The cutting up of an elephant is quite a unique spectacle. The men stand round the animal in dead silence, while the chief of the travelling party declares that, according to ancient law, the head and right hind-leg belong to him who killed the beast, that is to him who inflicted the first wound; the left leg to him who delivered the second, or first touched the animal after it fell; the meat around the eye to the English, or chief of the travellers, and different parts to the headmen of the different fires, or groups, of which the camp is composed; not forgetting to enjoin the preservation of the fat and the bowels for a second distribution. This oration finished, the natives soon became excited, and scream wildly as they cut away at the carcass with a score of spears, whose long handles quiver in the air above their heads. Their excitement becomes momentarily more and more intense, and reaches the culminating point when, as denoted by the roar of gas, the huge mass is laid fairly open. Some jump inside and roll about there in their eagerness to seize the precious fat, while others run off screaming, with pieces of the bloody meat, throw it on the grass and run back for more: all keep talking and shouting at the utmost pitch of their voices. Sometimes two or three, regardless of all laws, seize the same piece of meat, and have a brief fight of words over it. Occasionally an agonized yell bursts forth, and a native emerges out of the moving mass of dead elephant and wriggling humanity, with his hand badly cut by the spear of his excited friend and neighbour: this requires a rag and some soothing words to prevent bad blood. In an incredibly short space of time tons of meat are cut up, and placed in separate heaps around.[8]

It must be remembered that Livingstone was writing for a public as avid for information about Darkest Africa as people today are curious about outer space. But if he let himself go in his tale of this journey it was because he remembered it as a relatively happy interlude in the checkered story of the Zambezi Expedition. The worst of his troubles to date—Bedingfield, Baines, Thornton—were behind him, and those to come he could not foresee. He had left the accursed *Ma Robert* and, although sleeping every night on the ground under an open sky, at least enjoyed a dry bed. It was gratifying, too, to meet with such a friendly reception. Four years before, when following the same route in the opposite direction as the first white man ever to use it, some of the natives had been suspicious and their attitude threatening. But as one returning among them in fulfillment of a promise he was received with honors in every village, and toward the end the journey became a triumphal progress in which he was greeted everywhere with gifts and offers of help.

And yet we can see from his journal that it was not quite such plain sailing as appears in the *Narrative*. Desertions on the way increased the loads on the remaining porters and they "grumbled perpetually," making the journey "excessively disagreeable." On one occasion some of them refused to start in the morning, and only laughed when Livingstone threatened them with his stick, until he "applied it to two of their posteriors." On June 9, after they had been going for three weeks, he notes: "People are very obstinate and my brother keeping up his sulks ever since we left Tete." In an entry two days later he is evidently repeating some of the things said of him to his face by Charles.

Manners of a cotton spinner, of the Boers; didn't know how to treat men. An old filthy pillow that I got the benefit of it; that I cursed him, that I set the devil into him, etc., and asked if it was not his work to take time for me, and repeated again and again that I had cursed him. What part of Botany is Sunday cursing. Seemed intent on a row. Would be but a short time in the Expedition: regretted that he was on this journey. Would rejoice when he could leave it. So far my brother Charles.[9]

That there was a grain of truth, at least in the accusation that he did not know how to treat men—that is, white men, because nobody ever suggested that he could not handle blacks—made it all the more hurtful. It was Charles who had egged him on against the other members of the Expedition, and here he was suggesting that perhaps after all it was partly Livingstone's own fault that he had quarreled with them. Worse, however, to a sensitive man, was the revelation of his brother's true character and his capacity for hating his own kin. Charles had been engaged for the Expedition as its "moral agent"—that is, as the person who by teaching and example should be its principal advertisement for Christianity, but instead he was behaving like a vicious guttersnipe.

Soon, however, the regular routine of the long march was absorbing all the energies of the party.

We rise about five, or as soon as dawn appears, take a cup of tea and a bit of biscuit; the servants fold up the blankets and stow them away in the bags they carry; the others tie their fumbas and cooking pots to each end of their carrying sticks, which are borne on the shoulder; the cook secures the dishes, and all are on the path by sunrise. If a convenient spot can be found we halt for breakfast about nine a.m. To save time this meal is generally cooked the night before and has only to be warmed. We continue the march after breakfast, rest a little in the middle of the day, and break off early in the afternoon. We average from two to two-and-a-half miles an hour in a straight line, or, as the crow flies, and seldom have five or six hours a day of actual travel. This in a hot climate is as much as a man can accomplish without being oppressed; and we always try to make our progress more a pleasure than a toil. To hurry over the ground, abuse, and look ferocious at one's native companions, merely for the foolish vanity of boasting how quickly a distance was accomplished, is a combination of silliness with absurdity quite odious.[10]

After pitching camp one or two of the whites would set off to hunt, a regular supply of fresh meat being necessary both to themselves and the men. They liked to take a man with them to bring back the game, and if nobody volunteered because all were too tired, they were tempted to bring back only enough for themselves, thus, as Livingstone wrote (perhaps with memories of his own childhood in Blantyre), "sending the 'idle ungrateful poor' supperless to bed." "And yet," he adds, "it is only by continuance in well-doing, even to the length of what the worldly-wise call weakness, that the conviction is produced anywhere that our motives are high enough to secure sincere respect."[11]

On arriving at Zumbo, at the confluence of the Loangwa and the Zambezi, Livingstone's admiration was again aroused, as it had been at his first visit four years before, for the Jesuit missionaries who had founded the settlement three centuries earlier, and whose church still stood though "an utter ruin now." But he was horrified to find that the local chief, one Mpangwe, had recently been murdered by a Portuguese half-caste at the head of a band of armed slaves, and a usurper put in his place in return for a grant of land to the murderer. Some time later, after the English party had left, the same band arrived at Zumbo and, representing themselves to be Livingstone's "children," bought great quantities of ivory for a few coarse beads a tusk, and also, "at the same cheap rate, a number of good-looking girls."

Although it was only to be expected that others would take advantage of his pioneering, this was a major blow to Livingstone.

We were now so convinced [he wrote], that in opening the country through which no Portuguese durst previously pass, we were made the unwilling instruments of extending the slave trade, that, had we not been under obligations to return with the Makololo to their own country, we should have left the Zambezi. It was with bitter sorrow that we saw the good we would have done turned to evil.[12]

On August 9, nearly three months out from Tete, they stopped at the Victoria Falls, which Livingstone had discovered in 1855, and visited the island in the middle of the river from which a view could be obtained over the lip of the sheer drop. Livingstone was not easily frightened, but even for him the crossing in a crazy canoe, amidst rocks and swirling rapids, with the ever-present danger of being swept over the edge to certain death, was a terrifying experience. As it was, the trip nearly ended in disaster.

The canoe was conducted by a native called Tuba, reputedly the exclusive owner of the necessary "medicine" for ensuring a safe passage.

Never was canoe more admirably managed: only once did the medicine seem to have lost something of its efficacy. We were driving swiftly down, a black rock, over which the white foam flew, lay directly in our path, the pole was planted against it as readily as ever, but it slipped just as Tuba put forth his strength to turn the bow off. We struck hard and were half full of water in a moment; Tuba recovered himself as speedily, shoved off the bow, and shot the canoe into a still, shallow place, to bale out the water. Here we were given to understand it was not the medicine which was at fault; *that* had lost none of its virtue; the accident was owing entirely to Tuba having started without his breakfast. Need it be said we never let Tuba go without that meal again.[13]

The depth of the falls was measured by lowering a line with some bullets and a piece of white cloth attached to it. While one of the party lay with his head over a projecting crag to watch, the others paid out the line until the weights came to rest on a projection 310 feet below, but still fifty feet above the level of the seething caldron into which the water poured. From here it escaped by a cleft in the rock, running at right angles to the stream, which measurement by sextant showed to be only eighty yards across at its narrowest. "Into this chasm," wrote Livingstone with pardonable pride as the discoverer of one of the most spectacular scenic effects in the world, "of twice the depth of Niagara Falls, the river, a full mile wide, rolls with a deafening roar; and this is Mosi-oa-Tunya or the Victoria Falls." Mosi-oa-Tunya was a Makololo word meaning "thunder of smoke": the "thunder" being the noise made by the falls, and the "smoke" the permanent cloud of spray which rises for hundreds of feet above it.

On his first visit to Garden Island, as the natives called it after him, Livingstone had planted some peach and apricot stones and sown some coffee seed. He had also carved his initials on a tree with the date, November 17, 1855—"the only time," as he wrote, "I have been guilty of this act of vandalism." In spite of a hedge built round it by the natives, his plantation had been destroyed by hippopotami; but his initials were still there and below them his brother now carved his. For this there was much less excuse, since Charles was not even the second white man to see the falls. That honor belonged to a certain Mr. Baldwin, a trader from Natal, who had found his way to the place by compass, but had been detained by the local chief after taking a bath in the Zambezi and was still waiting to be ransomed. "If," said the chief, "he had been devoured by one of the crocodiles which abound there, the English would have blamed us for his death. He nearly inflicted a great injury upon us, therefore we said he must pay a fine." After Livingstone had intervened, Mr. Baldwin was allowed to depart.

They were now in Makololo country and a week later reached Sesheke, Sekeletu's new capital. There they heard that the chief had contracted leprosy, had executed various people whose witchcraft he suspected and was hiding himself away from his people on the other side of the river. However, he sent them presents, invited them to visit him and allowed the two doctors, Livingstone and Kirk, to treat him, which they did successfully.

Here also Livingstone learned the full details of the tragedy at Linyanti, of which he had already received a report on his way. Of the two missionary families, the Helmores and the Prices, consisting of four grown-ups, four children and an infant, all had died except one grown-up and two children. The survivors were Roger Price and two Helmore orphans, who had managed to struggle some of the way back to Cape Colony and were eventually rescued. Linyanti, lying in the swamps south of the Zambezi, was a notoriously unhealthy locality and the missionaries had arrived there in the hope that they would be allowed by Sekeletu to move to higher land north of the river. This he had refused, and according to Roger Price he had also kept them short of food and robbed them of their goods, so that they were reduced to near starvation before succumbing to fever. Sekeletu had appropriated the Helmores' wagon after their death and was still living in it in quarantine when Livingstone found him.

To Livingstone the chief told a different story. He had liked Helmore, he said, and had offered to take him to Sesheke to see if he liked that better than Linyanti, but while they were getting ready for the journey the wagon drivers came down with malaria. Within a few weeks both the Helmores, two of their children, Mrs. Price and her baby were all dead from the same cause. The medicines which might have saved them were only 100 yards away, in the wagon left by Livingstone several years before, which, as he discovered when he visited it, had never been disturbed.[14]

Livingstone accepted Sekeletu's explanation and in a letter to Tidman, Secretary of the London Missionary Society, written from Chicova on November 10, he sought to exonerate the Makololo, and also himself, from any blame for the disaster.

> On reaching the country of the Makololo in August last, I learned to my very great sorrow that our esteemed and worthy friends, the Helmores, had been cut off by fever after a very short residence at Linyanti.
>
> Having been unexpectedly detained in the lower parts of this river until May last, my much longed for opportunity of visiting the upper portion was effected only by performing a march on foot of more than 600 miles, and then I was too late to render the aid which I had fondly hoped to afford . . .
>
> From all I could learn the Makololo took most cordially to Mr. Helmore. They wished to become acquainted with him—a very natural desire—before removing to the Highlands, and hence the delay which ended so fatally.[15]

Tidman, however, preferred to believe the evidence of the survivors and in his reply did not conceal the indignation he felt both at the treatment meted out to the missionaries and at Livingstone's attempt to whitewash the Makololo.

> Sekeletu positively refused to allow them to leave his place, or to point out any healthy locality where they might await your arrival. Their settling down, therefore, in this scene of death was a necessity forced upon them by the will of a despot. . . . The only way in which we can reconcile the statement of your informants with these facts, is by supposing that Sekeletu and his people . . . apprehensive of your resentment, should the truth become known to you, purposely misrepresented the case.[16]

The detailed story of the Linyanti tragedy has been told by the biographer of Roger Price, the sole adult survivor, and leaves no doubt that Sekeletu behaved as badly as Price alleged.[17]

This being the case, Tidman's resentment against Livingstone is understandable. It was Livingstone who had proposed the mission to the Makololo, promising it would get a friendly reception, and who had pressed the London Missionary Society to go ahead with the project against their better judgment when they heard that Livingstone himself, having found something more interesting to do, was not prepared to go with it or even give it the benefit of his experience. All he had offered was his help in case he should happen to run into the mission on the Zambezi. He had made no special effort to do this, and it was pure coincidence that he should have arrived in Barotseland only a few weeks after the last victim had died, and that coming a few weeks earlier he might have saved them all simply with a few doses of quinine.

When the story reached England Livingstone was criticized for his part in it. This he bitterly resented and in a letter to his brother-in-law defended himself by throwing the blame on the victims and the Society. It was characteristic of Livingstone that, when thus attacked, he hit out in all directions—even against the dead who could not answer back.

It could be argued that he had severed his links with the Society, after they had refused to finance his Zambezi project, and was therefore entitled to wash his hands of anything they did subsequently. He could not, however, escape responsibility for having proposed a mission to the Makololo in the first place.

Had he gone himself all would have been well, but to send others in his place, as Robert Moffat predicted it would be, was fatal. It was not only that Livingstone was a much more experienced traveler, that he knew the Makololo country, had a cure for malaria and was known to and liked by Sekeletu. There was also a special reason, to which reference has already been made, why the latter wanted to have the Livingstones with him, and this was that Mrs. Livingstone—"Ma Robert" to the natives—was a daughter of Robert Moffat, and Moffat was a friend of Mosilikatse, the dreaded chief of the Matabele. The Makololo lived in fear of the Matabele and would not move from the swamps which were their protection against attack. But if the Livingstones took up residence among them, so they reasoned, all would be different.

As Gluckman has pointed out, Livingstone was not just a highly respected friend of the Makololo, he was the key figure in their foreign policy. This was why Sekeletu, when the explorer arrived penniless at Linyanti in 1853, had provided him with porters and goods—in other words financed his journey—first to the West Coast and then right across the continent. He was relying all the time on Livingstone's promise to return with his wife and set up a permanent mission. In consequence, when the other missionaries turned up, of whom he had never heard, he was bitterly disappointed, took no interest in them and allowed them to "languish, some to death, in the Linyanti swamps."[18]

Now that Livingstone had at last reappeared, Sekeletu appealed once more to him and also to Kirk, to whom he had taken a liking, to come and settle down. If they would only do this, he, Sekeletu, would move with the whole of his tribe to the Batoka Plateau and provide a section of the country for the special use of the English. On being warned that in all probability their descendants would cause "disturbance" in his country—an understated prophecy of what was to occur a century later in Rhodesia—he replied that "these would be only domestic feuds and of no importance." But Livingstone declined to commit himself. The refusal of the Makololo to move was only cowardice, he told them; "they ought to remove out of the valley to the Highlands but it must be their own act, for if not, any evil that might befall them in consequence would be imputed to me."[19]

Before parting with Sekeletu Livingstone took the opportunity of presenting his letter of accreditation as British Consul to the tribes living in the interior. In his reply, which was taken down by Livingstone in native dialect and then read out at a public meeting before being translated into English, the chief revealed something of the anguish in his heart, as he saw the Makololo empire, built by his father, Sebituane, crumbling under his own weaker rule and the assaults of its more powerful neighbors, and of his desperate longing for the protective presence of the white men.

Sekeletu rejoices at the words of the letter that has arrived, but the country has disabled him while fleeing from Mosilikatse. He finds great affliction where he is. People perish, cattle perish. The country (called Phori) and Mpakane (Highlands near the River Kafue) is beautiful, and people might dwell there properly, but how can I live alone? If I lived alone I should not even sleep in it. Had (Mrs. L) Ma Robert come, then I should have rejoiced, because Mosilikatse would let her alone, and us, she being a child of his friend Moshete (Moffat). And Sekeletu says to the Lord of the English, Give me of your people to dwell with me, and I shall cut off a country for them to dwell in.[20]

In his covering letter to the Foreign Secretary Livingstone did not preclude the possibility of his own return to the Makololo.

> The party which now returns with us [he wrote from Sesheke on September 6], consisting of sixteen persons, are instructed by their chief to lead us—in the event of our being able to bring up our goods at once—to the healthy Highlands. Sickness alone prevents Sekeletu from accompanying us part of the way to select a proper locality for the whole tribe.[21]

It would thus appear that Livingstone was still open-minded and that before leaving Sekeletu he encouraged him in the idea that he *might* come back and settle on the central plateau. It depended on whether he could "bring up our goods" and this in turn depended on whether, with a new steamer, he would be able to force a passage up the Kebrabasa Rapids, in accordance with the original plan of the Expedition. In fact, although continuing to maintain that it was possible, he never tried, and Sekeletu never saw him again. Left to the tender mercies of native doctors the health of the Makololo chief soon failed again, and early in 1864 he died. His death was followed by civil war and the destruction of the tribe. As Livingstone comments in the *Narrative*, "the Kingdom, of which under an able sagacious mission a vast deal might have been made, has suffered the usual fate of African conquests."[22] He might have added that he was perhaps the only man who could have saved it, had he not been drawn away by more ambitious projects.

Leaving Sesheke on September 17, 1860, the party paid another visit to the falls and planted some more seeds on Garden Island. From there they traveled to the village of a chief named Sinamane, from whom Livingstone bought two canoes and borrowed three others. Canoes were not only quicker now that they were descending the Zambezi, but they would enable Livingstone to test the navigability of the river.

The first danger spot was the rapids of Kariba, where the great dam stands today, but though the current was strong they passed through safely. At the next they were not so successful, and disaster was only averted by the pluck of the native paddlers, who jumped overboard to lighten the canoes and guided them by swimming alongside.

After this experience, when they came to the next rapid,

where the current was running at six knots, the canoes were unloaded and their cargo carried for 100 yards overland. Even so a man was nearly lost when the last of the canoes was being brought down close to the shore.

> The stern swung round into the current and all except one man let go, rather than be dragged off. He clung to the bow and was swept out into the middle of the stream. Having held on when he ought to have let go, he next put his life in jeopardy by letting go when he ought to have held on; and was in a few seconds swallowed up by a fearful whirlpool. His comrades launched out a canoe below, and caught him as he rose the third time to the surface, and saved him, though much exhausted and very cold.[23]

By this time it could have been expected that Livingstone had learned some caution—but not a bit of it. The most dangerous stretch of water of all, the Kebrabasa Rapids, still lay ahead. In deciding to try to shoot them Livingstone had a motive other than bravado: he was desperately anxious to prove that the gorge was navigable and to do this was prepared to risk the lives of a score of men in what Kirk, not given to panic or exaggeration, would describe as his "mad attempt." Of the two accounts the one given by Kirk in his diary and quoted by Coupland is the more vivid, and is also illustrated by a diagram which makes it clearer what happened.

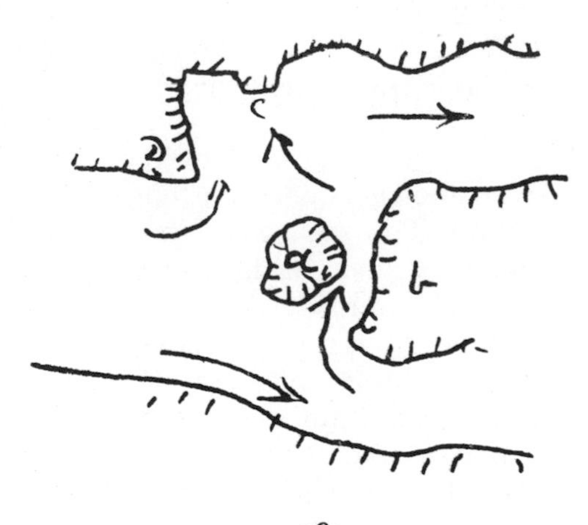

The water flowed along rushing hard on rock (a), part flowing by the channel between it and (d); a considerable body went down the right channel but a part returned by the passage between (a) and (b) to the left. The great danger was of being first dashed to pieces on (a), secondly of being carried against (c). As usual my canoe went first, for mine was the crew with most dash. We cleared (a) in fine style; the water ran hard as the men paddled and had complete command of the canoe. I then said, 'now avoid (c), the water runs hard on it.' They bent the head round and had given one stroke ahead; there was no danger and we could go through easily, but at this time we saw Dr. L's canoe carried up to the rock (a). Every second we expected to see it upset and all in the boiling water. To make things worse Mr C.L.'s canoe was running as if into them; both would be upset. The only hope was from us. We all looked. Had we paddled on we should have saved ourselves easily, but had the others capsized there was no hope of saving them, for the water boiled up and curved in eddies so that no man could survive.

The next thing I saw was the water rushing over our canoe. We were upset and all in the water. The other told me after that we struck with a loud crack. I heard nothing, the thing was instantaneous . . . we were all under water or clinging on. It is a great thing when these accidents happen suddenly; there is no danger of anyone losing presence of mind. The men behaved admirably. We were upset by being carried side on to rock (c).[24]

The crew managed to clamber ashore, the canoe was saved, but most of its contents were swept away and Kirk lost everything except his rifle.

The remainder of the journey is described by Livingstone in a single paragraph.

We now left the river and proceeded on foot, sorry we had not done so the day before. The men were thoroughly frightened, they had not seen such perilous navigation before. They would carry all the loads rather than risk Kebrabasa any longer; but the fatigue of a day's march over the hot rocks and burning sand changed their tune before night; and they then regretted having left the canoes: they thought they should have dragged them past the dangerous places, and then launched them again. One of the two donkeys died from exhaustion near Luia. Though the men eat zebras and quaggas, blood relations of the donkey, they were shocked by the idea of eating the ass: 'it would be like eating man himself, because the donkey lives with man and is his bosom companion.' We met two large trading parties of Tette slaves on their way to Zumbo, leading, to be sold for ivory, a number of Manganja women with ropes round their necks, and all made fast to one long rope.[25]

Normally slaves were bought in the interior and taken down to the coast to be shipped abroad. Now a traffic had started in the opposite direction, ironically as a result of Livingstone's efforts, first in protesting against the coastal trade and secondly in opening a route to the interior.

There was one other incident during the journey, not mentioned by Livingstone, but which convinced Kirk that Charles Livingstone was not only a mischief-maker but dangerous to the Expedition. It occurred after Charles, in a fit of ungovernable temper, had kicked the Makololo headman as the climax of almost continual quarreling with his brother.

I trust [Kirk confided to his diary] that if I am sent on an overland trip I may not have C.L. for a companion, for if he can break out and abuse, tearing with nails so as to draw blood, his brother, indulge in epithets such as 'the cursing Consul of Quelimane' repeated over and over again, act before the men in such a way as to make them look on him as mad . . . one who loses his temper suddenly so as to change from joking to kicking with iron nailed boots the chief man sent by a proud powerful savage chief, to conduct us safely through his dominions and ask assistance in the chief's name in front, is one on whom no reliance could be placed. Nothing but the high personal regard for Dr. L. averted bloodshed in that case. The spear was poised and needed only a stroke of the arm to send it to the heart. I never expected so much moderation among savages. For Dr. L's sake he held back but ordered Sekeletu's men to put down Mr. C.L's bedding in the field, that it should not be carried by any of them.[26]

From the wrangling of the brothers it also emerged that it was indeed Charles, as Kirk long suspected, who had poisoned Livingstone's mind against the other members of the Expedition.

This has been an unfortunate Expedition for quarrels and of all that has happened, the disclosing of the horrible childish utterly false assertions of Mr. C.L. have been the worst. The most disagreeable thing to me was Dr. L stating that he (C.L.) would not like to hear told the slanders he had raised on the other members of the expedition to which Dr. L had not listened, and that Mr. Rae, the engineer, going off with a good character, had been gall and bitterness to him in as much as he had taunted the Dr. for giving such a character. This so fully confirmed what I had observed both in my own case and in that of other members of the Expedition that it was painful to feel, for although Dr. L may know the truth of his brother's insinuations often being base and false, still they have a powerful influence, as often I have observed. For Dr. L., so remarkable in individual power, is deficient in administrative talent.[27]

In recording his travels Livingstone always understated the difficulties and dangers of the enterprise. Naturally modest he took a perverted pride in belittling the courage and endurance needed to overcome them. But this was not the only motive. By making his journeys look easier than they were, he hoped to persuade the British public that no special qualities were necessary for the successful colonization of Africa. In this instance, for example, he scarcely referred to the last and most painful stage of the journey, made on foot. Terrain and heat were exhausting, there was little food, and when one day Kirk and Livingstone lost the rest of the party they found that Charles had taken the men away and ignored the shots fired to recall them. Kirk had only the clothes which he had been wearing when the canoe sank and they were now reduced to rags. More, however, than the loss of his personal possessions, it was the loss of all his botanical notes, and of his diary for six months, that depressed him. The Expedition had already extended for longer than anticipated, he noted, and "without the whole concern being on a different footing as to accommodation and time for some sort of packing, or arrangement," he had no desire "to be any longer on it."

It was a relief to them all when on November 23, 1860, they struggled into Tete after an absence of just over six months. "We have kept faith with the Makololo," Livingstone wrote to

Murchison, "though we have done nothing else." In his dispatch of November 24[28] to the Foreign Secretary, however, he was able to claim as a positive result of the trip the discovery that the Zambezi was navigable between Kebrabasa and Victoria Falls. As for the Kebrabasa Rapids—the "only great difficulty"—he remained convinced in spite of everything that "at full flood, when the river in that part rises eighty feet, the cataract will be smoothed over" and that "it could be passed by a powerful steamer"—an opinion that was not shared by Kirk after his narrow escape from drowning, and that subsequent experience has proved untenable.

The negative result he kept for the last paragraph.

While entering into friendly relations with the people along our route, it was mortifying to find Portuguese traders in our footsteps reaping the benefit of our labours and employing assassination as a means of increasing their power.

This was sufficient reason, if there were no others, for turning his back once and for all on the upper Zambezi, accepting his defeat at Kebrabasa and seeking his fortune elsewhere.

10

The Bishop Goes to War

December 1860–July 1861

IT COULD TAKE up to six months for a letter sent from the Zambezi to reach London, the time depending on the date when the next man-of-war called at the mouth of the river. The same period would be required for the reply, so that Livingstone might have to wait a whole year for the answer to one of his dispatches, by which time it could well be out of date. It was therefore fortunate that his six-month journey in the interior gave the Government at home a chance to catch up with his correspondence.

The main decision they had to take was whether to extend the two-year period of the Expedition, which would expire in the spring of 1860, or cut their losses and call the whole thing off. Foreign Office officials were in favor of the latter. They were alarmed by the increasing animosity shown by Livingstone to the Portuguese, with whose Government the British Government wished to remain on friendly terms, and at the same time feared that Portugal would reap the benefit of any results achieved by the Expedition. As one of these officials noted in a memorandum dated December 1, 1859:

I firmly believe that the Portuguese will either appropriate to themselves any advantage derived from Dr. Livingstone's mission, or will throw obstacles in the way of our profiting by his discoveries of such a nature as to render the practical result insignificant.[1]

This, in fact, was already happening. A Portuguese customs house, manned by an officer and four soldiers, had been set up at the Kongone harbor, and a military post had been established at the confluence of the Shire and Zambezi. It was clear that there was no question of making either river free for the entry of legitimate commerce, as Livingstone constantly urged they should be. Worse still was the fact that the routes he had opened up, both to the interior and up the Shire, were now being used by Portuguese traders, usually half-castes, to increase the traffic in slaves. The method employed was to send out bands of armed slaves who would incite one tribe to wage war on another and make prisoners of all the able-bodied. They would then buy the captives in exchange for cloth or beads and march them off in chains: the men to the coast for shipment to the French island of Réunion, the women to the interior to be exchanged for ivory. In some cases these bands, when following in the explorer's footsteps, had the effrontery to represent themselves as Livingstone's "children," thereby implying they were under his protection.

Livingstone, moreover, was convinced that, although officially frowned on, the traffic was in fact connived at by local officials from the Governor General of the colony downward. They were so badly paid, even when they were paid at all, that they were forced to trade on the side in order to exist, and the only trade open to them was in slaves. Even his friend Major Sicard, commandant at Tete, who was tireless in his assistance to the Expedition and to whose "noble and generous nature" Livingstone would pay a glowing tribute, was not above suspicion in this respect.

All these were good enough reasons for the Whitehall realists to terminate the Expedition. But Lord John Russell, the Foreign Secretary, was reluctant to do so. Public opinion, which still expected great things of Livingstone, would be disappointed and blame the Government if his venture was cut short by their parsimony or apprehensions. Before taking any decision Russell sought the advice of Captain Washington, the Admiralty expert, who was asked to say (1) how far the original objects of the Expedition had been realized; (2) whether the advantages of more extensive exploration would warrant the additional expense; (3) what period was required to secure these advantages.[2]

In his reply, sent on December 9, Washington expressed the opinion that the objects of the Expedition had been accomplished to "some extent" by Livingstone's journey up the Shire and discovery of Lake Shirwa, "which promised to be a fertile country abounding in cotton which the natives would be willing to barter for European goods." He thought there were "fair grounds" for anticipating further advantages, and since the annual expense in the future would be only £2,500, chiefly for salaries (but omitting the cost of the new vessel), the public would "cheerfully see that sum expended even with a distant hope of seeing realised" the objects of the Expedition. As regards the extension of time, he considered five years the limit of a European's endurance in such a climate. At the end of it the Government could review the results and if necessary organize a new expedition.

So far so good, but Washington then added several warnings. In the first place the exploration of the Shire was not in the original plan; the river was too near the coast and would be claimed by the Portuguese. Much better if Livingstone stuck to his project of penetrating to the interior near the Victoria Falls and from there developing links with the British Cape Colony, which would make him independent of the Portuguese.

As for the Universities Mission, while its formation was a favorable sign of public interest in Africa, in Washington's opinion it would be "madness" for it to "attempt the Zambezi." He also deprecated Livingstone's proposal for a Scottish colony on the banks of Lake Shirwa as "a wild project which should not receive the sanction of H.M.G." Although later he was to modify his opposition on the grounds that missionaries made the best pioneers, Washington's advice about the Universities Mission was sound; had it been taken, a number of lives, including probably that of Livingstone's own wife, would have been saved.[3]

In a further report, drafted at the end of March after the receipt of further dispatches from Livingstone, Washington approved his plan to explore the Rovuma as a possible alternative route to Lake Nyassa "without even the semblance of passing through Portuguese territory," and suggested that the Expedition split into two parties, one to ascend the Shire and the other the Rovuma, with a view to joining up at the lake. He also thought the request for a new steamer which could be taken apart and carried in pieces past the Murchison Falls was "worth considering" but that the project for a white settlement was premature.

Dealing next with Livingstone's proposals for the suppression of the slave trade and his protests against the Portuguese plan to impose customs duty on the Zambezi, Washington showed himself a true Englishman in the liberal tradition speaking with the outraged accent of the Puritan conscience shocked by the wickedness of lesser breeds.

If we were dealing with a civilized country [he wrote in reference to Portugal], some scruple might be felt on the subject; but with a notoriously slave-dealing nation who have a few half-military, half-penal settlements, or rather posts, dotted here and there at wide intervals along 1200 miles of coast, it would seem monstrous that we should stand upon such punctilio as to permit ourselves to be debarred from trading with the native races in the interior. If however this right (to impose customs dues) is to be insisted on, the only alternative would seem to be to let the Zulus loose upon them. With slight encouragement they would soon clear the delta of the Zambezi and set it free. Considering the great object in view, the extinction of the slave trade, and the persons we have to deal with I consider we should be fully justified in adopting such a course.[4]

We do not know how Lord John Russell reacted to this outburst; probably he just ignored it. But in his letter to Livingstone of April 17, 1860, he made it clear that the Government did not share the xenophobic fervor of the fire-eating naval hydrographer. While recognizing that the Portuguese either connived in or were unable to check the slave trade, "still the Government of Portugal," he wrote, "is the Government of a friendly and civilised nation and entitled to be dealt with accordingly." For the rest the Foreign Secretary adopted Washington's recommendations; the exploration of the Rovuma was approved, but not the proposal for white settlement, which was thought premature; further consideration would be given to the request for a portable steamer, but sappers would not be sent to build a road for it (on which Palmerston, who as Prime Minister was shown a draft of the letter, as was Queen Victoria, commented in the margin: "But would not the sappers be useful as overseers or directors of the native workmen?"); finally Livingstone was urged to establish direct communication with the Cape Colony and "avoid Portuguese settlements."[5]

From this it is clear that the men in the Foreign Office were still as anxious to avoid a showdown with the Portuguese as Livingstone was keen to provoke it. However, that they foresaw that his activities might have that result—as in fact came to pass a few years later—emerged from another letter, sent by the Foreign Secretary to the Colonial Secretary, only two days later, and requesting that the Government of the Cape Colony be urged on its side to open direct communication with the Zambezi without passing through Portuguese territory. After expressing his belief that the evident intention of the Portuguese was to restrict Livingstone in his movements (which in fact they never did) or to profit by his discoveries (which was, of course, inevitable) Russell continued:

> H.M.Government have as yet refrained from any general discussions with the Government of Portugal as to rights of sovereignty in these parts and it is only with reference to the limits south of Lorenco Marques river that any decisive step . . . has as yet been taken.[6]

Thus the events which nearly led to war between Britain and her oldest ally and culminated in the Salisbury ultimatum of 1890 were already foreshadowed as one of the two most important results—the other being the eventual suppression of the slave trade—of the Zambezi Expedition.

Russell's letter on the whole was encouraging for Livingstone; although it did not give him all he had asked for, his past actions were commended and his future plans were broadly approved. Best news of all was the confirmation that the Universities Mission, headed by a bishop, was on its way to establish a permanent station in the Shire uplands on Livingstone's advice.

Before it reached him, however, there were already some second thoughts in London. Asked to report on the portable steam launch, Washington first drew up a specification: it should be seventy-five feet long, drawing two feet of water, with an engine of ten horsepower producing a speed of eight knots, and capable of being packed in forty cases of which "no part to exceed 3 cwt. in weight, or such as two natives, one before the other, could carry slung on a pole between them, and this might be carried wherever there was a footpath through the bush." The boat could be built in three months by Tod and McGregor of the Clyde Foundry, Glasgow, would cost £1,200 to complete, in addition to which there would be £100 for freight to the Cape, plus the "wages and expenses of a skilled workman to rivet the parts together, say £200," making a total of £1,500.

But Washington then went on to say:

Yet without further communication from Dr. Livingstone I am not prepared to recommend the sending out of such a vessel. The great utility of the steam launch would be to explore Lake Nyassa. Now without the slightest disposition to damp Dr. Livingstone's ardour, I think he has a higher object in view than geographical discovery. It is very well for Captains Burton and Speke, and men of that ilk, but Dr. Livingstone has already discovered more country and more people than he can deal with. To make friends with and instruct the natives in the valley of the Shire will be occupation enough for the next twelve months, and probably one steamer on his hands would be enough at once.[7]

This was the first warning signal, had Livingstone known of it, that the days of the Expedition were numbered. Enthusiastic admirer and supporter of its leader as he was, Washington already saw a danger that the whole thing would get out of hand, with Livingstone straying ever farther from the original objectives and becoming increasingly embroiled in ambitious projects for which the Government had no appetite.

Of this anxiety, however, which was to increase as the months went by, there was scarcely a hint in Russell's letter to Livingstone; and when he found it waiting for him at Tete, on his return from the trip to Sesheke, it gave a considerable boost to the morale of the Expedition. He now asked Kirk, who had intended going home, to remain, and the latter at once agreed. It seemed to them all that a new and more propitious chapter was opening.

Meanwhile the new paddle steamer provided by the Government to replace the ailing *Ma Robert* was on the way. Named the *Pioneer*, she had been built and fitted out at a cost of nearly £6,000 and carried, in addition to her normal stores, a "light boat" for navigating Lake Nyassa, implements for making a road past the Murchison Falls, and goods and articles of barter to pay the natives employed in constructing the road. Her complement consisted of a master, Mr. May, R.N.; a mate; a surgeon-naturalist; an engineer; and sixteen men; their salaries would cost another £2,500 per year. Leaving England at the beginning of September, she had been towed as far as Madeira and had then proceeded under her own power of sail and steam, first to Sierra Leone to coal, and thence to the Cape. In spite of some apprehension on the part of the master—she was after all designed as a river boat, not for ocean voyages—who wrote from Sierra Leone: "I cannot shake off a feeling of being neglected by having to proceed alone," the vessel arrived safely at Simonstown on December 11 and ten days later sailed for the Zambezi. Livingstone, therefore, had no time to lose in going down the river to meet her.

On leaving the *Ma Robert* at Tete in May he had intended to abandon her for good, but during his six-month absence the two sailors left on board had patched her up and it was therefore decided to attempt another journey with her. This proved to be the last. On December 21, 1860, a fortnight after leaving Tete, the leaking vessel grounded finally on a sandbank and immediately filled with water. She could neither be pumped out nor floated off. During the night the river rose and the next day all that was visible of the wreck was the top six feet of her two masts. Most of the goods on board were saved and removed to an island, where the Expedition spent a miserable Christmas, made worse by another row between the Livingstone brothers, till rescued by canoes sent from Sena by the friendly Senhor Ferrão. So ended the life of the vessel to whose defects Livingstone was wont to attribute all his misfortunes, but considering the way he used her, it was surprising that she lasted so long.

While awaiting other transport Livingstone took the opportunity to write to Thornton, making overtures for the latter's return to the Expedition. The Government had examined the two cases, Baines's and Thornton's, and while deciding, on Washington's advice, against Baines, had considered that Thornton ought to be reinstated and instructed Livingstone accordingly. It was, however, left to the leader of the Expedition to approach Thornton, since, as Washington wrote, "it was necessary to support him by allowing him to exercise the prerogative of mercy as well as of punishment." This was inviting Livingstone to admit that in dismissing the geologist he had been in the wrong, a thing he had never done in his life and was not going to start doing now. In his letter to Thornton he therefore sought to give the impression that it was he, not the Government, who had taken the initiative, and that while not withdrawing his previous charges he was prepared out of the goodness of his heart to take him back. At the same time he made it a condition that Thornton should hand over the results of the work he had done on his own, and which Livingstone needed to swell the somewhat meager scientific discoveries of the Expedition. The letter dated "Shupanga, 1st Jany, 1861" shows him at his worst: dishonest, smug, unforgiving and crafty.

MY DEAR SIR,

Towards the beginning of last year I took certain measures in your behalf and am happy to inform you that I have heard by a mail which we found at Tete on 23rd Novr last that your salary may be restored to you without deduction if I can give a recommendation to that effect. As I was influenced by seeing you engaged in work which I could not prevail upon you to perform for some eight months, my recommendation would come with all the greater force if accompanied with a proper report of your geological researches for the use of H.M.Government . . . I shall wait for an answer for some months before proceeding farther in the matter.

I am etc.
D. LIVINGSTONE.[8]

Thornton, who knew his Livingstone, was not taken in and replied with a firmness that did credit to his spirit. His letter, dated May 7, 1861, was sent from Zanzibar, where he was preparing to set out with the German explorer Baron von der Decken on an expedition to Mount Kilimanjaro.

On April 13th last I received a packet of letters from Quillimane, containing one from you dated January 1st, 1861. In this letter you not only do not moderate your former accusations against me but even repeat it in an aggravated form, and, as your letter is worded, I could not give you the report you wish without acknowledging that for some eight months you could not prevail on me to perform my duty.

From home I have not heard that you have stated anything publicly against me, but I heard that Sir Roderick Murchison 'implicitly believes your statement that I had grown idle and useless'. I therefore wrote to Sir Roderick Murchison on April 19, laying before him the main points of the case and of the circumstances under which I acted, and concluded with the following two charges against you—First, that you condemned mainly on the evidence of your brother C. Livingstone, without making a proper enquiry into the truth of that evidence, and without giving me an opportunity to defend myself; Second, that you condemned me for having done no work without even asking me what I had done. To this day you do not know what geology I did or did not whilst a member of the Expedition.

In conclusion I cannot accept a restoration of my salary in exchange for my geological work without an accompanying restoration of my character.[9]

To his brother George Thornton he wrote:

He has no confidence in me to give the recommendation without first seeing my work, and gives no guarantee that on receiving the work he will give the recommendation. If I will acknowledge that for eight months Dr. Livingstone could not prevail on me to perform my work, and will give him the result of any work since leaving the Expedition (which has cost me £115 in money, besides time and health) then if it pleases him so to do he will recommend the Government to restore my salary for some to me unknown period.[10]

This correspondence helps to explain why Livingstone was so disliked by all the men, including Kirk, who served in the Expedition under him. Although admiring his exceptional qualities, they felt he was not straightforward, was too clever at maneuvering others into a position of disadvantage, and while pretending to have their interests at heart would sacrifice any of them if it served his purpose.

Having hired canoes, the party continued their journey down river, arriving at the Kongone harbor on January 4. Here they put up in a hut, recently erected by the Portuguese as a customs house, and settled down to await the arrival of the *Pioneer*. Livingstone, who hated doing nothing, occupied his time in hunting and natural history.

In this focus of decaying vegetation [he wrote later], nothing is so much to be dreaded as inactivity. We had therefore to find what exercise and amusement we could, when hunting was not required, in peering about in the fetid swamps; to have gone mooning about, in listless idleness, would have ensured fever in its worst form, and probably with fatal results.[11]

When at the end of the month the *Pioneer* appeared, it was accompanied by two cruisers bringing Bishop Mackenzie and the advance guard of the Universities Mission. The Bishop, still in his thirties, was by all accounts brave, able and energetic. After a brilliant career at Cambridge, he had gone to South Africa as a missionary to the Zulus and had soon been promoted to Archdeacon in Natal. While on a visit home he was invited to head the new Mission and was consecrated Bishop in Cape Town just before leaving for the Zambezi. The other members consisted of two clergymen, H. C. Scudamore and L. J. Procter; another cleric, not yet ordained, Horace Waller; a carpenter and an agricultural laborer; and five colored men from the Cape. These were later joined by another clergyman, the Rev. H. Rowley. "It was a puzzle," wrote Livingstone, "to know what to do with so many men." When a few years previously, in his famous address at Cambridge, he had made a dramatic appeal for men to carry on his work after his death, he had no idea of provoking an immediate response and would have been appalled if any members of the audience had jumped to their feet and volunteered their services on the spot. And now that, as a direct result of his appeal, the first volunteers had already materialized, fired by his eloquence and raring to go, he was more dismayed than gratified. He had written to offer every assistance to the Mission—he could not have done otherwise—but it was already obvious that they were going to be another and heavy burden upon him and greatly complicate the task of the Expedition.

The missionaries had read the enthusiastic accounts given by Livingstone of the Shire highlands, some of which had been published in the *Journal of the Royal Geographical Society* and other places. In these he represented the Shire country as an earthly paradise, a land flowing, if not with milk and honey, with cotton and other products; enjoying moreover a healthy climate in which white men could live at peace with friendly natives, teach them the arts of civilization and sow the seeds of the Christian faith. It was natural therefore that to the Shire they wished to go, and as speedily as possible.

Livingstone, however, had other ideas. Since the only result of his exploration of the Shire valley had been an increase in the slave trade, he was more than ever anxious to discover a route to the interior removed from Portuguese influence, and for this purpose he had been authorized by the Government to explore the Rovuma River, 500 miles to the north. Should his hope be realized that this river led to Lake Nyassa, then it would be better for the Mission to settle near its headwaters, rather than on the Shire or Zambezi.

After some argument he persuaded the Bishop to adopt this plan, and it was arranged that H.M.S. *Lyra* should take the members of the Mission to Johanna, one of the Comoro Islands lying off the coast of Mozambique, where they should wait while Livingstone, accompanied by the Bishop, explored the Rovuma in the *Pioneer*.

There was a good harbor at the mouth of this river and no bar, but it soon started to shoal, and after ascending thirty miles, with the water level falling and a danger of being stranded until it rose again in the rainy season, it was deemed wise to beat a retreat. Had he not had to think of the Mission, Livingstone would have continued on foot or by boat, but he felt responsible for settling the missionaries safely before doing anything else and therefore decided to return to the Shire and "commence forthwith a road past the cataracts."

When they reached the coast most of the crew were down with malaria and there were scarcely enough hands to work the ship. Her master, Mr. May, being among the sick, Livingstone took over the navigation. As he wrote in the *Narrative:*

The habit of finding the geographical position on land renders it an easy task to steer a steamer with only three or four sails at sea; where, if one does not run ashore, no one follows to find out an error and where a current affords a ready excuse for every blunder.[12]

It was probably this experience, his first of navigating a ship at sea, that gave him the confidence to get rid of its commander at the first opportunity. After his quarrel with Bedingfield he was determined not to have in the Expedition any naval officer who might challenge his authority and had already turned down an application to join it by a Lieutenant Burlton. Washington's comment on this was significant.

I think we have seen enough of Dr. Livingstone during the last two years to judge that he does not easily brook a rival near the throne and I have great doubts if an officer of Lt. Burlton's rank might not be too near an approach to equality. For the new ship the naval officer in charge should be a tractable man of humble mind who has had some experience of African travelling.[13]

It seems that May was not of sufficiently humble mind since he now demanded the place of second-in-command. The request was logical, inasmuch as the commander of the *Pioneer*, on whom the Expedition entirely depended for transport and security, was next in importance to the leader; May also believed he had been sent to succeed Bedingfield. But this would have meant "exalting" him over the heads of Kirk and Charles Livingstone, which Livingstone was not prepared to do. May then preferred to resign from the Expedition and, after an "amicable" parting, returned to England, leaving Livingstone, much to the concern of other naval officers, in sole charge of the ship.

Livingstone's desire not to be trammeled by professional sailors was understandable: as leader of the Expedition he wanted to be free to follow his own bent and a ship's commander who was not willing to risk the ship could be a nuisance. It was nevertheless a great mistake to dispense with May without replacing him. Livingstone could not both command the *Pioneer* and lead the Expedition without neglecting one or the other. A ship's captain is much more than somebody who stands on the bridge giving orders to the helmsman. There are also such things as the order and cleanliness of the ship and the discipline of the crew to attend to. By all accounts conditions in the *Pioneer* after Livingstone took her over were those of utter confusion.

In other respects, too, it would have been better if occasionally he had listened to the advice of the Navy. They could have told him, for example, that his exploration of the Rovuma was a waste of time. Thus Captain Crawford of H.M.S. *Sidon* reported to the Admiralty that

> Dr. Livingstone seems to be under the impression that the Rovuma is navigable to a great extent towards Lake Nyassa, although the survey of Commander Owen gives a distance of about 45 miles and then only, probably, for boats.

Crawford was equally skeptical about the commercial use of the Zambezi.

> Many poor sailors [he wrote in the same report] have been lost in attempting to explore these dangerous lagoons. Whilst off the Kongone the *Sidon*'s anchorage was the open sea with a prevalent wind and a heavy ground swell setting directly on the shore; and altogether it would be difficult to discover a more unpromising position with a view to opening up a future communication and trade with the natives of Africa.[14]

This was the general opinion among naval officers who knew the coast, and it has been vindicated by the fact that the mouth of the Zambezi has never become a commercial port, as Livingstone envisaged, and that access to the interior continues to be through Quelimane, which the Portuguese had been using for several centuries before Livingstone's arrival, or the more modern port of Beira.

Very early in his life Livingstone boasted that he never allowed his judgment to be influenced by another man's opinion. This was sound enough in principle, but it led him increasingly, as the years went by, to believe only what he wanted to believe and to reject the evidence of those better qualified than himself if it happened to run counter to his prejudices or his plans.

After picking up the missionary party at Johanna the *Pioneer* sailed for the Zambezi. With a ship dangerously overloaded, no qualified skipper, and the monsoon season approaching, this was a perilous enough voyage for the fifty souls on board, which few men but Livingstone would have risked. However, they were lucky, and after seven days' steaming or sailing, the *Pioneer* arrived off the Kongone mouth. A first attempt to take her across the bar in heavy surf had to be abandoned as too dangerous, and at the second attempt she all but grounded and only just scraped over, iron nerve and overweening confidence in himself compensating for the navigator's lack of skill and experience.

Livingstone was at first full of praise for the new ship, which was larger, more powerful and more comfortable than the *Ma Robert,* but after entering the river he soon discovered that she had the same defect of drawing too much water. This was inevitable. To meet Livingstone's demand for a more powerful vessel, it had to be too big and too heavy to carry on the deck of another steamer, while the extra weight required to make it capable of the ocean voyage from England to South Africa added another two feet to the draught, increasing it from three feet to five feet. To make matters worse the *Pioneer* was now laden with the additional burden of the large missionary party and their immense quantity of stores and baggage. All this, as Livingstone wrote,

> caused us a great deal of hard and vexatious work, in laying out anchors and toiling at the capstan to get her off sandbanks. We should not have minded this much, but for the heavy loss of time which might have been more profitably, and infinitely more pleasantly, spent in intercourse with the people, exploring new regions, and otherwise carrying out the objects of the Expedition. Once we were a fortnight on a bank of soft yielding.[15]

How he must have kicked himself for ever making that speech at Cambridge!

When they left the Zambezi to enter the Shire, things got no better.

Although Sunday [Kirk wrote on June 16] we are forced to proceed to work to get the ship off. There being no passage we are forced to drag through sand. Three feet is the utmost of which the Shire is capable in order that a ship should proceed without constant labour. As to the Zambezi above Senna, it seems almost beyond the term of navigation unless vessels can be made of 18".[16]

After ten weeks' toilsome progress, at an average speed of three miles per day, on July 8, 1861, the *Pioneer* anchored off Chibisa's, the last village before the cataracts, otherwise known as Dakanamoio Island. Here she would have to stay till the following December, when the water would be high enough to carry her downstream. Meanwhile there was plenty of work to do, the first task being to find a site for the Mission.

In retrospect Livingstone was to represent this moment as the high-water mark of his achievement, as though everything up to then had gone according to plan, which was very far from being the case.

The Expedition [he would write in the *Narrative*] was up to this point eminently successful . . . we had opened a cotton-field, which, taking in the Shire and Lake Nyassa, was 400 miles in length. We had gained the confidence of the people wherever we had gone; and supposing the Mission of the Universities to be only moderately successful . . . a perfectly new era had commenced in a region much larger than the cotton-fields of the Southern States of America. We had, however, as will afterwards be seen, arrived at the turning point of our prosperous career, and soon came into contact with the Portuguese slave trade.

To discover a region capable of producing cotton was, of course, not quite the same as to open a cotton-field. Somebody had to grow the cotton. Livingstone's argument was that the natives would do so once the slave trade ceased, but there was not much evidence of this. Most of the missionaries considered that they had been badly misled by Livingstone's overenthusiastic accounts of the Shire valley. Henry Rowley, in the book he wrote later, was particularly bitter about this:

It never can be a suitable residence for Europeans and I think its fertility has been much over-rated . . . that it could ever have been thickly populated seems to me impossible.[17]

So lightly were the difficulties of the country estimated—and from the information we had received I cannot see that this favourable estimation was unwarranted—that it was determined that the Bishop's sisters and other ladies should come out to us as soon as our arrival and settlement in the country was known.[18]

This, however, was a judgment after the event, and at the start all were optimistic. When on July 15 the whole party, with Livingstone leading, set out for the hills to found the first mission station, it was in the eager spirit of men nearing the Promised Land.

You would like to see our picturesque appearance on march [wrote Mackenzie to the Bishop of Oxford]. Livingstone in his jacket and trousers of blue serge and his blue cloth cap. I with trousers of Oxford grey and a coat like a shooting-coat, a broad-brimmed wide-awake with white collar, which Livingstone laughs at, but all the same keeps the sun off. *He* is a Salamander. . . .

We were a strange party; Livingstone tramping along with a steady, heavy tread which kept one in mind that he had walked across Africa . . . I had myself in my left hand a loaded gun, in my right the crozier which they gave me in Cape Town; in front a can of oil, and behind a bag of seeds. . . .[19]

The missionaries must indeed have looked strange, and it is easy to laugh at them now as well-meaning innocents; and yet we should remember, when judging their subsequent behavior, that they were brave and devoted men of superior education who were risking their health and their lives for an ideal. They had been recruited from all levels—High, Broad and Low—of the Church of England, and their doctrinal differences afforded some quiet amusement to Livingstone, whose conception of Christianity was essentially nonsectarian, although with a bias against "frills" and Puseyism.

The mission is happy [he wrote to Moffat] in having various temperaments associated together. The Bishop is High Church and a strict disciplinarian in theory, but liberal and very lax in his control in practice. Waller, the lay member, very careful and somewhat anxious, does not believe in Apostolic Succession, Baptismal Regeneration, or any of the High Church tenets; argues briskly against them. Procter and Scudamore tend that way (High), if any way at all, while Parson Rowley is red-hot High Church. Scudamore and the Bishop work; Rowley writes to fill his purse with the fruits of his imagination. . . . They are on the whole a very happily constituted family. I think that active labour will work out the High Church bigotry which can only flourish in solitude.[20]

Their first test came very soon and was to have decisive consequences. While resting at a village on the second day out, they were informed by its chief, one Mbame, that a slave party would shortly pass through on its way to Tete. Livingstone had previously met other slave gangs but, although he had sufficient force to do so, had refrained from intervening, partly on the grounds that the rescue of slaves was not one of the official objects of the Expedition and could make difficulties for it both with the Portuguese and the natives, and partly because he would not know what to do with the rescued. Had he been alone with only the members of the Expedition present, his political instinct would probably have led him to remain neutral again; but in front of newcomers, who saw him as the great liberator of Africa, it was perhaps necessary to play a more heroic role. On the other hand the future of the Mission might be compromised if on its first encounter with the slave trade it failed to accept the challenge.

What happened next has been described by Livingstone in a famous passage of the *Narrative*.

'Shall we interfere?' we enquired of each other. We remembered that all our valuable private baggage was in Tete, which, if we freed the slaves, might, together with some Government property, be destroyed in retaliation; but this system of slave-hunters dogging us where previously they durst not venture, and, on pretence of being "our children", setting one tribe against another, to furnish themselves with slaves, would so inevitably thwart all our efforts for which we had the sanction of the Portuguese Government, that we resolved to run all risks, and put a stop, if possible, to the slave-trade, which had now followed on the footsteps of our discoveries.

A few minutes after Mbame had spoken to us, the slave party, a long line of manacled men, women, and children came winding their way round the hill and into the valley, on the side of which the village stood. The black drivers, armed with muskets, and bedecked with various articles of finery, marched jauntily in the front, middle and rear of the line, some of them blowing exultant notes out of long tin horns. They seemed to feel that they were doing a very noble thing, and might proudly march with an air of triumph. But the instant the fellows caught a glimpse of the English, they darted off like mad into the forest; so fast indeed that we caught but a glimpse of their red caps and the soles of their feet. The chief of the party alone remained; and he, from being in front, had his hand tightly grasped by a Makololo. He proved to be a well known slave of the late Commandant at Tete* and for some time our attendant while there. On asking him how he obtained these captives, he replied he had bought them; but on our enquiring of the people themselves all, save four, said they had been captured in war. While this enquiry was going on he bolted too.

The captives knelt down, and, in their way of expressing thanks, clapped their hands with great energy. They were thus left entirely on our hands, and knives were soon at work cutting the women and children loose. It was more difficult to cut the men adrift, as each had his neck in the fork of a stout stick, six or seven feet long, and kept in by an iron rod which was riveted at both ends across the throat. With a saw luckily in the Bishop's baggage, one by one the men were sawn out into freedom. Many were mere children about five years of age and under . . . Two

* Major Sicard. By mentioning that the chief of the party was himself a well-known slave belonging to Sicard, Livingstone gives the impression that the latter was somehow involved in the affair. But from the entry in his journal it is clear that the man left Tete secretly without the knowledge of his master. Whether or not he was ever engaged in the slave trade—and Livingstone believed that he was—on this occasion Sicard was innocent, and to insinuate the contrary was scarcely fair to an officer who had done more for the Expedition than any other Portuguese.

of the women had been shot the day before for attempting to untie the thongs . . . One woman had her infant's brains knocked out because she could not carry her load and it. And a man was despatched with an axe because he had broken down with fatigue . . .[21]

The Bishop, with Scudamore and Procter, had gone off to bathe and was not present during this drama, but on his return, after some hesitation, he gave his approval of the action taken. At the same time, when writing home, he made it clear that the decision to free the slaves had been taken by Livingstone and Livingstone alone.

There had been five or ten minutes' notice of their approach, so that Livingstone had time deliberately to take his course—a course which no one can blame; but surely all will join in blessing God that we have such a fellow-countryman.[22]

As to the propriety of clergymen using arms, which he realized would come in for some criticism at home, in a letter to Rowley, who had been left behind at Chibisa's, he wrote:

I am clear that in such cases it is right to use force, and even fire, if necessary to rescue captives. I should do so myself if necessary; but I think it more becoming our office to see the guns in the hands of others.[23]

The number of people liberated was eighty-four, mostly women and children. Told that they were free to go or stay, they mostly elected to stay and were then adopted by the Bishop to be attached to the Mission and "educated as members of a Christian family." During the next two days a further sixty-four were freed and similarly adopted, while Kirk was sent off to intercept another gang making for the Shire.

It now became urgent to find a suitable site where all these people, and the missionaries, could settle down. The Bishop was in favor of staying where they were, at a village called Soche's, which lay in fertile and well-watered country and was within easy reach of the Shire River. But while they were debating the question the paramount chief of the district, Chigunda, arrived with an invitation to the Mission to come to his own village of Magomero. This was some twenty or thirty miles farther on, near Mount Zomba, and lay unhealthily in a hollow only 1,000 feet above sea level. Chigunda told them that the Ajawa tribe, who had recently invaded the country from the north, were attacking the Manganja, plundering and burning their villages and taking prisoners to sell as slaves. All the other Manganja chiefs had fled with their people, but if the English came to live with him he would feel secure and stand his ground. For Livingstone this seemed to be a heaven-sent opportunity to stem the advance of the marauders. "We seem to be invited to stand in the gap and arrest a flood of slavery," he wrote in his journal. "May the Lord direct us."

Another advantage of Magomero in Livingstone's eyes was that it was well placed for communicating with Lake Nyassa, to which he was still hoping to find a route of access along the Rovuma River. This would enable the Mission to snap its fingers at the Portuguese in the event of their closing the entrance to the Shire. Furthermore Magomero could easily be defended, as it stood on a river and was surrounded on three sides by water.

Although the Bishop would have preferred Soche's, he bowed to Livingstone's judgment and allowed himself to be persuaded. "In a sanitary point of view it seemed the worst place that could be chosen," wrote Rowley, "it was enforced upon the Bishop by Dr. Livingstone for prudential reasons." Before proceeding farther, however, it was decided to call on the Ajawa chief to try to persuade him to "give up his warring and slaving activities, and turn the energies of his people to peaceful pursuits." Intended as a peace mission, the visit proved disastrous.

On the morning of the 22nd [of July, 1861] we were informed that the Ajawa were near, and were burning a village a few miles off. Leaving the rescued slaves, we moved off to seek an interview with these scourges of the country. On our way we met crowds of Manganja fleeing from the war in front. The villages were all deserted; one where we breakfasted two years before was burnt; the stores of corn were poured out in cart-loads and scattered all over the plain, neither conquerors nor conquered having been able to convey it away.

About two o'clock we saw the smoke of burning villages, and heard triumphant shouts, mingled with the wail of Manganja women, lamenting over their slain. The Bishop then engaged us in fervent prayer; and, on rising from our knees, we saw a long line of Ajawa warriors, with their captives, coming round the hill-side. The first of the returning conquerors were entering their own village below, and we heard women welcoming them back with "lillilooings."

The Ajawa headman left the path on seeing us, and stood on an ant-hill to obtain a complete view of our party. We called out that we had come to have an interview with them, but some of the Manganja who followed us shouted "Our Chibisa is come": Chibisa being well known as a great conjurer and general. The Ajawa ran off yelling and screaming, "Nkondo! Nkondo!" (War! War!). We heard the words of the Manganja, but they did not strike us at the moment as neutralising all our assertions of peace.

The captives threw down their loads on the path, and fled to the hills; and a large body of armed men came running up from the village, and in a few seconds they were all around us, although mostly concealed by the projecting rocks and long grass. In vain we protested that we had not come to fight with them but to talk to them. They would not listen, having, as we remembered afterwards, good reason, in the cry of "Our Chibisa." Flushed with recent victory over three villages, and confident of an easy triumph over a mere handful of men, they began to shoot their poisoned arrows, sending them with great force upwards of a hundred yards, and wounding one of our fellows through the arm.[24]

As the white men, still anxious to avoid bloodshed, slowly retreated up the hill, the tribesmen closed in to within fifty yards, yelling and dancing "hideously," while some went behind to cut the party off. Eventually it was necessary to open fire and drive the attackers off. Livingstone does not say that any of them were hit, but according to Kirk, who was not present and got the story second hand, "the rifles took down about six men." Another fact which Livingstone omits to mention is that after all the Ajawa had fled to the hills he burned—or allowed to be burned—their villages, which contained large quantities of booty. This was normal procedure in tribal war but scarcely what was to be expected of an English missionary.

For Livingstone the fight was a traumatic experience, implying a fall from grace which affected him profoundly, and gave a special significance to his subsequent remark that this was the "turning point of our prosperous career." Although he had often been in danger of attack, in all the years he had traveled in Africa he had never had to use a weapon in self-defense; by a combination of coolness, patience and force of personality he had always got himself out of an ugly situation without bloodshed. He was so little prepared for it on this occasion as to be unarmed himself, until the Bishop thrust his own rifle into his hands after a poisoned arrow had fallen between them. "Had we known better . . . the temper of these bloodthirsty marauders," he wrote in extenuation of the action, "we should have tried messages and presents before going near them."[25]

Livingstone was not a pacifist; although he had never used it before, he knew that a show of force was the best way of avoiding trouble. But he realized that to take sides in what was essentially a tribal struggle would be a fatal blunder and wreck the peaceful purpose of the Mission. It was one thing to release slaves from dealers who were strangers in the land and were detested by the whole population, but it was quite another to ally oneself with the Manganja against the Ajawa. For the former were no better than the latter; they were just as ready to take prisoners and sell them as slaves if they got the chance; the only difference was that, until the arrival of their new "Chibisa"—in the shape of an Anglican Bishop and other white men armed with Lee-Enfields—they were getting the worst of it. And to espouse the cause of the weaker was simply to make enemies of the stronger, whose cooperation was needed even more if the Mission was to succeed.

Thus when the Bishop, his blood up after this baptism of fire, wanted to pursue the defeated Ajawa and drive them out of the country, Livingstone strongly advised against it; and on the Bishop inquiring whether, in the event of the Manganja again asking aid against the Ajawa, he ought to accede to their request, "No," replied Livingstone, "you will be oppressed by their importunities, but do not interfere in native quarrels." Unfortunately this advice was to go unheeded, with what results we shall see.

11

Feminine Interlude

August 1861–March 1862

HAVING DISPOSED of the missionaries—for the time being—Livingstone was free to continue the work of the Expedition and turned his attention with relief to its next objective. This was the exploration of Lake Nyassa, for the special purpose of discovering whether at the northern end its waters flowed into the Rovuma River. Should they be found to do so, then the problem might be solved of obtaining an access route to the lake beyond control of the Portuguese.

Leaving the *Pioneer* in charge of the first mate, Mr. Gedye, Livingstone, with his brother and Kirk and a party of Makololo, set out on August 6, 1861. They took a four-oared gig, complete with sails and awning, which had to be carried by hired porters for forty miles past the Murchison cataracts before it could be launched on the smooth water above. This took three weeks. Another week, now using the boat for transport, brought them to the junction of the river with the lake, which they entered on September 2. They then sailed along the western shore, while the land party, carrying the goods for barter, followed on foot. In the boat, besides the three members of the Expedition, were an Irish sailor, called John Neil, and a black crew.

It was the season of equinoctial gales and the waters of the lake were frequently lashed by terrific storms which got up in a few minutes. On one occasion they were caught in a storm a short way off shore, dared not return through the breakers, and had to ride it out at anchor for six anxious hours, expecting every moment to be swamped by the waves. After this experience Livingstone was sensible enough to take the advice of John Neil, who had been a fisherman on the coast of Ireland, as to when it was safe to put out. At night it was necessary to beach the boat to prevent its sinking, and often they "sat cowering on the land for days together waiting for the surf to go down."

The first impressions of the lakeside people were favorable. Livingstone had never seen in Africa such a dense population; wherever the travelers stopped they were immediately surrounded by hundreds of natives, curious at seeing white men for the first time. There also seemed to be plenty of food, including fish obtained from the lake. But soon there was a change for the worse. The people became less friendly and were unwilling to sell food. One night, as the white men slept in their tents, thieves crept in and stole nearly all their possessions, with the exception fortunately of the firearms. It was the first time Livingstone had ever been robbed in Africa. Not long after, they came on the familiar signs of tribal war: burned villages and putrefying corpses showing that there had been savage raids only a few days before. Farther on, the ground was strewn with skulls and skeletons. The marauders, they learned, were the Mazitu, a Zulu tribe who had originally come from the south to settle round the upper end of the lake.

The land party now refused to go on without a European to protect them, so Livingstone left the boat, after giving orders for it to meet him later at another point. Unable to find a path along the rocky shore, from which the mountains rose abruptly, he had to strike inland over a succession of steep ridges and spent a whole day advancing only five miles. When at last he reached the rendezvous it was to see the boat disappearing; after being chased by Mazitu pirates in canoes, it was driven by bad weather to take shelter farther up the coast and could not return till four days later. Meanwhile Livingstone, deserted by all but two of his followers, wandered unarmed into a party of Mazitu warriors, who at first threatened him by rattling their spears on their shields but fled in terror when he showed them "the hideous white skin of my arms." Accompanied by one goat as their sole remaining provision, the three men struggled back to the shore. Here they found an abandoned canoe, but on attempting to launch it in a rough sea "it was nearly upset every time the goat moved and it soon filled with water from leaks besides."[1] They spent a cheerless night without a fire so as not to attract attention, and only the next morning, the fourth since their separation, sighted the boat returning to pick them up. "What on earth made you run away and leave us?" were Livingstone's first words to Kirk; on which the latter commented in his diary: "Nothing like taking the first word and laying the blame on someone." The mistake had in fact been made by Livingstone in refusing to believe it when told by natives that the inland path did not rejoin the shore for several days' march.

The party, although reunited, were now in a situation of some danger, which Kirk blamed on Livingstone's foolhardiness. Separated from their porters, in hostile country, with food running out, and several of them, including Neil, the only competent seaman, down with fever, it was obviously impossible to go on. As Livingstone tersely explained in his subsequent dispatch to the Foreign Secretary:

> She [the boat] reported the coast in front to be worse than that I had trudged over. Mountains formed a most inhospitable coast by precipices coming down 500 or 1000 feet perpendicularly to the water's edge; the peoples either fugitives from a slave war which is raging on the opposite coast to feed the Iboe slave trade, or pirates living on detached rocks and rushing out towards the boat. A fathom of calico was demanded for a fish's head. Our provisions were expended, the land party had gone back, so though the large land masses loomed in the distance in which Lake Nyassa ends we were obliged to return also.[2]

Livingstone estimated that the lake was 225 miles long, but could gain no definite information from the natives. One of them, who lived at the southern end, when questioned on the subject, replied: "Why, if one started as a mere boy to walk to the other end of the lake, he would be an old grey-headed man before he got there. I never heard of such a thing being attempted."[3] Lake Nyassa is actually 300 miles long, and he had gone nearly two-thirds of the way up it. Had he been by himself he might have pushed on, regardless, as was his habit, of all risks. But he had the safety of his companions to think of and was forced to register another disappointment. For the object of the exercise, which was to establish if there was any connection between Lake Nyassa and the Rovuma River, had not been achieved. Every native he questioned gave a different account: "One man declared positively that we could sail out of the Lake into the river, and another would assert with equal positiveness that the boat must be carried at least fifty miles or a hundred."[4]

In fact the headwaters of the Rovuma lie only thirty miles from the eastern shore of Lake Nyassa and nearly opposite the point on the western shore reached by Livingstone. Had he proceeded up the eastern side—which would also have been safer for the boat, since the prevailing wind was easterly and she would have been under the lee of the land—he would probably have solved the problem. To cross from one side to the other, over thirty miles of treacherous water, would have been too dangerous in that season; the only way it could have been done, as Livingstone told the Foreign Secretary, was to capture an Arab dhow which was being used to ferry slaves across the lake—"but we had no slave papers and the owners kept it well out of our way."[5]

Now the problem was to get the party safely back to their base, some 300 miles to the south. Weather permitting, the boat could carry them by day, but at night it had to be beached and they must then sleep ashore. Without the Makololo escort, all but two of whom had turned tail and were finding their own way home, the four white men had only their own weapons with which to defend themselves and their black companions. One evening their camp was invaded by hostile tribesmen. Realizing that they were in serious danger, Livingstone took precautions which probably saved the whole party from being massacred. With his usual understatement he describes the incident in his journal.

People became very impudent, imagining that we had been obliged to flee from the Mazitu. At last, during our meal, some sat close to us, making remarks and laughing at everything. Masega [one of the two remaining Makololo escort] spoke to them and they pointed their spears at him. This was not to be borne, and the Makololo made a general rush at them, mauling right and left with their sticks. They were 'slightly elevated'—threatened to attack us by night, which is the mode of warfare all arrow-weaponed people adopt. A battle axe stolen during the fray was brought back as an excuse for seeing how we lay. We burned off the grass around and set watches. I took the first, Dr. K. the second, and C.L. the third. At eleven, when the moon was down, I shifted all the camp to a sleeping place under a dark shady tree, leaving tent and grass of the men's beds standing: the goods all in the boat, the guard under its lee of the bank. About 1 A.M. a man came with his bow and arrow and saw that we had shifted. Dr. K. simply looked, ready to act if required. He seemed to have gone off and informed the others that we were on the alert, and none came.[6]

It is curious—or rather characteristic—that in his published *Narrative* Livingstone made no mention of this incident whatsoever. Other travelers, writing up their adventures, would have made the best of such an experience, and we should have been spared none of the details: the silent preparations for an attack, the nerve-racking watch in the moonlight, the stealthy shifting of the camp, the tense moments observing the movements of the enemy scout and the long wait till dawn brought relief.

Livingstone was vain of his achievements as an explorer, but only insofar as they contributed to geographical knowledge or the progress of mankind; of the courage and endurance which rendered them possible he made no account, as of things that were all in the day's work. It is not surprising, therefore, that he should have passed over this particular example of his coolness and resource in the presence of danger.

He had, however, other reasons for suppressing it. In the *Narrative,* as in his dispatches, he was trying to persuade the reader that the new countries he had discovered were suitable for British enterprise and British settlement. Having decided in his mind that Lake Nyassa was an ideal place for mission stations, he was not going to say anything that cast doubt on its fitness.

His companions generally were much less sanguine and found their leader's unshaken optimism not a little irritating. But the principal victims of it were the missionaries, who considered that they had been "led up the garden" by Livingstone's glowing accounts of the Shire valley and Lake Nyassa. As one of them wrote in his diary, after hearing the story of the forestalled night attack: "Yet this is the place proposed for a mission station!!"[7]

Frequent gales delayed the return journey, and when the wind dropped, the heat of the sun became almost unendurable.

The exposure to the sun we have endured is very great [grumbled Kirk to his diary]. The awning has very seldom been up, for the least wind that moved Dr. L. ordered up the mast and sail, when it would have been far better to pull under the awning. We must attribute the great amount of fever we have had to want of exercise, exposure to the sun and bad food.[8]

On October 26 they reached the outlet at the southern tip of the lake which they had entered eight weeks previously, and after crossing the smaller sheet of water, Lake Malombe, which lies just below, commenced the descent of the Shire. Here the land party, who had rejoined the main body after their desertion, went off again, this time to hunt elephant, without telling Livingstone, and he decided not to wait for them. They were probably desperate for food, but he chose to regard it as a second mutiny; and, as Kirk observed, the remainder of the Expedition—four white men and three blacks, two of them slaves from Sena—got on better alone. They still had some goods for barter, since one of the reasons why they had gone hungry on the lake was that the calico supplied by the Government was so inferior—"being of the flimsiest quality, deficient in breadth and plastered over with starch"—that the natives, accustomed to dealing with Arab slave traders, refused to accept it in payment; and they used what was left to reward some tribesmen who helped them to sling the boat from the branches of a tree at the head of the Murchison cataracts, for recovery should they ever come back. The remaining forty miles having been covered on foot, they reached the *Pioneer* on November 8, after an absence of just over three months, all of them "in a very weak condition, having suffered more from hunger than on any previous trip."[9]

For Kirk the greatest relief was to step ashore and see the last of the gig.

> Sitting in the stern of that boat exposed all day to the sun has made an impression not easily forgotten. The inactivity and the pains in the bones and joints, the gradual emaciation, the fevers and the starvation of that Nyassa journey combine to make this the hardest, most trying and most disagreeable of all our journies. It is the only one I have no pleasure in looking back on. The insubordinate state of the Makololo, and the treacherous people who robbed us and attempted a night attack, did not add anything to our enjoyment.[10]

And Kirk was not one to exaggerate.

But for Livingstone it was not the dangers and hardships endured, nor the failure to trace the source of the Rovuma, that remained in his memory, but the grisly evidence, in rotting corpses and whitening bones, that Lake Nyassa was the nerve center of the slave trade.

> Would that we could give a comprehensive account [he was later to write in the *Narrative*] of the horrors of the slave trade, with an approximation to the number of lives it yearly destroys! For we feel sure that were even half the truth told and recognised, the feelings of men would be so thoroughly roused that this devilish traffic in human flesh would be put down at all risks.[11]

Nobody did more to rouse those feelings than Livingstone; yet nearly a quarter of a century would pass before the last stronghold of the Arab slavers on Lake Nyassa was destroyed.

The trip to the lake had procured one blessing for Livingstone, if only temporarily; it had taken him away from the missionaries and their problems. Now he was back in the thick of them and did not like the look of it. His last words of advice to the Bishop were not to allow himself to be persuaded to take sides in a tribal war and not to engage in fighting except in self-defense. He had scarcely left them, however, before the missionaries had proceeded to do these very two things. At the head of an army of Manganja they had gone on the warpath against the Ajawa, routed them and burned their village; and in a second punitive expedition, possibly more justified, they had burned another village where two of their company had been attacked and robbed and some attendants taken prisoner. The folly of the action lay in the fact that in the matter of slave dealing there was nothing to choose between the Manganja and the Ajawa. For example, after the battle was over, Kirk tells us, "the Bishop found the Manganja, for whom he had been fighting, making captives of Ajawa children for sale as slaves." Worst of all, from its leader's point of view, some men from the Expedition, who were staying with the Mission for their health, had taken part.

Livingstone heard the story from the lips of the Bishop, who came down from Magomero to the *Pioneer* a week after Livingstone's return from Lake Nyassa. Appalled by the news, and realizing what effect it would have at home, where the doings of the Mission would inevitably be linked with his own name, he sat down immediately to write to the Foreign Secretary in order to absolve himself of all responsibility.

SHIRE, 15 NOVR, 1861.

I beg leave to state, for your Ldp's private information, that Bishop Mackenzie told me that he went and attacked another body of Ajawa near Mount Zomba, drove them away and burnt their town. I had sent the Engineer, quarter-master and one seaman of the *Pioneer,* who were much reduced by fever, up to the highlands for a month for a change of air . . . They were invited by the Bishop to go with the missionaries to the fight and inconsiderately went. They recollected afterwards that they had no orders to do so, nor indeed to fire a shot unless they were attacked, but are to be excused in consideration of the position of the gentleman who asked them to go . . . The blood was shed by the mission party alone. The Bishop seemed rather proud of the affair . . .

After reporting his own rejection of a similar request from Manganja chiefs to go against the Ajawa, Livingstone concluded the dispatch as follows:

A missionary ought in all lawful things to identify himself with the interests of his people, but it is doubtful whether this should extend to fighting for them. I shall keep carefully aloof from the policy adopted by this new mission, not so much because my explanations of the policy usually pursued by philanthropists have been stultified by the fighting after I left, but because it has made the Ajawa enemies of the English, and they will continue so. The first affair could easily have been got over, as we were able to say, 'You began it,' 'You attacked us,' but not the second and third by the Bishop.[12]

If Livingstone a year earlier could write that the sending of the Universities Mission was the best news ever for Africa, he must have felt now it was just about the worst. For, whoever was to blame, the fact was that as a result of the Bishop's action, all his own work among the tribes in the Shire valley was undone and all his plans for the country were fatally compromised. And the irony of it was that but for that speech at Cambridge none of this would have happened, and that he was merely reaping the whirlwind of his own enthusiasm and eloquence. The chickens were coming home to roost and this was only the first of them.

There was, however, consolation in the news that now arrived that a ship was on its way from Cape Town, bringing the Bishop's sister, Miss Mackenzie; the wife of another missionary, Mrs. Burrup; and Livingstone's own wife, Mary. We last heard of Mrs. Livingstone, it may be remembered, when she was dumped at the Cape from the *Pearl,* having been found pregnant on the voyage from England besides suffering atrociously from seasickness. After the birth of her child, she had returned to Scotland to join her other offspring. How she came to leave them again, in order to be reunited with her husband, is explained by his Victorian biographer in a passage which, in spite of its discreetness, tells us enough about her motives.

Some of them [the children] were at school. No comfortable home for them all could be found, and though many friends were kind, the time was not a happy one. Mrs. Livingstone's desire to be with her husband was intense; not only the longings of an affectionate heart, and the necessity of taking counsel with him about the family, but the feeling that when over-shadowed by one whose faith was so strong her fluttering heart would regain its steady tone, and she would be better able to help both him and the children, gave vehemence to this desire. Her letters to her husband tell of much spiritual darkness; his replies were the very soul of tenderness and Christian earnestness.[13]

In other words the wretched woman was at the end of her tether. With a growing family to care for, no husband, no home and no relations to turn to (her own were in South Africa and she had quarreled with his), having lost the religious faith which might have sustained her, she could no longer face her life alone in England and was willing to take any risk to see Livingstone again. Only his awareness of her desperate need for him, one assumes, could have induced him to authorize a journey from which by now he must have known that the odds, at any rate for a woman, were against survival.

But there was another reason for letting her come, and it appears in a letter of his to her mother, Mrs. Moffat, after her death. "I regret," he wrote, "as there always are regrets after our loved ones are gone, that the slander which, unfortunately, reached her ears from missionary gossips and others had an influence on me in allowing her to come, before we were fairly on Lake Nyassa. A doctor of divinity said, when her devotion to her family was praised: 'Oh, she is no good, she is here because her husband cannot live with her.' The last day will tell another tale."[14]

Although they had in fact been separated for half their married life, there is no evidence that Livingstone preferred to live apart from his wife, and those who knew them best did not believe it. In her reply to his letter Mrs. Moffat wrote:

As for the cruel scandal that seems to have hurt you both so much, those who said it did not know you *as a couple*. In all *our* intercourse with you, we never had a doubt as to your being comfortable together. I know there are some maudlin ladies who insinuate, when a man leaves his family frequently, no matter how noble is his object, that he is not *comfortable* at home. But we can afford to smile at this and say, 'The Day will declare it.' . . .[15]

To the Victorians, of course, the word "comfortable," when applied to a married couple, did not mean what it would today, i.e., moderately well off financially. It implied that they had a happy relationship in the fullest sense, including the sexual; and in this case it would seem to be confirmed by the frequency, considering the little she saw of her husband, of Mrs. Livingstone's pregnancies.

The news of her approach, and that of the other two ladies, was brought by Mrs. Burrup's husband, a young clergyman who had come out to join the Universities Mission and found his own way from the coast by canoe—quite a feat for a newcomer to Africa. He also reported the arrival, in parts carried on the deck of another ship, of the *Lady Nyassa,* the new portable steamer ordered by Livingstone for carriage past the Murchison Falls (which in fact were a series of shallow cataracts extending for thirty miles) and launching on the lake she was named after. She had been built at Livingstone's own expense—the Government having rejected a suggestion of Washington's that they should contribute half the cost—for the sum of £6,000, which was about all that remained of the fortune he had made from his book after setting up a trust to provide for his family. The safe arrival of the boat, accompanied by Rae, the former engineer of the *Ma Robert,* who had supervised her construction, was probably the best news of all for Livingstone.

The Bishop, delighted by the news about his sister, was keen to go and meet her at the coast, a proceeding of which Livingstone privately disapproved.

The Bishop does not realize his position [he wrote in his journal], as he intends leaving his most important post at this time to bring up his sisters! He seems to lean on them. Most high church people seem to lean on wives or sisters, I would as soon lean on a policeman.[16]

Eventually it was arranged that Mackenzie, accompanied by the new recruit, Burrup, should return to the mission station at Magomero and from there explore a way by land to the mouth of the Ruo River, a lower tributary of the Shire, where the *Pio-*

neer, carrying the ladies, would meet them in January, that being as far up the river as it was thought advisable to bring her. The two men, whom they were never to meet again, then took leave of the *Pioneer* and her crew, receiving "three hearty English cheers as they went to the shore," and the ship steamed off on her journey down the river.[17]

The water should have been high, but the rains stopped early and it started to fall. After only twenty miles the ship ran aground. All the usual methods employed to move her, such as laying out of anchors, etc., were unavailing, and there she remained, on and off, for the next five weeks, from the beginning of December 1861 till the first week in January. Stuck in the most unhealthy section of the river, known as Elephant Marsh, one after the other came down with malaria. It was now that the Expedition suffered its first fatal casualty with the death of the ship's carpenter, "a fine healthy young man," who, as Livingstone assured his readers, "had enjoyed perfect health all the time he had been with us."

During the long and dreary wait for the water to rise again, Livingstone was tormented by the thought of his wife arriving on the coast and not finding him there to meet her. He considered going on in a boat but decided that his duty was to remain with the ship. Finally it got off, and on January 7 passed the Ruo River, where, as there was no sign of the Bishop, Livingstone concluded that he had heard of the detention of the *Pioneer* and deferred his journey. He therefore continued on his way to the coast, arriving at the Luabo mouth of the Zambezi on January 23.

In fact the Bishop did not know of the delay and had set off with Burrup, as arranged, to keep the rendezvous at the mouth of the Ruo. Finding the land route impracticable owing to the unsettled state of the country, they took a canoe at Chibisa's, where they had said goodbye to the *Pioneer,* and on January 8 started down the river. On the following night the canoe capsized in shallow water; although nobody was hurt the two missionaries were soaked to the skin, lost their change of clothing, most of their provisions and, worse still, all their medicines. When they arrived the next day at the Ruo, it was to find that the *Pioneer* had passed by a few days before. To return to their base at Magomero, a distance of more than 100 miles, was considered impossible in their destitute and weakened condition. They therefore decided to await the return of the ship, meanwhile taking up their residence on an island where a hut was provided for them by the local chief.

There was no lack of food, but both men were exhausted by their journey and ill; the Bishop was also depressed by the difficulties he foresaw in getting his sister to Magomero if Livingstone was not prepared to take the *Pioneer* above the Ruo, and generally by the difficulty of maintaining communications between the mission station and the sea. Livingstone had advised that the missionaries should have their own ship, but there had not been time to provide one and instead they had relied on his. Now they realized they could no longer depend on this—he had, after all, his own program to carry out—the future of the Mission looked bleak.

After a fortnight, during which he daily became weaker with fever and diarrhea, the Bishop went into a coma. Five days later he died without having regained consciousness and was buried by his companion. Burrup, himself in very poor shape, then struggled back to Chibisa's, where he collapsed. He had to be carried to Magomero, arriving on February 14, and a week later he too was dead.

The indirect cause of the double tragedy was the anxiety of the two men to meet their womenfolk in order to conduct them from the Ruo to Magomero. But of course women should never have come to such a country at that stage, and for their doing so the other missionaries blamed Livingstone for misrepresenting its conditions.

The probable arrival of the ladies [wrote Rowley] was a great cause of anxiety to us; under happiest circumstances their presence would have been, at so early a period in the history of the Mission, a mistake, a great mistake, involving them and us in much trouble, even if they found those to whom they came alive. Bishop Mackenzie did not write for his sisters until he was told he might safely do so by Dr. Livingstone, who expected his wife to join him, and for whom we proposed building a house at our Station.[18]

If it was true that Livingstone had encouraged the Bishop to send for his sisters, it must have been before the misfortunes which had befallen both the Expedition and the Mission. Before women could safely come out it was essential, firstly, that a healthy and secure mission station be established in the highlands, and, secondly, that there be swift and dependable communication with the coast. With his usual optimism Livingstone may have assumed that these conditions would be fulfilled, for otherwise it was madness to let the women come. But it was now too late to stop them, and in the case of his own wife it is doubtful whether he would have tried anyhow, since the unhappiness of her life at home made even the pestiferous Zambezi seem preferable.

Meanwhile the ladies in question, accompanied by a bevy of clergymen, were making slow progress toward the goal of all their hopes, little realizing what was in store for them. The sailing brig *Hetty Ellen* conveying them from Durban had arrived off the mouth of the Zambezi on January 8, 1862, and not finding the *Pioneer*, which was still aground in the Shire, had put to sea again, been caught in a tornado and nearly foundered before finding shelter at the island of Mozambique. There it was met by a British warship, H.M.S. *Gorgon*, which had orders to conduct it back to the Zambezi. Among the officers of the *Gorgon* was a young assistant paymaster called Devereux, who kept a diary which was afterward published as a book under the title *A Cruise in the "Gorgon."* He was a shrewd observer with a lively pen, thanks to which we get an intriguing picture of what must surely have been one of the oddest collections of people ever to set foot in primitive Africa.

On the feminine side it consisted of Mrs. Livingstone, "a motherly-looking lady about thirty-eight or forty"; Miss Mackenzie, sister of the Bishop, "a pleasant, humerous, good-natured elderly Scotch lady"; Mrs. Burrup, soon to be widowed; and "two maid-servants, or lady's maids, who are rather fond of dress, but a little steadied by being attached to the mission." There were also several new members of the Universities Mission, and an independent visitor, the Reverend Dr. James Stewart, sent out by the Free Church of Scotland, who is described by Devereux as "a manly looking fellow, not thinking too much of himself to take a turn at the wheel, or anything else when necessary, knowing something of curing the body as well as the soul, and, in fact, one of those rare missionaries who like to see whether the object to be gained is worth the risk of a number of valuable lives—a most sensible plan of the Presbyterian Church, a good example to our own Mackenzie mission, which is not content to push a part of people blindfold and almost purposeless into the wilds of South Africa, but adds to their distressing position by allowing a lot of helpless females in their blind devotion to accompany them."[19]

Carried in the hold or on the deck of the *Hetty Ellen* were the several hundred parts of the *Lady Nyassa*, the new steamer ordered by Livingstone for launching on Lake Nyassa. They were in charge of Rae, Livingstone's faithful engineer, who had been supervising the construction of the vessel and now had the responsibility, to quote Devereux again,

> first, of taking the brig and her cargo to Quillimane river (a place reeking with fever), crossing its dangerous bar, putting the steamer together (a work of three weeks), taking her to Congoni,* steaming up the shallow and comparatively unknown river of Zambezi, unshipping her at the Murchison Falls, carrying the *Ladies*, maid-servants, steamer and gear, weighing 140 tons, through a country full of obstacles, tribes, jungle, and brutes of the wilds, and to push his way to the Lake Nyassa, where, perhaps, he may find the mission located. If the engineer carries all safely to its destination, and floats the "Lady Nyassa", as his piecemeal steamer is called, on the lake, he will deserve a monument in the Institute of Civil Engineers . . .[20]

Devereux seems to have been rather a cynical young man, but with his skepticism he was only reflecting the attitude of the Navy generally to the whole crazy scheme. For four years now they had been risking the lives of their boats' crews crossing the murderous bars of the Zambezi in support of Livingstone, and although their help was never lacking, their patience was wearing thin. To have now to cart women around in these dangerous waters and fever-

* Devereux's spelling of the Kongone.

infested swamps, which he had represented as no serious obstacle to European settlement and commerce, must have been almost the last straw.

However, they set about their task cheerfully by inviting the ladies to transfer from their uncomfortable quarters in the brig to the more commodious *Gorgon*. For weeks the five women had shared the *Hetty Ellen's* only cabin, where "their first sleep," if we are to believe Devereux, "was generally disturbed by the midnight consultation of captain and mate laying off the distance, and arranging the course on the thumb-stained chart, the huge legs of the worthy skipper frequently spanning the tender forms beneath him like the Colossus at Rhodes." The invitation was also extended to the missionaries, but only the "high church" party accepted; the "low" remained where they were, "thinking the discomforts of mingling with the other party greater than those on board the brig." The invitation was likewise refused by Mrs. Livingstone, who perhaps preferred the companionship of the man who had escorted her out from England. In the brig also stayed the wagon and two mules, which were to transport the *Lady Nyassa* past the cataracts, and Miss Mackenzie's donkey, Alice.

Of the new arrivals, James Stewart was the most interesting, both in his own right and because of his connection with the Livingstones. Born in 1831—eighteen years junior to Livingstone—he had been at Edinburgh University and then at St. Andrews, later returning to Edinburgh to study divinity under the aegis of the Free Church. Having read Livingstone's *Missionary Travels*, he was inspired—like so many of his earnest young contemporaries—to emulate its author, and with two fellow students proposed to the Foreign Mission Committee of the Free Kirk that they should found a mission station in Central Africa, with the dual purpose of converting the heathen and developing cotton production, as urged by Livingstone in his lectures. Some businessmen in Glasgow, Liverpool and Manchester were interested and formed a committee to provide finance. It was decided that as a first step Stewart should go out to the Zambezi and prepare a report, and with the help of money he obtained himself by selling some of his inheritance, including the family plate, a sufficient sum was raised to pay for his journey. During these preparations he had been in correspondence with Livingstone, who had encouraged the project, had met Mrs. Livingstone and for a time acted as tutor to their son Thomas. He had also helped her, or tried to, with her "religious difficulties," and delayed his passage to South Africa, at her request, so that they could travel together. In return she secured his passage in the brig by refusing to go without him when the High Church party tried to keep him off it. It was, therefore, almost inevitable that malicious gossip should have linked their names together; and it was to this no doubt that her mother, Mrs. Moffat, was referring, in the letter to Livingstone already quoted, when she wrote of "the cruel scandal that seems to have hurt you both so much."*

Leaving Mozambique on January 22, the *Gorgon,* with the brig in tow, called first at Quelimane for the latest news of Livingstone and then continued to the East Luabo mouth of the Zambezi, where they arrived on January 31—the very date, if the passengers had known it, of Bishop Mackenzie's death. From the deck the ladies gazed eagerly at the shore, still several miles away, in the hope of spotting some sign of the explorers, and this time they were not disappointed. There, plainly visible, was a little white steamer with a red cross on her paddle box, which could only be the renowned *Pioneer.* Embarking in his gig Cap-

---

* The origin of the scandal, which first arose when Mrs. Livingstone was living alone in Scotland, as told to Kirk by Stewart himself, is revealed in the following passage from a letter written by Kirk to his brother Alick, dated July 25, 1862.

> I suspect that all this came out of scandal caused by the injudicious conduct of both. No doubt he hoped to gain influence with Dr. L. through her. Certainly he did so and as he knew her character and professes (confidentially to me, so don't speak of it) to have found out early in the day that she drank very freely, so as to be utterly besotted at times, I think any prudent man would have drawn off from such a person, instead of risking his character by going at late hours into a married woman's bedroom and to prevent the people becoming aware, studiously keeping even the landlady of the house out, lest she should find out the secret. Of course the truth soon became well known and Mr. Stewart's visits had an interpretation placed upon them and quite naturally too. Now I believe that he only did all this to gain capital with Dr. L. and perhaps, as he says, also with a view to hiding such a scandal.[21]

tain Wilson, commander of the *Gorgon,* immediately set off for the vessel and, in spite of mistaking the passage and capsizing on the bar, finally succeeded in boarding her. The return of the gig, which did not appear until the next day, with "information concerning their loved ones up country," was anxiously awaited by the two ladies, Miss Mackenzie and Mrs. Burrup, sitting in the gangway through the night. Of more interest to the professional sailors on board, who had seen their much-loved captain narrowly escape drowning in his eagerness to obtain news for his frail and forlorn guests, was their conclusion from the gig's experience that "a long sharp-bowed craft of her size is unfit for a heavy surf" and that "it is highly dangerous to cross under sail."

The great moment came at 8 A.M. the following morning, when the *Pioneer,* piloted by Livingstone, came out across the bar and steered for the *Gorgon*'s anchorage.

The great African traveller is on her paddle-box, dressed as usual in the consul's faded gear. He lifts his silver-laced cap to the ladies, and having passed us makes for something more interesting—the ladies in the brig astern.[22]

For Stewart, perhaps, more than any, it was a great moment, thus to meet for the first time his hero, who was also the world-famous husband of the woman to whom for many weeks, in the cramped confinement of shipboard life, he had been not only close companion but spiritual adviser. The impression it made on him is recorded in another of those ostensibly private journals which (fortunately for future historians) every self-respecting Victorian traveler in Africa felt obliged to keep.

LUABO MOUTH, FEBRUARY 1ST, 1862. This morning early the white funnel and hull of the *Pioneer* were seen making way across the bar towards us. The expedition of seven months were now brought to a climax in what the next few minutes will reveal. About 8 o'clock the *Pioneer* glided in between the *Gorgon* and the brig. We thought she was going on board the *Gorgon* and Mrs. Livingstone's countenance fell. But she glided on and I could not help remarking to Mrs. Livingstone that the Doctor seemed to be a great swell. It must be confessed that in his white trousers, frock coat and naval cap he looked uncommonly smart and really had a commanding air. All the troubles and work of many years seemed compensated for in the romance of this morning . . . Mrs. Livingstone has not seen him and I disturb or perturb her by saying, 'There he is'. I allow her emotion to subside and then add, he is, etc. She gives me a gratified slap for so speaking of the great pioneer and prince of travellers on whom I have just set my admiring eyes, with much though apparently little reverence.[23]

On being introduced to the great man, Stewart seems to have behaved as though he was in the presence of royalty. "I shake hands," he confesses, "and continue my backward progress under the awning. 'I am glad to see you here, Mr. Stewart.' 'Thank you, Doctor,' was all my reply, except the hearty goodwill and admiration with which I looked at the man."

In spite of this friendly welcome Stewart was not invited to breakfast in the *Gorgon,* an omission which he accepted "in a state of contented acquiescence," while noting with some satisfaction that when a more pushing individual, the Reverend Edward Hawkins, a member of the Universities Mission, climbed over the side and invited himself to join the Livingstones, "they look at him as if they wished him overboard."[24]

No doubt Livingstone was pleased to see his wife, but with enough trouble over the Mission already on his hands he must have been appalled by this onslaught of new recruits and womenfolk, with their maidservants, mountain of luggage and donkey, all totally inexperienced in African travel and all looking to him, whose first duty should have been to the Expedition, to provide for their safety, comfort and entertainment. Nor could it have been any consolation to remember that they had come in response to his past writings and speeches and that he was therefore being hoisted with his own petard.

Early the next morning the brig, with all the passengers on board, and the two paddle-box boats of the *Gorgon* attached to her stern, was taken in tow by the *Pioneer* and brought safely to anchor inside the bar, where the water for once was relatively smooth. With them went fifty armed officers and men from the *Gorgon,* under her commanding officer, Captain Wilson, who, as he explained in a report to the Admiralty dated April 25, had responded to an "earnest request" by Livingstone to assist the Expedition in transporting "at one trip (whilst the river was in flood) the hull of the *Lady Nyassa* to the foot of the Murchison Falls."[25] A further object of the naval party was to relieve the mission station at Magomero, in case it should be found, as Livingstone feared, to be under attack by the Ajawa.

It was a bold, even a rash, decision by Wilson, only justified by the fix he saw Livingstone was in. The *Gorgon* was short of provisions and was lying off a notoriously unhealthy coast at an unprotected anchorage which was quite untenable when the wind blew hard from the south—its prevailing direction for nine months of the year. And yet he realized that with his own resources Livingstone would never get his new steamer into the water, whereas with the help of the Navy "he calculated that one year's time would be saved."[26]

The first job to be done was to transfer the sections of the *Lady Nyassa,* the wagon, the mules, and the missionaries' baggage and stores, as well as the ladies and *their* abundant belongings, from the deck and holds of the brig to those of the *Pioneer.* A start was made with the mules, who, after refusing to let themselves be hoisted out of the ship, were blindfolded, pushed overboard and made to swim for the shore. As the pile of ironwork grew ever higher on the deck of the *Pioneer,* and every available space was fast filled up, it soon became obvious that even without the missionaries and their possessions it would be impossible to carry all the pieces of the steamer in one trip, and that at least three would be needed. As it was, most of the goods for the Mission, which included "wearing apparel, household furniture, provisions, agricultural instruments, cooking utensils, nicknacks of every kind, necessaries and luxuries lavishly furnished," were simply dumped on the shore where they remained "half buried in sand," for anyone to steal.[27]

On board the overcrowded and overladen *Pioneer,* everything was in confusion; but for the wardroom officers of the *Gorgon,* who had not enjoyed feminine society for many months, the presence of the ladies was a welcome distraction, observed with disapproval by the brooding and introspective Stewart, already worried by Livingstone's failure to observe the Sabbath.

The talk was of the lightest kind generally. Sometimes riddles and 'finding a word' formed the amusement of an hour or two. I can't say I found any pleasure in any of these evenings. I was alone and solitary and very friendless, fighting my way to a distant but certainly great aim, and my thoughts generally took flight to the past or future.[28]

Stewart had had one interview with Livingstone, shortly after his arrival, and recorded it verbatim in his journal.

On producing Dr. Candlish's* letter, he said: 'I don't want any certificate. I suppose you are the man Dr. Tweedie† wrote about.'

J.S. 'It is not a certificate. I did not mean to refer to these things. As an honest man yourself, you must know the pain it gives to be constantly suspected.'
DR. L. 'I think all that behaviour on their part was madness. It seems to me they were acting in the most nonsensical way imaginable.' And a good deal more followed in the same strain.

Of what could it be that Stewart was "constantly suspected" if it was not of having had an affair with Mrs. Livingstone?‡ As has been said, no evidence of this has ever been produced and neither Livingstone nor anybody in his family believed it. But the scandalous talk, started in missionary circles at home, where Livingstone had many enemies, spread far, and had now reached the mouth of the Zambezi.

The company [noted Kirk on February 3], in addition to our former number, is Mrs. Livingstone, a coarse, vulgar woman whose behaviour with a missionary (Mr. Stewart) seems to have caused some scandal.[29]

---

* Dr. Candlish was a prominent leader in the Scots Free Church secession.
† Dr. Tweedie, Convener of the Free Church, had written to Livingstone more than a year before, proposing to send out Stewart, and Livingstone had replied with an enthusiasm which evidently he no longer felt.
‡ Another story, put about by the Portuguese Consul at Cape Town, was that Stewart was not a missionary but a trader in disguise; but this was too ridiculous for any sensible man to take seriously.

And a few days later:

The Mr. Stewart who came prospecting for an industrial self-supporting mission will accompany us. He is A.1 in the Lady's books and thus stands sure in those of the Doctor. He seems to be an active man, but if there is truth in the stories he will make mischief yet. As to Mrs. L. she seems cut out for rough work but she is a queer piece of furniture.[30]

However much he believed in Stewart's innocence, it could have been scarcely pleasant for Livingstone to have the subject of such gossip living in close quarters with himself and his wife. However, he does not seem to have allowed it to affect their relations and when the two men later quarreled it was over other matters.

After a week's intense activity the *Pioneer* was so loaded she could hold no more. Some privacy was provided for the ladies by improvising a cabin for them out of the stern section of the *Lady Nyassa* which was carried on the deck, with the other supernumeraries finding a place where they could amidst the jumble of iron plates, boilers, machinery and stores, not to mention the mules and the donkey. On February 9 the ship weighed anchor and headed up the river.

It was only now that Livingstone's real troubles began, of which his summary account in the *Narrative* gives barely an idea.

We steamed off for the Ruo on the 10th of February, having onboard Captain Wilson and a number of his officers and men to help us discharge the cargo. Our progress was distressingly slow. The river was in flood, and we had a three-knot current against us in many places. The engines of the *Pioneer* were of the best quality, but had been entirely neglected by the engineer—the packing not having been renewed during twenty months. These causes delayed us six months in the delta, instead of, as we anticipated, only six days; for finding it impossible to carry the sections up to the Ruo without great loss of time, it was thought best to land them at Shupanga, and, putting the hull of the *Lady Nyassa* together there, to tow her up to the foot of the Murchison Cataracts.[31]

A typically misleading passage! It was true, as Rae, the other engineer, confirmed, that the engines of the *Pioneer* had been badly neglected by her own engineer, Hardesty. But this was not the only, or the most important, cause of delay. At the best of times the *Pioneer* drew too much water for the Zambezi, and now, with her enormous top-heavy load, she was aground more often than ever. It was the old story of wild miscalculation, blind optimism and refusal to take any advice, on the part of Livingstone, that had wrecked his plans again and again.

Dr. Livingstone [wrote Devereux] is the only one of the Expedition who has sanguine expectations of getting to the Murchison Falls; all the others (good authorities) think there will not be sufficient water; and if we do ground badly what will become of the "Lady of the Lake", of the live ladies, and all their baggage —is dreadful to contemplate.[32]

No sooner [Stewart wrote] was the boat got off one bank by might and main, and steady hauling by capstan on anchor laid out ahead got a few miles of fair steering, than again we heard that sound abhorred by all of us—a slight bump of the bow, and rush of sand along the ship's side, and we were again fast for a few hours, or a day or two, as the case might be.[33]

After a week's snaillike progress covering a bare eighty miles, it was clear that the *Pioneer* would never reach her destination. Captain Wilson then decided to go on by boat, taking with him Miss Mackenzie and Mrs. Burrup, who were increasingly anxious to be united, the former with her brother and the latter with her husband, not yet knowing that both men were dead; and on February 17 he set out in the *Gorgon*'s gig, with the two ladies and Dr. Ramsey, the ship's surgeon, on board. Kirk and Sewell, the *Gorgon*'s paymaster, followed in a whaler.

It was about 120 miles to the mouth of the Ruo River, where it was hoped to meet the Bishop, and they had been told by Livingstone that the return journey could be made in ten days. This estimate, as usual with Livingstone, was overoptimistic, and in fact it took ten days to reach the Ruo. Here the whaler was sent back with Sewell, and Kirk joined the party in the gig. Of what conditions must have been like in that open boat, in which some twenty people, including a crew of bluejackets and two women, had been living, eating, sleeping, and everything else for ten days, while constantly devoured by mosquitoes, we get some idea from a brief entry in Kirk's diary.

In the gig I found matters much less comfortable than in the whaler, where we two had made ourselves rather jolly. Now we had the stern completely occupied by the Bishop's old invalid sister who has followed him through some sort of fanatical infatuation. She was unable to place one foot before the other. If she decided to shift her position, she had to get assistance and to have herself supported with pillows. The daily ablution was a serious job; a bower or shelter had to be constructed (on shore) and she carried to it. Mrs. Burrup on the contrary was full of life, talked nautical and jumped about.[34]

On the island where the Bishop had died, the people, out of fear, pretended they had never heard of him, so it was decided to press on. Another five days, rowing and sailing, brought them to Chibisa's, just below the cataracts. Here were now settled the Makololo tribesmen with whom Livingstone had parted company after their desertion at Lake Nyassa; they had helped themselves to the prettiest of the slave girls rescued from the Ajawa and were living comfortably by hunting combined with occasional raids on their neighbors. It was from one of these men they first heard the news of the Bishop's death. There were also several letters addressed to Livingstone from the mission station at Magomero, which Kirk opened. They represented the missionaries as in such dire straits from famine and disease that he and Wilson decided immediately to go to their rescue, accompanied by a party of sailors. As only Kirk knew, it was a highly risky venture.

Nothing but what seemed an absolute necessity would have induced me to go off thus without medicines, proper food, or sufficient supply of cloth, during the wet season and with a large body of untried Englishmen . . . Had we known that some of them [i.e., the missionaries] were now healthy and strong and possessed not only goats but preserved meats, coffee and tea, I should have remained quietly awaiting their appearance.[35]

As it was, the journey nearly proved fatal. After two days, when they were barely halfway, Kirk and Wilson both collapsed with fever and were unable to go any farther. Kirk then sent on a native messenger to the mission station with an urgent request for medicines. Two days later the man returned, bringing news that Burrup too was dead, and soon after, three of the missionaries arrived. "To our surprise," wrote Kirk, "instead of haggard, starved men, they seemed all in tolerable health."

On starting to return to the boat Wilson was again overcome by weakness and had to be carried by his coxswain. After losing their way for some hours in the dark, the party reached a village where Wilson was put to bed and, watched over by an anxious Kirk, lay between life and death.

It was a chance which way the case would turn. As I went outside the hut, I could not help seeing by the starlight the rocky soil. It seemed all stone and rock and the idea which came with this was the difficulty of digging a grave. Scudamore [one of the missionaries] stuck to us throughout. He remained while we lost our way and quietly did his best to get the path. He would have taken his lot with us that night without a single word of murmur. His conduct contrasted with that of Rowley who looks after writing his journal and making himself comfortable.[36]

In the morning the Captain rallied sufficiently to be carried in an improvised hammock on the shoulders of four men, and by afternoon they were back at Chibisa's. Mrs. Burrup had already received a note from Kirk informing her of her husband's death and seemed to have borne the news stoically. As for Miss Mackenzie, Kirk tells us, "We found her very well indeed. She stood the shock very well, her behaviour deserves the greatest admiration." Livingstone, when later he met the lady, took a more cynical view: "Miss Mackenzie bears up very well; people who have a competence hold out wonderfully."[37]

Afterward, however, both women collapsed, as much from exposure and exhaustion as grief, and when they reached the ship they were carried on board barely conscious by seamen who themselves could scarcely stand.

With its cargo of bereaved women and commanding officer not yet recovered from his illness, the gig started the return journey on March 11. Helped by the current and stopping only for a brief visit to the Bishop's grave, where Kirk and Wilson erected a rude cross, the boat made a swift descent of the river and three days later, after an absence of nearly four weeks, reached the *Pioneer*, now at anchor off Shupanga.

The effect on Livingstone of the bad news it brought has been described by Stewart.

It was difficult to say whether he or the unhappy ladies on whom the blow fell with the most personal weight, were most to be pitied. He felt the responsibility, and saw the widespread dismay which the news would occasion when it reached England, and at the very time when the Mission most needed support. 'This will hurt us all,' he said, as he sat, resting his head on his hand, on the table of the dimly-lighted little cabin of the *Pioneer*.[38]

But Livingstone was not one to take misfortune lying down. After absorbing the first shock, he lost no time in writing off to England in order to clear himself with the Government and place the blame for the disaster firmly on the shoulders of the victims.

I feel extremely sorry [he told the Foreign Secretary in a dispatch of March 15] on account of this loss because of the effect it will produce at home on our enterprise, but we all feel persuaded that had these men exposed themselves in England as they did here, they could not have lived. We cure the fever so readily that they could not realize the danger of the climate, and all our warnings were thrown away when Mr. Burrup succeeded in ascending the Shire in a common canoe unscathed and referring to my travels it was maintained that 'what one man has done another may do.' And coarse living and rash exposure have ended in the sad loss of life.[39]

As Kirk had already noticed, there was nobody quicker than Livingstone at getting his word in first. Nor had he any patience with what he regarded as amateurism. Thus to Stewart a fortnight later he wrote:

This sad loss will have one good effect: better men will be sent and no one hereafter come for a lark or to make a good thing of playing the missionary for a few years and then reaping laurels.[40]

It was a scathing epitaph on Mackenzie, whom he liked personally, and generously defended in the *Narrative,* but privately considered deficient "in judgement and strength of decision," and on Burrup, who had annoyed him with the silly remark that what had been done by Livingstone could be done by others. He had no better opinion of Rowley, who spent most of his time writing and boasted of the articles he would sell to the press, or of Procter, who would "make an excellent parish priest." Only Scudamore, "a brick," earned his respect, and later Horace Waller, the layman of the Mission, who became a close friend.

And Livingstone of course was right: better men *did* come, but much later, and established missions in the Shire highlands and on Lake Nyassa just where he always thought they ought to be.

12

The Last Phase

March 1862–December 1863

THE DEATH of the Bishop was only the first of a series of blows which were now to befall the Expedition. It was as if some unseen opponent with whom Livingstone had been battling for four years—and just holding his own—had decided that the time had come to move in for the kill.

At the beginning of the year 1862 three problems faced Livingstone. The first was the revival, with the encouragement of the Portuguese, of the slave trade in the Shire valley, with its accompaniment of tribal war, which threatened to wreck all his plans and destroy the good he had done in opening up the river for legitimate trade; the second was the presence of the missionaries, who were both encumbering the Expedition with their requirements and embarrassing it by their misguided intervention in native politics; the third, and by far the most urgent, was how to get his new steamer up to the Murchison Falls.

On February 22, before he knew of the deaths of Mackenzie and Burrup, he wrote to the Foreign Secretary to say that he would be employed for the next twelve months in transporting the steamer to the lake, and asking whether he had authority, first, to "issue a formal protest or order to the Bishop not to engage in hostilities and thereby endanger my progress . . ." and second, "to take possession of new discoveries such as Lake Nyassa, in the name of Her Majesty."[1] In seeking permission to acquire territory he was also thinking of the Rovuma River, which the Governor General of Mozambique had asked the Sultan of Zanzibar to accept as the boundary between his possessions and the Portuguese. The Sultan had been persuaded by the British Consul, Colonel Rigby, to refuse, and to fix the border at Cape Delgado, several miles south of the Rovuma; but the incident showed that the Portuguese were only waiting to proclaim their sovereignty over any new area adjoining their colony explored by Livingstone.

Lord Russell's reply, which was not received till the end of October, gave it "as his opinion" that Livingstone should not interfere with the Mission except by "using your best efforts to persuade them to keep at peace with the Natives." He should point out "that such hostilities as those which they appear to have been engaged in endanger not only the success but the safety of both Expeditions and should not be undertaken except when absolutely necessary for self-defence." As for his second request, the answer, approved by Palmerston, was a blunt refusal: " I have to acquaint you that Her Majesty's Government cannot authorise you to take possession in their name of any new territory you may discover in Central Africa."[2]

They must have seen this coming and the last thing they wanted was to become involved in *any* colonial venture, especially with the added risk of international complications.

Nearly thirty years were to pass before the mood of England changed in this respect. Meanwhile it was a bitter thought to Livingstone that his own country might never benefit by his work, and all the fruit be reaped by the hated Portuguese. His only consolation was to learn that Her Majesty's Minister in Lisbon had been instructed to make strong representations against the continuance of the slave trade.

As for the *Lady Nyassa,* the steamer having arrived in parts, Livingstone had hoped to ship them to the Murchison Falls in one trip; but when it became clear that because of their weight and bulk and the lack of water this would not be possible even with several trips, he decided to carry the bits and pieces only as far as Shupanga, eighty miles from the mouth of the river, where they could be assembled and the vessel launched for steaming or towing to the foot of the falls.

The effect of this decision, which there was no avoiding, was to throw the whole of his timetable for the year out of gear. It would take three months for the transport of the parts, and another two for the assembling and launching, by which time the river would have fallen so low that it could not be navigated until the following January, and it would be the end of March 1863 before the *Lady Nyassa* at last reached the falls. Thus fifteen months were to be spent simply in moving the vessel to the point where she would have to be taken apart again for carrying past the cataracts—an operation which Livingstone had estimated would require a further twelve months.

These first three months of the year 1862, spent chugging up and down between the coast and Shupanga and endlessly loading and unloading the parts of the *Lady Nyassa,* were probably the unhappiest—although worse was still to come—of the whole Expedition to date. Livingstone had always dreaded spending any time in the delta, which invariably took its toll in fever and dysentery, and now he had his wife to consider too.

After the return of the *Gorgon*'s gig with Miss Mackenzie and Mrs. Burrup, Captain Wilson was impatient to return to his ship, which he knew to be seriously short of provisions and had not seen for more than six weeks. But when, accompanied by the *Pioneer,* he arrived at the coast, there was no sign of the vessel. She had been driven to sea by a gale, had gone to Mozambique to provision and only returned to the Kongone a fortnight later. The two bereaved women had then to be carried on board, while the officers and men who had escorted them were in little better shape; scarcely one had escaped malaria.

Captain W——— [Wilson] first arrives, and shakes our hands cheerfully; he appears a mere skeleton of his former self. Next two dark objects are borne on the crossed arms of two bluejackets; not a word comes from them . . . they are the ladies, not dead but next to it. . . . The boats' crews bring up the rear; pale, thin, and worn out, some of them too weak to walk.[3]

After the departure for the Cape of the *Gorgon* and the *Hetty Ellen,* there only remained of the band of pilgrims whom they had

brought to the Zambezi Mrs. Livingstone and James Stewart.*
Their friendship continued to provide food for gossip.

> This trip [wrote Kirk on April 7] will take half the goods but we have to leave half. There are a good many cases of Mission stuff. Mr. Stewart too has a good load when his luggage is all together. Mrs. L. looks after his and keeps small things in her cabin. Dr. L. does not see how he has been thoroughly humbugged by this fellow. If he only knew the use he made of his wife, he would change his tune. Instead he thinks his wife a brick to insist on bringing this man with her and if he were refused a passage, remaining behind herself.[4]

The entry shows what four years of the Zambezi could do even to so levelheaded and judicious a man as Kirk, who normally was not the man to take much notice of such gossip. That Mary Livingstone was attracted to the handsome Stewart is by no means improbable, and had she given way to her inclination during the long separation from her husband when she had no other friend to turn to, it would have been almost excusable, although highly unlikely given her Victorian background. But a much more plausible explanation is that she had asked him to delay his departure from England in order to accompany her on the voyage—a very natural request for a woman traveling alone in that age; that having done so she could not decently abandon him at Cape Town, when the other missionaries were trying to prevent him from joining Livingstone; and that having arrived together in the midst of the Expedition, where the atmosphere at first was hostile to Stewart, she took him under her protection. Moreover, considering that Stewart had come, if not at the invitation, with the encouragement of Livingstone, it was clearly the duty of both of them to make him as comfortable as possible.

With the boilers of the *Lady Nyassa,* each weighing two and a half tons, loaded on her deck, and her hold filled with machinery and other goods, the *Pioneer* left the Kongone on April 10 and arrived at Shupanga four days later. The relatively fast passage

* Stewart's enemy, the Reverend Edward Hawkins, who had tried to stop him getting a passage in the brig, had thought better of joining the Mission and turned tail.

in spite of the heavy load was probably due to the presence on board of the *Gorgon's* gunner, Mr. Young, who had volunteered his services to the Expedition and now took charge of the vessel, much to the relief of other members, who had no great opinion of Livingstone's seamanship.

Mrs. Livingstone had kept pretty well during her three-month sojourn in the delta, although having frequent slight attacks of fever; but on April 21 she was taken seriously ill and a few days later was removed from the *Pioneer* and was put to bed in the only house of Shupanga, a long, low building bare of furniture or other comforts, but where there was at least more space and quiet than on board.

The state of her mind [wrote Kirk, who was attending as her doctor] has been such as to predispose her to any disease . . . and what must undoubtedly prey upon her mind has been the stories relating to her and Mr. Stewart, which the latter has most unwisely repeated to her and thus the whole thing has been before her husband. Now these were of such a nature as to cause much anxiety, for although untrue, still a woman could not be expected to be indifferent to her character.[5]

In the time between the date of this entry and that of the one previously quoted, Kirk had discovered that the malicious reports had first been spread by Miss Mackenzie and repeated to everyone by Rae, an inveterate gossip, and he was now persuaded that there was no more in it than a "great want of discretion." But the harm had been done and it was too late to repair it.

The patient became weaker and weaker as she could not take any medicine, while "blisters" and injections proved unavailing. At 6 P.M. on April 17 Livingstone sent for Stewart, who was having his tea in the *Pioneer*.

I went at once, but hardly guessing for what. When I went into the room Dr. L. said that the end was evidently drawing near and he had sent for me . . . There was considerable stertor, fixedness of feature, and slight coldness of extremities. The Dr. was weeping like a child. I could not help feeling for him and found my own eyes full before I was aware. He asked me to commit her soul to her Maker by prayer. He, Dr. Kirk, and I kneeled down and I prayed as best I could.[6]

As she lay on an improvised bed made of three tea cases with a mattress on top, Livingstone leaned over his dying wife and stammered through his sobs: "My dearie, my dearie, you are going to leave me. Are you resting on Jesus?" They were his last words to her. Since she was long past speech he awaited anxiously for a sign that she was reconciled with her faith and thought he detected it when at the last moment "she looked up thoughtfully towards Heaven."[7] At 7 P.M. Mrs. Livingstone was dead. They buried her next day under a large baobab tree, near the remains of two English naval officers who had died during the Owen Expedition in 1826. The coffin was carried by four seamen from the *Pioneer*, and the funeral service at his own request was read by Stewart. For several days a guard was mounted by men from the *Pioneer* to protect the grave until it had been built up with bricks.

The fact that of Livingstone's companions, most of whom had been with him for several years, he alone, with the exception of Kirk attending as doctor, was summoned by Livingstone to join him at the deathbed gave intense satisfaction to Stewart, who had been made by the others to feel like an interloper.

Out of all the ship's company [he entered in his journal], I alone was sent for to be with the Dr. in this hour of sorrow and trouble. This so far set my mind at rest as to the position I occupied. I who was supposed by most on board to be *nobody*, come in at the trying hour.[8]

Livingstone was shattered by his loss and poured out his grief to his journal and in his letters. He had loved his wife, but in the seventeen years of their married life they had only been together for eight, and only for four had owned a proper home. Now the home they had looked forward to together would never be granted, and the children, already separated from both their parents, would be forever motherless. He blamed himself for allowing his wife to come, and yet there were strong reasons for giving the permission at the time, one of them, as he told her mother, being to put a stop to the talk that he could not live with her, which was making her miserable.

Above all he blamed the "culpable negligence" of the *Pioneer*'s engineer, Hardesty, whom he held responsible for the fatal delays in the pestiferous delta. Ironically Hardesty himself, after nearly dying of malaria, had been nursed back to health by Livingstone and then had been sent home in disgrace. Livingstone had also quarreled and parted with the *Pioneer*'s mate, Mr. Gedye, whom he called to his face "useless trash," so that until Young took charge there was nobody but himself to exercise any supervision in the ship, for which he had neither the time nor the necessary competence. Thus to some extent he was paying for his own prejudice against having any naval officer on the Expedition who might dispute his authority.

But there was, of course, no question of allowing the death of Mrs. Livingstone to affect his plans in any way. The only change it made was in his relations with his children, which now grew closer. This is shown in his letters to them, which become more human: less like sermons, more intimate and "newsy." For the rest it was in work that he found his chief solace.

The loss of his wife was followed swiftly by a blow of another kind, when it was learned that the missionaries had abandoned their station at Magomero and had withdrawn to the Shire at Chibisa's. The whole district was now engulfed in the war between the Ajawa and the Manganja, and the missionaries, having reverted to a policy of neutrality, did not feel, according to Rowley, that they could stay and see "the country desolated" and the Manganja "reduced to extremity" without being compelled to help them again. So to avoid being put in the position of having to go to war for people who they now realized were no better than their opponents, they decided on retreat. Another consideration mentioned by Rowley was the loss of nearly the whole of their second year's supply of stores. These had been left at the Kongone in charge of the Reverend Edward Hawkins, but abandoned by him when he was taken ill and removed to the *Gorgon*, after which anybody who passed could help himself.[9]

However, the real reason for the withdrawal may have been that they were scared. There were constant reports of the Ajawa coming to attack the settlement and a watch had to be set at night. There were only a handful of white men, with three or four always sick, and nowhere they could send for help. At Chibisa's, unhealthier even than Magomero as it was, they could at least be reached by water and could send a canoe with a message down the river if necessary.

It was Livingstone who had persuaded the Mission to settle at Magomero, against their inclination to be nearer the Shire, in the hope that their presence would stem the slave trade. Its failure to do so was a sad disappointment, and when the missionaries complained that the place was unhealthy he blamed their own sanitary, or rather lack of any sanitary, arrangements.

At Magomero [he wrote to his father-in-law], about 200 people were allowed to deposit about the place and no scavenger beetles had philanthropy enough to aid in cleansing the air. The consequence was this cess pool became, in the language of the missionaries, a 'pest hole' . . . The venerable Dr. Pusey says that 'not even defensive warfare is lawful, for it prevents a missionary getting the martyr's crown. Suffering, not doing, is the rule for missionaries'. Here then was 'suffering not doing', breathing fetid effluvia, and when the heavy rains descended and washed their deposits and that of thousands into the streams around them and above their drinking places, over thirty natives became martyrs, or rather easy victims, to their own abominations.[10]

Early in May Kirk and Charles Livingstone were sent up to Tete to collect goods and baggage left there by the Expedition two years earlier. The highhanded action of Livingstone in releasing the slaves at Mbame's—which he defended on the grounds that there was nothing else he could do after their guards had run away—was deeply resented by the Portuguese traders, who considered themselves as robbed. However, they reserved their dislike for Livingstone; and when Kirk called on the Governor, Tavares de Almeida, he was hospitably received and was invited to make the Governor's house his own.

While Kirk and Charles were away Livingstone made two more trips to the coast to bring up the rest of the gear, returning to Shupanga with the last load on June 12. On June 23 the *Lady*

Nyassa was successfully launched into the Zambezi River, from ways made of palm trees laid on the bank. With no equipment other than what was brought from England; with all the hazards of improvisation and loss of essential material, such as iron screw bolts stolen by natives; with frequent interruptions from fever and dysentery; working in overpowering heat relieved only by torrential rainfall; in all these conditions the assembling and launching of the vessel was a feat of blood, sweat and tears which kept Livingstone in a constant state of anxiety.

None of this, however, appears in the *Narrative*, where we are allowed only to see its picturesque side, as in some colored brochure prepared for tourists, while admiring the author's pawky humor.

Natives from all parts of the country came to see the launch, most of them quite certain that being made of iron she must go to the bottom as soon as she entered the water. Earnest discussions had taken place among them as to the propriety of using iron for ship-building. The majority affirmed that it would never answer. They said, "If we put a hoe in the water, or the smallest bit of iron it sinks immediately. How then can such a mass of iron float?" The minority answered that this might be true with them, but white men had medicine for everything. They could even make a woman, all except the speaking; "look at that one on the figurehead of the vessel." The unbelievers were astonished, and could hardly believe their eyes when they saw the ship float lightly and gracefully on the river, instead of going to the bottom as they so confidently predicted. "Truly," they said, "these men have powerful medicine."[11]

But five months had been spent in bringing the parts from the coast, putting them together and getting the vessel into the water, and the river was now too low to get up the Shire and would not be high enough till December. They would have to wait for another six months, which Livingstone now decided to employ by combining a trip to Johanna for provisions and draft oxen (to replace the mules, which had died) with a second exploration of the Rovuma River. Although everyone else was convinced that the latter was a waste of time, since the Rovuma at best was only navigable by boats, Livingstone was not yet ready to abandon his hope that it would provide the alternative route to Lake Nyassa outside Portuguese control, which he was so desperately anxious to find.

Just before the Expedition set out on this forlorn venture, it was rejoined by Thornton, back from his journey to Mount Kilimanjaro. Livingstone, it will be remembered, had offered to take the geologist back on condition he handed over his scientific report. This Thornton refused to do, and he was then accepted on his own terms, which included restoration of all his pay (but not his expenses) and freedom to work how and where he wished. Although it represented a considerable climb-down, Livingstone seems to have been quite happy about the arrangement, which improved the statistics of his leadership in the matter of dismissals and resignations. On the other hand Thornton had shown by his initiative and enterprise that he was a valuable man to have with one.

The voyage to the Comoro Islands, of which Johanna was the principal port and a naval base, started on August 6, 1862, and lasted three weeks. Although the distance was only 600 miles, contrary winds and currents and the need to conserve fuel made progress slow, taxing even Livingstone's patience.

Dr. L is uncomfortable at sea and looks so. When the weather gets foul or anything begins to go wrong, it is well to give him a wide berth, most especially when he sings to himself, but the kind of air is some indication. If it be 'Happy Land' then look out for squalls and stand clear, if 'Scots wha hae' then there is some general vision of discovery before his mind which, having been puzzled how to realise, he is indulging in; but on all occasions humming of airs is a bad omen. Of late there has been a deal of this. The tedious voyage in part accounts for it. Probably letters received about his wife's goings on at home have vexed him, but he is above all annoyed at being boxed in the works for getting on with the *Lady Nyassa*.[12]

With Mr. Young, the *Gorgon*'s gunner, in charge on deck during the day, while the members of the Expedition shared the night watches, things went more smoothly in the *Pioneer*. The unhappiest person on board was the engineer, Rae, who "having been twice wrecked shudders at the sight of each dark cloud and dreads every sea that comes rolling on."

On arriving at Johanna they found in harbor a large man-of-war, H.M.S. *Orestes,* whose commanding officer, Captain Alan Gardner, offered them a tow to the Rovuma. Running into heavy weather both towing hawsers parted and the *Pioneer* had to get up steam and complete the voyage on her own.

Gardner also offered to accompany the exploring party part of the way up the river and took some officers and men from the *Orestes* in two of her boats. Livingstone traveled with the Captain in his galley, and they both slept ashore in tents made from the boat's awnings. "I had taken my hammock," Gardner recorded in his journal, "which was slung along the ridge of our tent and in which I slept as comfortably as I should have done onboard, between sheets and blankets and with a good pillow." The resourceful officer had also taken his cook, who "served us capitally—in fact we had every meal as comfortably as I should have had onboard the *Orestes.*"[13]

After reaching the point—about thirty miles from the mouth of the river—where the *Pioneer* had been forced to turn back two years before, and with the water rapidly diminishing, Gardner had seen enough to convince himself that the river, even if it connected with Lake Nyassa, was unnavigable, and that it was unlikely that Livingstone would get much farther up it. The naval party then separated from the Expedition and returned to their ship, taking with them Rae, who was sick.

During the last few days I had seen a great deal of Dr. Livingstone [Gardner wrote], and got to like him very much. He is modest, gentle and quiet and utterly fearless, and thus inspires confidence among the native tribes with which he is thrown into contact.[14]

The two Livingstones and Kirk went on in two boats, manned by native paddlers brought from the Zambezi. The river was at its lowest and so shallow in places that the boats had to be dragged over the shoals. When the depth of water fell to ten inches Kirk could see no point in going farther. He foresaw the boats being stranded and unable to return, and deplored such risks being taken with men's lives "all for the empty glory of geographical discovery"; he could only conclude "that Dr. L. is out of his mind." But when he expostulated, pointing out the danger of being left high and dry, he was told by Livingstone that "if he risked nothing he would gain nothing."[15]

On the very next day, September 19, Kirk's fears seemed likely to be realized when the explorers were attacked from the bank of the river by a large body of tribesmen firing musket bullets and arrows. Most of the arrows flew overhead, but four bullets passed through the sail of Livingstone's boat, whereupon Kirk aimed his rifle and shot dead one man at a range of 150 yards. A second was killed by the English coxswain of his boat. The enemy then fled and were not seen again. Needless to say these casualties would not be mentioned in the *Narrative*.

The incident occurred soon after the boats had passed a village where the chief tried to stop them. After a long palaver Livingstone had agreed, against his invariable principle, to pay for permission to proceed through the territory, and had made the man a gift of two large pieces of cloth—"preferring," as he wrote, "the disgrace of paying to shedding blood." It was therefore thought that the matter was settled, when suddenly another crowd of natives appeared from out of the bush and launched the attack. Livingstone attributed their hostility to the fact that they lived on one of the slave routes used by the Arabs between Lake Nyassa and the coast. "It is only where the people are slavers," he wrote in the *Narrative*, "that the natives of this part of Africa are bloodthirsty."*

For a week more they struggled on through the shoals, with Kirk, not easily scared, increasingly apprehensive, fearing for the line of retreat, and more convinced every day that Livingstone

* It has been noted in our day that when there is trouble in an African country it often occurs in a region where slaving was formerly rife. One example is the eastern provinces of the Congo, where the Mulelist rebellion raged in 1964–1965. Another is the northern district of Mozambique, where the guerrilla fighters currently at war with the Portuguese belong to the same tribe, the Makonde, whose ancestors attacked Livingstone.

was off his head and "a most unsafe leader." At last they reached a point where the river was strewn with rocks, and even Livingstone could see that further progress was impossible. They had traveled 156 miles from its mouth (114 in a straight line) and were within three days of N'gomano, where the river divided, one branch diverging in a southwesterly direction and the other continuing westward toward the northern end of Lake Nyassa. Some reports maintained that this branch actually flowed out of the lake, "but in a small stream and down mountains"; in any case it was now clear that the Rovuma was unnavigable by anything larger than a boat. With his habitual optimism Livingstone reported to the Foreign Secretary that "having now visited this river in flood and at its lowest ebb it is probable that a lucrative trade might be developed on it by a steamer drawing when loaded only eighteen inches of water."[16] But this was mere face-saving; in his heart he now wrote off the Rovuma as an alternative access route to Lake Nyassa, at any rate as far as the immediate future was concerned.

Thus at whatever cost to the nervous system of his companions, he had answered his own question to his own satisfaction, and one is inclined therefore to agree with the oft-quoted verdict of an eminent geographer that although this journey was apparently fruitless its results were far-reaching.

It had much to do with the decision of British missionaries and traders that, after all, the Shire was the only practicable approach to Nyasaland. . . . the Nyasaland of today is largely the result of that negative but supremely important journey, and in his uncouth way Livingstone showed finer qualities of leadership in pressing on against the wishes of all his men than in most of the other subsidiary journeys of this period.[17]

Furthermore, although it never proved suitable for water transport, the valley of the Rovuma, as Livingstone instinctively perceived, was a natural highway from the coast to the interior, and did eventually become one of the recognized access routes to Lake Nyassa, which was used by Livingstone himself on his last journey and later by the Universities Mission operating from their base in Zanzibar.

The return journey was uneventful, no further trouble being met with from the river dwellers. This suggested that Livingstone was justified in the risk he had taken, which was that of having to leave the boats and return on foot, without food or the means to procure it (since there were no porters with the party to carry provisions or goods for barter), through possibly hostile territory. As it was, the only other untoward incident, which occurred after reaching the coast, was an encounter with a hippopotamus which charged one of the boats, lifted it out of the water "with ten men and a ton of ebony onboard" and stove in the bottom. A second attack was only forestalled by a lucky shot from Kirk's rifle.

However, it was neither bloodthirsty tribesmen nor enraged wild animals that were now Livingstone's chief concern, but the behavior of his own men.

> In thinking of success [he wrote], people cannot realize the worry that the head of the expedition has to endure from the carelessness and selfishness of underlings—an engineer taking the pet or neglecting his work—or playing when he ought to be working—sickness made most of . . .[18]

When the *Pioneer* arrived at Johanna to take on board the oxen and provisions, there was trouble between the white and black members of the crew and he had to issue an order that no man should strike a native without his orders. At Quelimane, where the ship put in to cut wood for fuel, several of the white crew went on a drinking spree and had to be rounded up and brought back by Portuguese soldiers. It was almost a relief to return to the unhealthy but familiar waters of the Zambezi, and to drop anchor again at Shupanga, which was reached on December 17.

Here, however, the news was not good. The water was still too low to go up the Shire. There had been a severe drought followed by famine and whole villages were starving. Mariano, the half-caste slave trader who had been detained for a time by the Portuguese and then set free, was on the warpath again and was ravaging the Shire valley. Another bandit called Belchior was scouring the country for slaves. The Ajawa, having decisively defeated and plundered the Manganja, occupied the highlands, while Livingstone's former followers, the Makololo, who had become masters at Chibisa's after the murder of the former chief, with a large establishment of women and slaves, were reported by the missionaries to be behaving not much better. Stewart and Thornton were both away—the former prospecting for a site for a Free Church mission station—but Procter, who was in charge of the Universities Mission pending the appointment of a successor to Mackenzie, had just arrived from Chibisa's, where the missionaries were temporarily settled. Until the new bishop arrived they could make no permanent plans.*

One way or another things looked blacker than at any time since the Expedition first entered the Zambezi nearly five years ago, and the prospect of introducing legitimate commerce, civilization and Christianity to the African tribes seemed more remote than ever. It was not surprising that Livingstone's mood was increasingly bitter. His had been a labor of love, but now that it seemed doomed to failure, he began to count the cost. He had spent £6,000 of his own money—twice as much as he bargained for and all that he possessed—on the *Lady Nyassa*. He did not grudge the money, but it was "taking too much from his children," and if the Government were not willing to pay half, considering that he could earn much more by writing for the press, he thought that his salary should be raised.

Burton has £700 [he wrote to Murchison], one commissioner at Loanda, in the same latitudes as I work in, had £1,000 and the other £1,500, while I, doing ten times more work than any fine Commissioner, get £500, the salary of one of the under-clerks at the Foreign Office. It is true I do all *con amore* and will continue so to do.[19]

And yet there was still one hope left. If he could only get the steamer launched on Lake Nyassa all could still be saved: a mortal blow struck at the slave trade, legitimate commerce introduced and a suitable country found for mission stations.

The river having at last begun to rise, on January 10, 1863, the

* William George Tozer, Rector of Burgh, Lincolnshire, who succeeded Mackenzie, was consecrated in Westminster Abbey early in 1863 but did not arrive on the Shire till the following June.

Pioneer with the *Lady Nyassa* in tow left Shupanga and headed for the Shire. The tow was necessary because Rae had refused to install the engines of the *Lady Nyassa,* knowing that they would have to come out as soon as the foot of the cataracts was reached, when the vessel would have to be taken to pieces again. Subsequently he changed his mind for the reason, according to Kirk, that "then he could leave and say that he had put together the vessel."[20] But Livingstone, anxious not to lose any more time, refused his consent.

Torn between his desire to quit and fear of what would be said if he did so, Rae gave way to one of his periodic bouts of persecution mania, refused to sit with the others in the cabin of the *Pioneer* and ate his meals separately.

The voyage began inauspiciously with a serious accident on the first day, when the *Pioneer* went aground and the *Lady Nyassa* towing astern ran into her "like a battering ram," carried away a davit and smashed in a boat. After that it was decided to lash the two vessels side by side, in which position they went better. However, there was still not enough water—there never was for the *Pioneer*—progress got slower and slower, until on February 1 both vessels became firmly stuck in the old mud trap of Elephant Marsh, where they remained on and off for the next six weeks.

All around was the evidence of war and famine.

Dead bodies floated past us daily and in the morning the paddles had to be cleared of corpses caught in the night. It made the heart ache to see the widespread desolation; the river banks, once so populous, all silent; the villages burned down, and an oppressive stillness reigning where formerly crowds of eager sellers appeared. . . . The sight and smell of dead bodies was everywhere. Many skeletons lay beside the path, where in their weakness they had fallen and expired. Ghastly living forms of boys and girls with dull dead eyes, were crouching beside some of the huts. A few more miserable days of their terrible hunger and they would be with the dead.[21]

Prolonged inactivity in these depressing surroundings was disastrous for the morale of the Expedition. "There seems to be a different feeling throughout the ship," Kirk noted, "which does not make all work together with a will as they did. Their very shabby treatment seems to be the cause with most . . . fever plays a great part in making the ship a dull growling hole."

While the two steamers lay immobilized in Elephant Marsh, news reached them of the death from malaria of the Reverend H. C. Scudamore—"poor dear Scudamore," as Livingstone wrote—of the Universities Mission. He was their best man and was generally respected for his devotion, quiet courage and patient acceptance of hardship.

A few weeks later—still immobilized—they received a message from the Mission urgently requesting medical help. The Mission doctor, Dickenson, was seriously ill and its tanner and shoemaker, by name Clark, was delirious and raving. Livingstone and Kirk set off immediately by boat but arrived a quarter of an hour after Dickenson had died. While Livingstone returned to the ship, Kirk remained to nurse Clark and eventually pulled him through.

The Mission being seriously short of food, Thornton volunteered to go to Tete to try to procure meat. Accompanied by one missionary, Henry Rowley, he accomplished the double journey of 100 miles each way in a month and brought back a large flock of sheep and goats. But the effort of the march through difficult and waterless country exhausted his strength. Soon after his return to the Shire he was taken ill with dysentery and fever and died on April 21. Thus to the missionaries of Linyanti, to Mackenzie, Burrup, Mary Livingstone, Scudamore, Dickenson, and perhaps a dozen drowned sailors, was now added on the death roll the name of the youngest and perhaps the most promising of all the victims of Livingstone's idealism.

By this time, three months after leaving Shupanga, the two steamers had at last been extricated from Elephant Marsh and brought safely to the foot of the cataracts, where the *Lady Nyassa* was to be taken apart again and the work of building a road for the ox wagon begun. Since all of this was going to take some time, during which there would not be much for them to do, Livingstone was now prepared to release his brother and Kirk, both of whom had had enough of the Expedition. Kirk indeed had been wishing to leave for many months and had only remained at Livingstone's pressing request.

Through five years of danger, hardship, sickness and frustration he had been the one consistently reliable member of the Expedition: willing, levelheaded, tactful, cool in a crisis and (except in the privacy of his diary) uncomplaining. While increasingly critical (but only to himself) of Livingstone's leadership—even to the point of considering him insane—he had only once, when on the Rovuma, openly questioned his decisions, and had always carried them out loyally. Such service merited some acknowledgment when it ended, but from Livingstone there came no word of appreciation and only some last-minute demands. For Kirk these were the last straw and brought to a head his dislike of a man whom, while admiring his "energy and force of mind," he was to describe as "about as slippery and ungrateful a mortal as ever I came in contact with," as well as dishonest, untruthful and devoid of kindly feelings.

APRIL 27, 1863. In the morning Dr. L spoke to me and said that his brother had requested to be allowed to go home and that he had consented, as it would be selfishness to keep him and that as I desired to go, he would feel it the same in my case, that therefore I might pack up a small bundle of clothes and accompany him to Quelimane and that he would send down my baggage by the return canoes, i.e. in about 7 or 8 weeks. . . . I objected decidedly to the detail but expressed a desire to go away. I said I preferred accompanying my baggage. Dr L consented reluctantly. . . . Shortly after he desired me to go down to Quelimane to arrange the supply of stores there, saving him the necessity of going. I objected again to going without my baggage.[22]

Considering that their contract was for two years only and there had been no formal extension, it was obviously impossible for Livingstone to prevent any members of the original Expedition from leaving after five years. Moreover, since provisions were running short it was necessary to send away all who could be spared. To make a virtue of this necessity and take credit for unselfishness in releasing Kirk and his brother (whom in any case, according to Kirk, he was "sick tired of . . . as ever any man could be"[23]) was a characteristic example of the hypocrisy which not only Kirk found so irritating.

During the following days his suspicions of Livingstone increased.

APRIL 29. Dr. L proposed that . . . I leave some boxes and he will take them in December when he goes down with the *Pioneer*. Knowing how much his words and arrangements are to be depended on, I declined this and told him I would send up a canoe myself and await its return.
Dr. L busy writing despatches. His manner still very distant, in fact there is no doubt he will help me only if he thinks I can and will do so to him.[24]

When at last the arrangements for Kirk's departure were completed, Livingstone became seriously ill with dysentery and Kirk felt he must stay and nurse him. Finally on May 19 he said goodbye to the *Pioneer* and, with Charles Livingstone, the ship's carpenter and three seamen, all of whom were being sent home to save feeding them, set off down the river in a convoy consisting of "the large whaler, Thornton's boat and the Mission canoe." There were left behind, besides Livingstone himself, no more than half a dozen white men: Young, Rae, two stokers, a seaman and the ship's steward. The rest of its crew were natives either from Johanna or the Zambezi.

Livingstone was now in one of those situations whose hopelessness was obvious to everyone but himself. To begin with, the *Lady Nyassa* was too big for land transport, at any rate without a proper road being made, which Young estimated "would take at least 100 natives a year."[25] But owing to famine and war there was no labor available. A start was made on the road by clearing the ground of trees for a few hundred yards—exaggerated to "a few miles" in the *Narrative*—but at the first gradient the six oxen could or would not pull the wagon, and one of them "took a stubborn fit and obstinately pulled back." For keeping them tied up all day without food or drink the Johanna man in charge of the beasts was given by Livingstone "one stripe with a rope to let him taste how it felt," with a promise of "ten of the same next time."[26] So poor appeared the prospect of ever completing the road, or if it was ever completed of transporting the *Lady Nyassa* over it, that the work of dismantling the vessel was suspended and she remained afloat in the river.

But the most urgent problem was that of provisions. Even with a depleted crew there was enough food only till June, none could be purchased locally because of the famine, and it would not be possible to take the *Pioneer* down the river till December. Livingstone could have got food sent up from Sena or Tete, but rather than have to ask the Portuguese to supply it, he decided to try to obtain it from Lake Nyassa, and on June 16 set off northward with Rae. They hoped to use the boat which had been left behind after the last trip to the lake, nearly two years previously, but on arriving at the place where they had slung it up from a tree found the boat destroyed by fire. They then returned to the *Pioneer,* where Bishop Tozer had just arrived, bringing a letter from the Foreign Secretary dated February 2, 1863, ordering the withdrawal of the Expedition.

Her Majesty's Government [wrote Russell] fully appreciate the zeal and perseverance with which you have applied yourself to the discharge of the duties entrusted to you. They are aware of the difficulties which you must necessarily have met with and they have deeply regretted that your anxieties have been aggravated by severe domestic affliction.

Her Majesty's Government cannot, however, conceal from themselves that the results to which they had looked from the expedition under your superintendence have not been realized.

After acknowledging the interesting results obtained "in a geographical and scientific point of view," the letter went on to express doubt whether these results could be "made serviceable either for the interests of British Commerce or of humanity in general by diverting into a legitimate channel the energies of the native population at present embarked in the Slave Trade." In any case it was clear that the Zambezi route was "one which would be attended by serious if not insuperable difficulties," and Her Majesty's Government learned "from your last despatches the failure of your attempt to find an independent route by means of the River Rovuma." In consequence their motives for extending the period of the Expedition had ceased to exist, and while the "heavy charge* entailed on the public" could no longer be justified, it was moreover "undesirable to continue to impose on the naval service at the Cape the duty of keeping up a communication attended with serious difficulties and occasionally involving loss of life." Her Majesty's Government had therefore decided to withdraw the Expedition "within as short a period as may be practicable," which it was hoped would be the end of July.†

Instructions were then given for the withdrawal. A warship would call at the mouth of the Zambezi within three months after the receipt of the dispatch and all personnel would be given free passage home. Their salaries would cease on their reaching England and would not "under any circumstances be continued longer than the 31st December." If the Expedition was not withdrawn by July, the *Pioneer* must in any case be sent down to the bar while there was water to float her on the upper part of the river, and there be handed over to the naval authorities.[27]

The Government had sponsored the Expedition in response to popular demand and they were withdrawing it largely for the same reason. Public opinion, for whom Livingstone once could do no wrong, no longer supported him uncritically. In five years he had made too many enemies, both inside and outside the Expedition. Of its original members three had been dismissed, two had left at their own request, and none had a good word for the leader at the time of parting. Only the neurotic and sycophantic Rae remained and he also was to go after a quarrel. If Livingstone had not openly quarreled with the missionaries it was only because he avoided them, but he could not conceal his disapproval of their conduct, especially in disregarding his advice not to become involved in war with the Ajawa. For this they had been formally censured at home, and they had defended themselves on the grounds that their action was an inevitable consequence of his in releasing the captured slaves; this led to mutual recrimination, some of which found its way into the press.

---

* Washington estimated the total cost of the Expedition, including salaries, the cost of vessels and all other expenses, at £30,000, spread over six years, which was a paltry sum to spend on such a project even in those days.

† Livingstone only received the dispatch on July 2.

There was criticism of his management of the Expedition, especially at the Cape, and one of the bitterest critics was James Stewart, who turned against Livingstone after being brought close to him over the deathbed of Mrs. Livingstone. Stewart had fallen in love with the idea of mission work in Africa after reading Livingstone's *Missionary Travels,* but was so disillusioned with what he saw on the Zambezi and the Shire that he threw away his copy of the book into the river and wrote in his diary that he had "no wish whatever" to meet its author again—and this in spite of the fact that Livingstone had offered him £150 a year of his own money to stay on and learn the job of a missionary.*[28] And then too, there were the heavy death roll and the growing dislike of the Navy for the support operation.

The reaction against Livingstone, which had been gathering strength in England, reached a climax when the *Times* published an article of biting sarcasm at his expense.

> We were promised cotton, sugar, and indigo . . . and of course we get none. We were promised trade; and there is no trade, although we have a Consul at 500 l. a year. We were promised converts to the Gospel, and not one has been made. . . . In a word, the thousands subscribed by the Universities and contributed by the Government have been productive only of the most fatal results. To say nothing of the great mistake of attempting to establish a mission and a colony among remote savages, the first great blunder was to attempt to plant them in the foreign territory of a European nation, for wherever Dr. Livingstone attempted to set himself down he found that he was on what had been Portuguese territory almost from the time of Vasco da Gama.

After a withering analysis of his report on the Rovuma the *Times* concluded that

> Dr. Livingstone is unquestionably a traveller of talents, enterprise, and excellent constitution, but it is now plain enough that his zeal and imagination much surpass his judgement.[29]

---

* After Livingstone's death, however, Stewart had a second conversion and was instrumental in founding the great mission station of Livingstonia, on Lake Nyassa, as a memorial to him.

A few days later, Washington, now an admiral, on being asked for his opinion on the withdrawal of the Expedition, declared that

it has added very little to what was already known in a geographical point of view and that whatever results might have been anticipated had Dr. L adhered to the plan sketched out for him of establishing himself at some centre or base of operations, next to nothing has come of the desultory operations he has undertaken including his unsuccessful expedition to the Rovuma.[30]

This was a facile judgment unworthy of the naval hydrographer, but he had probably seen which way the wind was blowing in Whitehall, and may also have been influenced by unfavorable reports from the Navy at the Cape.

The only person who stuck up for Livingstone was Palmerston. The Prime Minister had always been his strong supporter and was not entirely happy about the decision to recall him.

Is it quite clear [he minuted on January 28] that Dr. L. has done all that can be usefully done and that his reports and discoveries have opened no available road for British Commerce? Is there no interesting geographical knowledge he could acquire and communicate? Being on the spot he is far better able than any other man would be to do what remains to be done in order to complete our knowledge of the country and its resources.[31]

It was doubtless in consequence of this advice that Russell enclosed in the same dispatch a second letter suggesting a "short postponement" of the withdrawal of the Expedition "to enable you to put in order the results of the geographical knowledge which you have acquired." If Livingstone desired this, he was to seek permission from the Governor of Cape Colony, but not to embark in any further proceedings "which could interfere with your ability to carry out your instructions in case the immediate withdrawal of the Expedition should ultimately be decided upon."[32]

The order of recall could not have come as a surprise to Livingstone, but rather brought relief by saving him from the need to concede defeat. It is not inconceivable, given the iron determination of the man and his refusal ever to acknowledge when he was beaten, that he would eventually have succeeded in placing his ship on Lake Nyassa—it was done, after all, with another, only twelve years later—but it would have needed far greater resources than were presently available to him, especially of labor. Livingstone's companion, E. D. Young, the man who eventually accomplished this great feat with the screw ship *Ilala,* was of the opinion that the *Lady Nyassa* was "too cumbrous by far" and that "the time had not arrived for the transport of such heavy sections as those which formed her hull."[33]

In any case it would have been a truly Herculean labor which Livingstone, sick and dispirited after endless disappointments, was now scarcely fit to undertake. In fact he had abandoned the whole plan as early as May 1, when he wrote to the Foreign Secretary to say that "unless this desolating slave trade is suppressed the objects of our mission cannot be attained" and offering the *Lady Nyassa* to the Government of India for the development of the cotton trade on the Upper Godavera River.*[34]

His discouragement appears in a dispatch of April 28, 1863, the last before receiving the order of recall and the shortest he ever wrote. It also marked the nearest he ever came to throwing in the sponge.

No words of mine [the dispatch begins] can convey a correct idea of the widespread devastation produced in one year by the slave trade and famine by drought in this Shire valley.

After briefly reporting the impending departure of his brother and Kirk, and the commencement of work on the road, he concludes with unwonted candor:

The spirits and health of the Expedition are low. The blight on our prospects reacts on us.

---

* Seaver's statement that "given only one month's longer grace, Livingstone could have launched his little ship on the lake and have anticipated by thirty years the suppression of the slave trade on the East Coast and the British colonization of Nyasaland" does not bear examination. Not even Livingstone believed it, as is proved by his letter of May 1 and the fact that he had suspended the dismantling of the *Lady Nyassa* before the order of recall came.

On which the Foreign Secretary noted:

A melancholy story—the Expedition leaves the slave trade stronger and more prevalent than ever in the district.[35]

But if he was resigned to being recalled, Livingstone was furious that the news should have been known to everybody before himself.

I take the liberty [he wrote to Russell] to complain of the use made of your Ldp's despatch before it reached its destination. When Bishop Tozer arrived at the Mission Station seven miles below this, the servant sent up hailed the ship's company from shore in strong Surrey dialect: 'No more pay for you *Pioneer* chaps after December—we brings the letter as says it!'

I have always considered the despatches of a high Officer of State as even more sacred than private correspondence, and as this could not have been degraded to the purposes of gossip with your Ldp.'s sanction, notwithstanding the courteousness of its style, I submit that at second hand my companions and self have been treated with very unmerited humiliation.[36]

This was an inauspicious introduction to the new Bishop, whom he met a few days later and took an immediate dislike to.

Bishop a non-resistance man, vegetarian, and inclined to leave the country: prays for their Majesties of Portugal . . . has made up his mind to try Morambala instead of Highlands here, in order to avoid expense of carriage up Shire, but will take the women and children of mission with him to Morambala.[37]

Morambala was the name of the mountain which stood on the left bank of the Shire, just above its confluence with the Zambezi. Its crest was frequently in cloud, and for this reason it was considered by Livingstone even more unhealthy for a mission station than the Shire River. He also suspected—rightly—that the move to Morambala was only the first step in the withdrawal of the Mission from the country, "Bishop Tozer," as he told Russell, "being as remarkable for caution as his worthy predecessor was for the want of it." The women and children were the released slaves whom the missionaries had taken under their protection two years before.

Livingstone had now to decide what to do with himself. The death of his wife had left him freer than he would have been, and he no longer looked forward to a home of his own. His children were growing up; they scarcely knew their father except through letters which too often read like sermons, and would need him less and less. Their education was left to trustees appointed by Livingstone, and the only home they knew was that of his aging relations. Robert, the eldest son, who refused to work at school, was to have joined his father in Africa but went to America instead; pressed into the Federal Army, he died of wounds received in battle at the age of eighteen. The only one to whom Livingstone was really attached was his daughter Agnes, and she would soon be of an age to marry. Thus there was nothing pulling him toward England.

Since the death of his wife he had a premonition that he too would die in Africa, and it was there that he now saw himself spending the rest of his days. In August he wrote to Horace Waller, one of the three surviving missionaries, with whom he had struck up a friendship which was to last his life:

> I guess that I shall work alone in Africa yet. £100 a year would do to support one. . . . I don't know whether I am to go on the shelf or not. If so, I make the shelf Africa. If *Lady Nyassa* is well sold I shall manage. . . . If the work is of God it will come out all right at last.[38]

In any case, and whatever the future might hold, he was in no hurry to return to England. The *Pioneer* could not descend the Shire until the river rose in December, and this was a good excuse for exercising the discretion given him by Russell to postpone "for a limited period" the withdrawal of the Expedition. In the meantime he would make one more journey; its aim, to explore the eastern and northern shores of Lake Nyassa—thus perhaps at last solving the problem of the source of the Rovuma—and also to verify the "information collected by Colonel Rigby*

* British Consul at Zanzibar.

that the 19,000 slaves who go through the customs-house at Zanzibar annually, are chiefly drawn from Lake Nyassa and the Valley of the Shire."

The journey was to have been made by boat, but the boat was swept away and lost while being warped past the cataracts. The plan was then changed to an exploration of the country to the west of Lake Nyassa, going as far north as Lake "Moele" (Mweru) if time permitted, and including a visit to Kota Kota, the headquarters of the Arab slavers.

Livingstone had proposed to go alone, but he was persuaded to take another European and chose the steward of the *Pioneer,* to "improve his health." There were also his usual retinue of African attendants. Leaving on August 10 the party reached their farthest point five weeks later, before turning back. In spite of illness among his followers, a recurrence of his own dysentery brought on by eating nothing but native meal, and the fact that a slave war was raging in the region, Livingstone would have gone on and worked his way round Lake Nyassa but for fear of being late in returning and holding up the *Pioneer.* As it was they reached the ship on November 1, after covering more than 700 miles on foot, much to the benefit of the steward, who "having performed his part in the march right bravely rejoined his companions stronger than he had ever been before."[39]

Apart from the usual grisly evidence—burned villages, skeletons, hostile tribesmen—that raiding for slaves was more prevalent than ever, thus confirming that Lake Nyassa was the principal source of the trade, this last journey did not add much to what was already known. Livingstone's regret that in order to be back on time he had missed an opportunity to "secure a geographical feat" was aggravated by the fact that the water in the Shire was still too low for navigation and he might have stayed away another six weeks.

It was while waiting for the rains to break, with nothing to do during the month of December 1863, that he heard that Bishop Tozer, after trying out Mount Morambala, had decided to withdraw the Mission from the mainland altogether and retreat to the island of Zanzibar, 700 miles to the north. In view of the recall of the Expedition, on which the Mission had always depended to some extent, and of the general state of the country, this was a sensible decision which later events fully vindicated; but to Livingstone it was the most bitter blow of all, the final and irrevocable seal of failure, signifying victory for the slavers, triumph for the Portuguese and the abandonment of the people he had tried to save, who were left in a worse condition than that in which he had found them.

This, I believe [he wrote to Maclear],* is the first instance in modern times in which missionaries have voluntarily turned tail . . . now the last ray of hope for this down-trodden people vanishes. . . . a grevious disappointment to me and much more so than our own recall . . . I would fain write to your good bishop† and pour out my distressed feelings to him, but I feel as if I could sit down and cry rather than write.[40]

Livingstone did not easily give way to despair and had only done so once before, on the death of his wife; but at this moment he could not see any light at the end of the tunnel, and if he had not believed that everything that happened to him was in accordance with the will of God, and must therefore have a good reason, however well concealed from himself, he would have given way to it now.

---

* Sir T. Maclear, Astronomer Royal at Cape Town.
† Bishop Gray of Cape Town.

Epilogue

By the third week in January 1864 there was enough water in the river to float the two steamers, and on the 19th the remnants of the Expedition started on their last journey to the coast. Except for a broken rudder the voyage was uneventful. A stop was made at Morambala to pick up about "thirty orphan children and a few helpless widows" who would otherwise have been abandoned when the Mission withdrew to Zanzibar. These were all that remained of the rescued slaves adopted by Bishop Mackenzie; the rest had been encouraged to become self-supporting by cultivating the soil and now formed a little community of their own.

On February 13 the ships arrived at the mouth of the Zambezi and were there met by two men-of-war, H.M.S. *Orestes* and H.M.S. *Ariel,* which had been sent from the Cape to evacuate the Expedition. The *Pioneer* was taken in tow by the *Orestes,* and the *Lady Nyassa,* with Livingstone on board, by the *Ariel.* Captain Chapman, of the *Ariel,* invited Livingstone to take passage in her, but he did not like to leave the *Lady Nyassa* so long as there was any danger. He, however, did accept the invitation for Waller, the missionary, "who was so dreadfully sick and woebegone I could not look at him without laughing."[1]

On the 16th the little fleet ran into a storm, which nearly put an end to Livingstone but proved the seagoing qualities of the

Lady Nyassa. A dramatic account of the incident is given in the *Narrative.*

A hurricane struck the *Ariel* and drove her nearly backwards at a rate of six knots. The towing hawser wound round her screw and stopped her engines. No sooner had she recovered from this shock than she was again taken aback on the other tack, and driven stem on towards the *Lady Nyassa*'s broadside. We who were on board the little vessel saw no chance of escape unless the crew of the *Ariel* should think of heaving ropes when the big ship went over us; but she glided past our bow and we breathed freely. Captain Chapman, though his engines were disabled, did not think of abandoning us in the heavy gale, but crossed the bows of the *Lady Nyassa* again and again, dropping a cask with a line by which to give us another hawser. We might never have picked it up had not a Krooman jumped overboard and fastened a second line to the cask; and we then drew the hawser on board and were again in tow.

There followed a terrible night, with the *Ariel* pitching so badly that at one moment a large portion of her copper bottom was showing and the next her stern bulwarks were level with the water, and a boat hanging from its davits was smashed. Fearing for the life of Livingstone Chapman offered to lower a boat for him, but, as he afterward wrote to his daughter Agnes, "the waves dashed so hard against the sides of the vessels it might have been swamped, and my going away would have taken heart out of those who remained." However, the *Lady Nyassa* did "wonderfully well, rising like a little duck over the foaming billow; she took in spray alone and no green water." When the weather abated, Chapman repeated his invitation, which Livingstone this time accepted "with a good conscience." Even then the boat transferring him to the *Ariel* was damaged.[2]

It took three days to clear the screw of the *Ariel,* with men diving nine feet under water and cutting at the entangled hawser with long chisels made on board for the occasion. During the towing, two more hawsers parted, each eleven inches in circumference, and only superb seamanship on the part of the warship's Captain and crew brought the two vessels safely into the harbor of Mozambique, where they arrived on February 24. The other two ships, from which they had become separated in the storm, limped in several days later, the *Orestes* having split eighteen sails.

Having handed the *Pioneer* and her crew over to the Navy, together with the survivors of the Bishop's flock, who were being given passage to the Cape, Livingstone had discharged his last duty as leader of the Expedition and was free to consider his own next steps. The first was to dispose of the *Lady Nyassa,* in which all his capital was tied up. After the Government had refused to pay half the cost of the vessel, and he had abandoned hope of launching it on Lake Nyassa, he had offered to sell it to them for use in India. The Government had declined and suggested he should dispose of it at the Cape. But Livingstone thought his chances were better in Zanzibar, which was also nearer; and after spending several weeks in Mozambique, where the *Lady Nyassa* was beached for scraping and painting, he sailed for the island on April 16, arriving a week later. There, however, no satisfactory offer for the ship was forthcoming and he then decided, rather on the spur of the moment, to sail her across the Indian Ocean and try his luck in Bombay.

It was a risky enterprise which few others would have attempted. The distance to be covered was 2,500 miles and only a few weeks of good weather could be counted on before the monsoon broke at the end of May. Although sturdily built to stand up to the violent storms on Lake Nyassa, the *Lady Nyassa* was never intended for ocean voyages. She carried only fourteen tons of coal and when steaming burned three tons in twenty-four hours, so that she could only afford to use her engines for five of the eighteen days which Livingstone estimated for the passage. For the rest of the time she would be relying on sail and, if delayed by calms, might be caught by the monsoon. Her complement consisted of seven native Zambezians and two boys, none of whom had seen the sea before volunteering, three other white men—a stoker, a sailor and a carpenter—and Livingstone himself, who, although a skilled navigator with some experience of handling ships, was far from being a professional seaman. Had he been one he would probably never have contemplated such a voyage.

Livingstone was counting on Rae to come as engineer, but almost at the last moment the latter announced that he was going back to Johanna, in the Comoro Islands, where an Englishman, Mr. Sunley, who was also British Consul, had offered him a partnership in his sugar business. Rae had spoken of this to Livingstone when they were at Mozambique, and Livingstone had approved his plan, but as nothing more was said he apparently assumed that Rae would not leave him until the *Lady Nyassa* was sold. Rae, however, had not bargained to cross the Indian Ocean and, after two shipwrecks and his recent experience of a hurricane in the *Lady Nyassa*, was "terror-struck" at the thought of it.* By that time it was too late to find another engineer, so Livingstone decided to do without one, in spite of being told by the sailor, Pennell, that there was "something wrong with the engines."[3]

Leaving Zanzibar on April 30 Livingstone followed the coast northward, in order to profit by the current, to a point about ten degrees above the equator, before altering course to the east. He had hoped to avoid the calm belt as shown in Maury's wind chart, but found himself still in it and for many days the *Lady Nyassa* lay becalmed. This was followed by six days of strong breezes; then "calms again tried our patience, and the near approach of that period, 'the break of the Monsoon,' in which it was believed no boat could live, made us sometimes think our epitaph would be 'Left Zanzibar on 30th April, 1864, and never more heard of.' "[4]

Livingstone devotes only a page of the *Narrative* to this, probably the most dangerous of all his adventures. (Perhaps because it had nothing to do with the Zambezi Expedition; perhaps because he was nearly at the end of his book and was tired of writing it; perhaps also because his pride, as already noted, took the form of belittling his own feats of courage.)

But from his diary we can see what his anxieties were. The black men of the crew, although totally inexperienced, quickly picked up the ropes, and Livingstone taught three of them to

* Rae returned to England with the intention of marrying before taking up work as a trader in Zanzibar, but died suddenly of a chronic ulcer of the stomach, probably the result of his five years with the Expedition, in the autumn of 1865.

steer by compass, so that he had some relief from "watch and watch" at the wheel. But two of the white men were ill and unfit for duty, each for a week, while the third was inclined to be mutinous. When nearly three weeks out, and scarcely making any progress, Livingstone's heart began to fail him.

I feel [he wrote on May 20] as if I am to die on this voyage and wish I had sent my accounts to the Government, and also my chart of the Zambezi. Often wish that I may be permitted to do something for the benighted of Africa. I shall have nothing to do at home; by the failure of the Universities Mission my work seems vain. No fruit likely to come from J. Moffat's mission either. Have I not laboured in vain? Am I to be cut off before I can do anything to effect permanent improvement in Africa.[5]

A week later, with an estimated fifteen days still to go and the monsoon due to break any day after that, he decided that the margin of safety was too narrow and turned the ship's head, intending to make for Aden. But with the wind from the west she would only sail north or south, so he returned to the old course.

Enquired how much water we had and found it as much as on short allowance will last ten or twelve days. I am shut up to one course, so turned her head E.N.E. for Bombay. May the Almighty be gracious to us all and help us.[6]

The vessel's screws when at rest acted as a drag on her, and even in a stiff breeze her speed was only three and a half knots.

How Rae could say that on the trial trip she went between 5 and 6 with two little trysails I dont know. She is a good seaboat . . . but dreadfully slow.[7]

At last, on June 12, the land of India was sighted 100 miles to the south of Bombay. Livingstone thought of going in but decided to press on in spite of damage to the feed pump and frequent squalls, one of which tore the foresail to ribbons. The next day he sighted the lightship off Bombay and brought the *Lady Nyassa* safely to anchor in the harbor. The voyage, which was to have taken eighteen days had lasted forty-five days and ended just before the monsoon broke. "The vessel was so small," Livingstone wrote in the *Narrative,* "that no one noticed our arrival."

However, the next day two British officers called with an invitation from the Governor of Bombay, Sir Bartle Frere, who was staying upcountry at Dapuri. Here Livingstone spent a happy week, resting after his exertions, meeting all the notabilities and inspecting various mission schools. He also discussed with the Governor, who was a great admirer of his exploits, his future plans for the suppression of the slave trade. It was probably as a result of the encouragement he received from Frere that he changed his mind about selling the *Lady Nyassa.*

'Oh man of feeble mind' you may say [he wrote to Maclear], for with the sale, which many people seemed ready to effect, came the idea most vividly, 'You thereby give up future work in Africa,' and I could not do it. By Tozer's dastardly retreat, decided upon before he had landed, all our work up Shire is cast away. I must therefore do what I can to get an English settlement away from the Portuguese. Bombay merchants profess willingness to try, if a feasible spot can be pointed out. I therefore resolved to run home by this mail of 24th June and consult with friends and, if matters can be made favourable, I shall be out again in four months to go up and examine the Juba and other two rivers near.[8]

The Juba (Giuba) is a river in Somalia which runs into the Indian Ocean 500 miles north of Zanzibar and nearly 1,000 miles from Lake Nyassa, so it is difficult to see what connection it had in Livingstone's mind with his antislavery plans. In fact he would never go near it. However, what mattered was his decision, come what may, to return to Africa.

After placing the *Lady Nyassa** in charge of a friend, and paying off the crew, Livingstone embarked for England on June 24, 1864. With a brief stop at Aden and traveling by land from Suez

* She was sold a year later for less than half her cost to Livingstone. He deposited the money in a Bombay bank which subsequently failed, so he lost it all.

to Alexandria, the journey took almost exactly a month, and on July 23 he was back in London.

In spite of the apparent failure of the Expedition and the tragic fiasco of the Universities Mission, his reception in England, although less enthusiastic than on his first return from Africa, was still highly flattering. On the night of his arrival he was taken to a party at Lady Palmerston's, had two conversations with the Prime Minister about the slave trade and was invited to dinner. Although Russell's manner was "very cold, as all the Russells are," other members of the Government said "very polite things" and were "all wonderfully considerate." Several grand houses reopened their doors to him and he received an invitation from the Lord Mayor to "dine with Her Majesty's Ministers."[9] But although he recorded these events with satisfaction in his diary, he could not conceal from himself that his return was the reverse of triumphant and that the cost of the Expedition, especially in lives, was generally considered to be out of all proportion to its results. Even his loyal friend and patron Sir Roderick Murchison was found by Kirk to be "downdeath on the Expedition." Livingstone had offended too many people and would henceforth walk as a man alone, regarded by an increasing number as slightly mad, until his death raised him again to the status of a national hero.

If the Foreign Secretary in particular was less than friendly it was partly, as Coupland has pointed out, because Livingstone's attacks on the Portuguese had created a delicate diplomatic situation.

The Prince Consort was King Pedro's cousin and he made no secret of his displeasure at any interference with Portuguese rights. At the time of its inception he had questioned the propriety of intruding the Expedition into Portuguese territory at all; and on the same ground he had refused to be patron of the Universities Mission. During the course of the Expedition, moreover, personal events had multiplied the interchange of courtesies between the courts of Lisbon and St. James's. King Pedro's marriage in 1858, the visit of the Prince of Wales to Lisbon in 1859, the King's death in 1861 and the accession of his brother, Luiz I, another royal wedding in 1862—it was these matters with all their paraphernalia of ceremony and compliment that occupied the diplomatists and filled their despatches. And it was difficult to thrust the gaunt realities of far-off Africa into that glittering picture, difficult to present His Most Faithful Majesty with the Garter on one day and to box his ears on the next for the sake of Livingstone and the Slave Trade.[10]

For British diplomats, in fact, Livingstone's behavior for the past six years had been that of a bull in a china shop, and they could only be relieved that he had at last been removed from his stamping ground and could only hope that the damage done was not irreparable.

On their side the Portuguese were long since convinced of what they had suspected all along, namely that the Expedition was simply a cover for British imperialism. As early as May 1859 the Overseas Minister had written to the Governor General of Mozambique warning him of Livingstone's plan

to set up in the neighbourhood of Tete a British factory to the end that he may subsequently demand the right of free access from the said factory to the mouth of the Zambezi River, thus ill repaying the generous assistance given him by the Portuguese Government and the good faith in which that Government subsequently procured for him the Royal *Exequatur* for his appointment as British Consul at Quelimane

and containing instructions to the Governor General

to take, with the utmost discretion, every possible measure to find out what the plans of Dr. Livingstone may be and to prevent him carrying out the suspected scheme or any others which he may attempt to put into execution without the previous consent of His Majesty's Government, so that he may not under cover of the Gospel or of Science, change his status of explorer for that of conqueror.[11]

Letters to the Governor General from the Governor of Quelimane and the Military Commander of Tete, which are in the Portuguese national archives, show that these officials did their best to discover and report on Livingstone's real intentions, but with little success. While accepting their help he never told them his plans, and they had to rely on odd bits of gossip picked up from other members of the Expedition or natives. All they knew for certain was that he was friendly with their enemies, such as the rebel bandit Bonga, and this naturally aroused their resentment. They also objected to his shipping "slaves" out of the country—the "slaves" in question being the orphans and widows rescued from Morambala—without taking them through customs and in any case against the law. Otherwise they seemed to have behaved with astonishing forbearance, especially when one thinks of what the British reaction would have been if a Portuguese expedition accompanied by a Catholic mission had arrived, for example, in Australia or Canada.

Feelings in Lisbon, however, were much stronger; and after Livingstone had repeated all his accusations in an address given at Bath to the British Association for the Advancement of Science, the Portuguese Government retaliated by issuing an English translation of a series of articles written by a Dr. D. F. de Lacerda and published in their official journal. The burden of these was that Livingstone's claims as an explorer were false, that he had discovered nothing which had not been known before to the Portuguese, and that "under pretext of propagating the Word of God (this being the least in which he employed himself) and the advancement of geographical and natural science, made all his steps and exertions subservient to the idea of . . . eventually causing the loss to Portugal of the advantages of the rich commerce of the interior, and in the end, when a favourable occasion arose, that of the very territory itself."[12]

If the questioning of Livingstone's discoveries was unjustified in the sense that whether or not he was the first white man to see them he was certainly the first to map and describe them accurately, de Lacerda's other accusation was only the truth. There is abundant proof in Livingstone's dispatches, journals and private letters—some of which have been cited in this book—that he did not recognize Portuguese claims on the Zambezi and the Shire and wanted the British Government to challenge them with a view to the establishment of British commerce, British settlements and ultimately of British authority over territories which

Portugal regarded as her own. And that it was all in a good cause, as he considered, did not alter the fact. Indeed it is the essence of imperialism to believe that it is acting righteously and that the end justifies the means.

Livingstone had not intended to write another book—his plan was to return to Africa as soon as he could arrange it—but the storm provoked in Lisbon by his address to the British Association stung him into replying, and it was thus that he came to write his *Narrative of an Expedition to the Zambesi and Its Tributaries.* The book was based chiefly on his own journals and dispatches, but also on notes supplied by his brother, less for their value than to justify the signature of Charles as part author and the concession to him of profits from sales of the book in America. He also had some help from Kirk and Stewart, both of whom, after quarreling with him in Africa, resumed friendly relations when he returned to England.

Although it did not obtain the sensational success of *Missionary Travels,* the book went into five editions and brought a considerable sum of money to Livingstone. Since the author was a born writer it still makes good reading, but as a travel book it is spoiled by a preponderance of propaganda. In fact it is less an account of the Zambezi Expedition than an exercise in public relations, vindicating Livingstone's leadership, justifying his views on the suppression of the slave trade and putting all the blame for the failure of the Expedition on the Portuguese.

The publication of the *Narrative* brings our story to an end. With what followed—Livingstone's return to Africa to solve the problem of the sources of the Nile, his seven years' solitary wanderings, famous encounter with Stanley, death at Chitambo's and burial in Westminster Abbey—with all this we are not concerned here. The story, however, would not be complete without some assessment of the results of the Expedition.

At the time, as we have seen, they seemed small. The main object—of opening a route to the interior of Central Africa for the entry of commerce, civilization and Christianity—had not been achieved. The slave trade had not received a setback; on the contrary it had been stimulated by Livingstone's proceedings. The attempt to found a mission station had failed miserably, and the great cotton field which he saw in his dreams as replacing that of America had never seemed likely to materialize.

And yet the discoveries made during the Expedition, and Livingstone's repeated attempts to solve the problem of access to the interior, were to bear fruit with decisive consequences for the whole future of Central Africa. Twelve years after Livingstone's death, Lieutenant E. D. Young, R.N., his former shipmate in the *Pioneer*, succeeded in doing with another vessel, the *Ilala*, exactly what Livingstone had tried and failed to do with the *Lady Nyassa;* that is to say, he unloaded the pieces from a larger ship at the mouth of the Zambezi, put them together on a mudbank, steamed up the Shire River to the foot of the Murchison Falls, took the vessel apart, had the parts carried in fifty-pound loads by 800 native porters over sixty miles of bush paths, put them together again, launched the vessel on the upper Shire and steamed triumphantly into Lake Nyassa.

This magnificent feat, which Livingstone had had the imagination to conceive but not the means to carry out, led to the establishment on Lake Nyassa of Livingstonia, the great mission station founded as a memorial to him, and of other missions at Blantyre and Zomba in the Shire highlands; the introduction of legitimate commerce by the African Lakes Company (1878); the proclamation of the British Central African Protectorate over Nyasaland (1891); and the final defeat of the Arab slavers (1895), followed by the extinction of the slave trade. Thus everything Livingstone worked for came to pass almost exactly as he planned it. It was above all in realizing, after his check at Kebrabasa and on the Rovuma, that the Shire valley held the key to the interior, that his genius as an explorer and prophetic vision were revealed, since it is there that the railway runs today.

Nor were his own countrymen the only, or even the principal, beneficiaries. The latter, of course, were the natives, who knew freedom from fear for the first time in their history, and together with it peace and the beginnings of a process of evolution which was to change them in less than 100 years from a collection of primitive and warring tribes into a sovereign independent nation with all the trappings of modern statehood. But the Portuguese also benefited. The extinction of the slave trade was followed, just as Livingstone predicted, by a great expansion of agriculture in the Zambezi valley; and although the mouth of the river never became the thriving commercial port which he alone envisaged, the problem of its navigation was solved by the building of vessels drawing not more than eighteen inches, propelled by stern paddles as on the Mississippi, and carrying their own wood fuel in barges lashed alongside.

And all this was still not all. It was the Zambezi Expedition, and all the publicity attending it, that put the idea in the heads of the people at the Cape that there was a vast vacuum to the north of them waiting to be filled and that it extended to the Victoria Falls and beyond. Hence Rhodes with his Cape-to-Cairo railway project; the colonization of Bechuanaland, Rhodesia and Northern Rhodesia (today Zambia); the "scramble for Africa" and all that followed. It may be said indeed that the development and present status of the countries south of the Sahara, with all that is happening in that part of the globe today, derives largely from the movement which Livingstone set going when he embarked with his little band in the S.S. *Pearl.* Whichever way you look at it, whether for good or bad, there can be no question of the immensity of his influence, and it is certainly without parallel in the history of Africa.

It only remains to examine Livingstone himself. What sort of man is he shown to be by the Zambezi Expedition? Much has been written about his failures as a leader. He was certainly unloved by the men who served under him, but this is no criterion: Wellington was not loved, although Nelson was. It is not necessary for a leader to be liked, as long as he is respected and trusted. The trouble was that Livingstone, although respected, was not trusted, either in his judgment or his dealings. This was partly through his failure to take others into his confidence: as a result they never knew what he was really trying to do and were expected to follow blindly, however stupid or dangerous they considered the course he was taking. This was the case of Kirk on the second exploration of the Rovuma, and Kirk was the man he came nearest to sharing his thoughts with. During the whole six years of the Expedition there is recorded only one council of war, and that was held in the very early days to decide what was to be done with the *Pearl.* Thereafter Livingstone never called a meeting of his colleagues and his intentions could only be guessed from his behavior and from odd remarks.

He had of course his reasons for being secretive, inasmuch as some of his plans, if revealed to them, would not have had the approval of the other members of the Expedition. They did not, for example, share his prejudice against the local Portuguese, who were generally friendly and helpful people, and would have disliked the idea of plotting against them behind their backs, as Livingstone did not scruple to do, while accepting their hospitality and assistance.

As for his dealings with his own people it is a fact that, rightly or wrongly, and with the possible exception of Rae, who himself was a liar and a mischief-maker, he was distrusted by every member of the original Expedition, including his own brother, and that there was not one who had any faith in his honesty or fairness where their own interests were concerned. It is probable that Kirk was only expressing what they all felt when he wrote in a letter to Stewart:

I find that in an underhand way Dr. L. has given me no cause to thank him: he simply said one thing, or wrote it, to me and another to the Foreign Office. He is about as ungrateful and slippery a mortal as ever I came in contact with, and, although he would be greviously offended to think that anyone doubted his honesty, I am sorry to say that I do. I think the explanation to be that he is one of those sanguine enthusiasts wrapped up in their schemes whose reason and better judgement is blinded by headstrong passion. I don't think he would exactly say what he knew was untrue, but for all practical purposes the result is the same, and in him I believe all kindly feelings to be absolutely extinct. For the first two years I had great respect for him, and for his energy and force of mind have so still . . .[13]

There is no evidence that Livingstone did what Kirk accused him of with the Foreign Office, and the fact that they soon became reconciled again and that Kirk was one of the two people to see him off at Dover when he left England for the last time suggests that by then he realized he had been mistaken. But that he, who was not given to be suspicious or jump to conclusions, should have thought Livingstone capable of such underhand behavior is significant.

Kirk also considered that Livingstone was ungrateful: after six years of devoted service as second-in-command he was entitled to a word of thanks which he never got. It never occurred to Livingstone to praise a person merely, as he saw it, for doing his duty. What he failed to realize was that the others were working for *him:* for any success achieved by the Expedition he would be given all the credit, but he would owe at least some of it to their labors and ought therefore to show some appreciation. Moreover, the hardships they all endured were much easier for the leader to support: with his eye constantly fixed on the distant goal, his mind ever seething with plans and calculations, his leisure time fully occupied writing letters and dispatches, he had something always to distract him from boredom and discomfort, while the rest of them must simply grin and bear it.

Then there was what Kirk called his stinginess. Livingstone was generous with his own money when it could be used to advance any of the causes he had at heart: for example he paid his brother-in-law an annuity to enable him to become a missionary and footed the whole bill for the *Lady Nyassa,* but he never spent a penny more than was necessary on himself and boasted that he could live in Africa on £100 a year. Having been brought up in the utmost penury he was accustomed to do without luxuries, scarcely missed them and had a Puritan disapproval of those who did. The Government had provided ample funds for the Expedition, but Livingstone was so averse to spending money that its members were frequently on short rations and had to go without such items—essential to health and morale in a tropical climate—as tea, coffee, sugar, wine and spirits.

There has been general agreement with Kirk's verdict that Livingstone had little administrative talent. He had no idea of organizing the work of others so as to get the best out of them, but simply left them to their own devices. He could handle Africans, but not white men, with whom he was gruff, faultfinding and inconsiderate. They followed him to begin with willingly, later grudgingly and finally with a reluctance verging on mutiny; but always they were overawed by the force of his personality, and shamed, in spite of themselves, by certain qualities in the man—pre-eminently his physical courage—into grumblingly putting up with his demands on them.

If Livingstone's companions had all been worthless, their dislike and distrust of him would not have been significant. But this was not the case, as they proved in their later careers: Bedingfield, in spite of his difficult temperament, was an able officer who rose to the rank of admiral; Baines, so unjustly dismissed, was a simple man whose sterling qualities were generally recognized afterward, and a charming artist to boot; Thornton, who made good on his own after being dismissed, also unjustly, might have done great things but for his premature death; while Kirk, the most outstanding, became British Consul General at Zanzibar and was knighted for his distinguished services in connection with the suppression of the slave trade. Even Charles Livingstone, for whom nobody in or connected with the Expedition ever had a good word, ended his days in the respectable post (obtained for him, like Kirk's, by Livingstone's influence) of Consul at Fernando Po.

In assessing the reasons for Livingstone's unpopularity with all the men who worked under him, allowance must be made for the physical and mental strain imposed on them by danger, disease and discomfort, in a barbarous country where for long periods they were cut off from all contact with civilization or any news of the outside world. Livingstone's own health was permanently affected for the worse, and even Kirk toward the end was not the same rational being that he had always shown himself formerly. This may partly explain his bitterness against Livingstone, of which he afterward repented.

But when everything has been said against Livingstone's leadership, his conduct of the Zambezi Expedition remains an extraordinary performance of imaginative enterprise, grit and dogged perseverance, eclipsing all his other exploits. For on those he was only driving himself and it is much easier to do that than to drive a team.

Considering the all but insuperable difficulties—the sickness, the strandings, the breakdowns, the endless toil dragging the steamers through shallows or cutting wood for their fuel—it is astonishing that the Expedition achieved as much as it did. And at the end of it all, what one remembers is not the tortuousness, the spite, the egoism, the self-righteousness, but the indomitable spirit and glorious recklessness of the man who dared to shoot the Kebrabasa Rapids in his canoe and gambled on sailing his little craft, with a scratch crew, across the vast expanse of the Indian Ocean just before the monsoon broke. With all his faults he towers over ordinary men.

Let the final word, therefore, be with one of Livingstone's most devoted disciples, a man who knew him at close quarters for two years on the Shire, and afterward edited his *Last Journals.*

With all his grand qualities [Horace Waller wrote to Stewart], those who know him make allowances for the unrounded qualities of his character. His heart's in the right place and he's the bravest man I ever saw or ever expect to see, which for one who has longed to have a tithe of his pluck, is a go-and-do-likewise object to gaze on and not pick to pieces. So I always stick up for him tho', I confess, with more tact in dealing with his companions, he might make a much greater and more lasting mark.[14]

Principal Sources

BOOKS AND PUBLICATIONS

Blaikie, W. G., *The Personal Life of David Livingstone,* 6th ed. Murray, 1917.
Chamberlin, D., ed., *Some Letters from Livingstone.* Oxford University Press, 1940.
Coupland, Sir R., *Kirk on the Zambezi.* Oxford University Press, 1928.
Debenham, F., *The Way to Ilala.* Longmans, 1955.
de Lacerda, D. F., *Reply to Dr. Livingstone's Accusations.* London, 1865.
Devereux, W. Cope, *A Cruise in the "Gorgon."* London, 1869.
Gelfand, M., *Livingstone the Doctor.* Blackwell, Oxford, 1957.
Goodwin, H., *Memoir of Bishop Mackenzie.* London, 1865.
Jackson Haight, M. V., *European Powers and South-East Africa.* Routledge, 1967.
Kirk, J., *The Zambesi Journal and Letters,* R. Foskett, ed. Oliver & Boyd, 1965.
Livingstone, D., *Zambezi Expedition, Journals, Letters, and Dispatches,* J. P. R. Wallis, ed. Chatto & Windus, 1956.
Livingstone, D. and C., *Narrative of an Expedition to the Zambesi.* Murray, 1865.
Rowley, H., *The Story of the Universities Mission.* Saunders, Otley and Co., 1866.

Royal Geographical Society (R.G.S.), *Journal of the,* Vols. 30, 31, 33, 35.
Schapera, I., ed., *Family Letters of D. Livingstone, 1841–1856.* Chatto & Windus, 1959.
Seaver, George, *David Livingstone, His Life & Letters.* Lutterworth Press, 1957.
Shepperson, George, ed., *David Livingstone and the Rovuma.* Edinburgh University Press, 1965.
Smith, E. W., *Great Lion of Bechuanaland.* Independent Press, 1957.
Stewart, James, *The Zambesi Journal of James Stewart,* J. P. R. Wallis, ed. Chatto & Windus, 1952.
Thornton, Richard, *The Zambezi Papers,* E. C. Tabler, ed. Chatto & Windus, 1963.
Wallis, J. P. R., *Thomas Baines.* Cape, 1941.
Young, E. D., *Nyassa.* Murray, 1877.

MANUSCRIPTS

State Papers in Public Record Office, London (F.O. Series).
London Missionary Society, London (Livingstone Correspondence).
Bodleian Library, Oxford (Clarendon Correspondence).
Livingstone Memorial, Blantyre, Scotland (Journals and Letters).
National Library of Scotland, Edinburgh (Journals).
Arquivo Historico Ultramarino, Lisbon (Official Correspondence).
Central African Archives, Salisbury, Rhodesia (Bruce Collection).
Livingstone Museum, Zambia (Miscellaneous).

Notes

Note: All works referred to are denoted by the name of the author followed by the number of the page, except where Livingstone is the author and then only the abbreviated title is given, e.g., *Narrative, Journals.* Manuscript sources in the Public Record Office, England, are denoted by the serial number, e.g., F.O. 63/842, but where extracts from manuscripts have already appeared in print the reference given is to the publication.

CHAPTER 1

1 *Journals,* 7.
2 Schapera, Vol. 2, 182.
3 Blaikie, 254.
4 Seaver, 286.
5 Schapera, Vol. 2, 150, 151.
6 *Ibid.,* 116.
7 Chamberlin, 160.
8 Coupland, 35.
9 Chamberlin, 25.
10 Schapera, Vol. 1, 13.
11 *Ibid.,* 14.
12 *Ibid.,* Vol. 2, 160, 161.
13 Chamberlin, 201.
14 Seaver, 108.
15 Schapera, Vol. 2, 162.
16 *Ibid.,* 54.
17 Seaver, 133.
18 Chamberlin, 155.
19 *Ibid.,* 157.
20 *Ibid.,* 207.
21 Schapera, Vol. 2, 224.
22 Chamberlin, 257.

CHAPTER 2

1 Seaver, 268.
2 *Ibid.*
3 *Journals,* xvii.
4 Chamberlin, 259.
5 *Ibid.*
6 Schapera, Vol. 2, 289.
7 *Ibid.,* 280.
8 *Journals,* xvii.
9 *Ibid.,* xxii.
10 Seaver, 297.
11 *Journals,* xx.
12 Seaver, 299.
13 *Ibid.,* 372.

14 Chamberlin, 255.
15 Smith, 23, 24.
16 L.M.S. Archives.
17 Seaver, 312.
18 L.M.S. Archives.
19 Seaver, 300.
20 *Journals*, xxv.
21 Seaver, 287.
22 F.O. 63/842.
23 The *Times*, Dec. 12, 1857.
24 Blaikie, 194.
25 F.O. 63/842.
26 *Journals*, xxv.
27 F.O. 63/842.

CHAPTER 3

1 Schapera, Vol. 2, 284.
2 Seaver, 257.
3 Coupland, 85.
4 *Ibid.*, 267.
5 *Narrative*, 407.
6 Blaikie, 160.
7 Coupland, 87.
8 Seaver, 308.
9 F.O. 63/843.
10 Coupland, 93.

CHAPTER 4

1 Coupland, 95 *et seq.*
2 Gelfand, 13.
3 F.O. 63/842.
4 Kirk, 3.
5 *Ibid.*, 4.
6 *Journals*, 412.
7 *Ibid.*, 2.
8 Kirk, 13.
9 *Journals*, 4.
10 Smith, 43.
11 Thornton, 22.
12 *Journals*, 4.
13 *Ibid.*
14 *Ibid.*, 6.
15 *Journals*, 8.
16 Kirk, 32.
17 *Journals*, 9.
18 Seaver, 301.
19 Kirk, 45.
20 F.O. 63/843, Part 1.
21 *Journals*, 9.
22 Kirk, 34.
23 *Journals*, 10.
24 Kirk, 40.
25 *Journals*, 12.
26 *Ibid.*, 24.
27 *Ibid.*, 13.
28 *Ibid.*, 15.
29 *Ibid.*, 16.
30 *Narrative*, 28.
31 *Ibid.*, 26.
32 *Journals*, 16.
33 F.O. 63/842.
34 Kirk, 43, 44.
35 *Journals*, 17.
36 *Ibid.*, 18.
37 *Ibid.*, 24.
38 *Ibid.*, 272.

CHAPTER 5

1 *Narrative*, 27.
2 *Ibid.*, 33.
3 Kirk, 55.
4 *Journals*, 34.
5 *Narrative*, 33.
6 *Journals*, 37.
7 *Ibid.*, 39.
8 *Ibid.*, 42.
9 Kirk, 106.
10 *Narrative*, 44.
11 Kirk, 66.
12 *Ibid.*, 113.
13 *Ibid.*, 80.
14 *Ibid.*, 87.
15 *Journals*, 46.
16 Kirk, 91.
17 *Ibid.*
18 *Journals*, 52.
19 *Ibid.*
20 Kirk, 111.

CHAPTER 6

1 Kirk, 115.
2 *Journals*, 59.

3 *Ibid.*, *n.*
4 *Ibid.*, 60, 61.
5 *Ibid.*
6 *Ibid.*, 63.
7 Kirk, 124.
8 *Ibid.*, 128.
9 *Ibid.*, 127.
10 *Ibid.*, 134.
11 *Ibid.*, 136.
12 *Journals*, 70.
13 F.O. 63/843, Part 2.
14 Kirk, 139.
15 R.G.S. *Journal*, Vol. 31, p. 87.
16 F.O. 63/871.
17 *Ibid.*
18 *Journals*, 80.

CHAPTER 7

1 *Journals*, 71.
2 *Narrative*, 74.
3 *Journals*, 75.
4 *Ibid.*, 305.
5 *Ibid.*, 78.
6 *Narrative*, 76.
7 Kirk, 76.
8 Kirk, 153.
9 F.O. 63/871.
10 Wallis, 167.
11 *Journals*, 85.
12 *Ibid.*
13 Kirk, 156.
14 *Narrative*, 80.
15 *Journals*, 98.
16 F.O. 63/871.
17 *Ibid.*
18 Kirk, 209.
19 *Ibid.*
20 *Ibid.*, 213.

CHAPTER 8

1 *Journals*, 109.
2 *Ibid.*, xli.
3 Thornton, xiv.
4 *Journals*, xl.
5 *Ibid.*
6 *Journals*, 115.
7 *Ibid.*, 118.
8 F.O. 63/871.
9 *Ibid.*
10 Kirk, 221.
11 *Journals*, 117.
12 Kirk, 221.
13 *Journals*, 125.
14 *Ibid.*, 120.
15 F.O. 63/871.
16 *Ibid.*
17 *Ibid.*
18 F.O. 63/871.
19 *Journals*, 137.
20 Kirk, 125.
21 *Journals*, 125.
22 Wallis, 179.
23 *Journals*, 134.
24 F.O. 63/871.
25 Seaver, 354.
26 *Ibid.*, 355.
27 F.O. 63/871.
28 Seaver, 354.

CHAPTER 9

1 *Journals*, 136.
2 Kirk, 271.
3 Blaikie, 226.
4 F.O. 63/871.
5 Kirk, 283.
6 *Journals*, 160.
7 *Ibid.*, 163.
8 *Narrative*, 167.
9 *Journals*, 252.
10 *Narrative*, 179.
11 *Ibid.*
12 *Ibid.*, 241.
13 *Ibid.*, 252.
14 *Ibid.*, 280.
15 Seaver, 376.
16 *Ibid.*
17 Smith, Ch. 5.
18 Seaver, 377.
19 *Journals*, 262.
20 *Ibid.*, 395.
21 *Ibid.*, 392.
22 *Narrative*, 273.

23 *Ibid.*, 329.
24 Coupland, 168.
25 *Narrative*, 335.
26 Kirk, 310.
27 *Ibid.*
28 F.O. 63/894.

CHAPTER 10

1 F.O. 63/871.
2 *Ibid.*
3 *Ibid.*
4 *Ibid.*
5 *Ibid.*
6 *Ibid.*
7 *Ibid.*
8 *Journals*, 177.
9 *Ibid.*
10 Thornton, 221.
11 *Narrative*, 343.
12 *Ibid.*, 350.
13 F.O. 63/871.
14 *Ibid.*
15 *Narrative*, 351.
16 Kirk, 345.
17 Rowley, 77.
18 *Ibid.*, 4.
19 Seaver, 388.
20 *Ibid.*, 394.
21 *Narrative*, 355–357.
22 Goodwin, 325.
23 Rowley, 127.
24 *Narrative*, 361.
25 *Ibid.*, 363.

CHAPTER 11

1 *Journals*, 206.
2 *Ibid.*, 406.
3 *Narrative*, 389.
4 *Ibid.*, 404.
5 *Ibid.*
6 *Journals*, 208.
7 Stewart, 56.
8 Kirk, 393.
9 *Narrative*, 400.
10 Kirk, 396.
11 *Narrative*, 391.
12 F.O. 63/894.
13 Blaikie, 251.
14 *Ibid.*, 256.
15 *Ibid.*, 257.
16 *Journals*, 213.
17 *Narrative*, 401.
18 Rowley, 323.
19 Devereux, 164.
20 *Ibid.*
21 Kirk, 569.
22 Devereux, 170.
23 Stewart, 1.
24 *Ibid.*
25 F.O. 63/894.
26 *Ibid.*
27 Devereux, 182.
28 Stewart, 5.
29 Kirk, 415.
30 *Ibid.*, 416.
31 *Narrative*, 408.
32 Devereux, 190.
33 Blaikie, 247.
34 Kirk, 419.
35 *Ibid.*, 423.
36 *Ibid.*, 428.
37 Stewart, 208.
38 Blaikie, 248.
39 F.O. 63/894.
40 Stewart, 208.

CHAPTER 12

1 F.O. 63/894.
2 *Ibid.*
3 Devereux, 251.
4 Kirk, 434.
5 *Ibid.*, 439
6 Stewart, 57
7 Seaver, 413.
8 Stewart, 58.
9 Rowley, 340.
10 *Journals*, 240.
11 *Narrative*, 423.
12 Kirk, 469.
13 Shepperson, 175.

14 *Ibid.*
15 Kirk, 475.
16 F.O. 63/894.
17 Debenham, 201.
18 Shepperson, 130.
19 *Journals,* 379.
20 Kirk, 495.
21 *Narrative,* 450.
22 Kirk, 514.
23 *Ibid.,* 595.
24 *Ibid.,* 516.
25 Stewart, 226.
26 *Journals,* 231.
27 F.O. 97/322.
28 Stewart, 79, 187, 190.
29 The *Times,* Jan. 20, 1863.
30 F.O. 97/322.
31 *Ibid.*
32 *Ibid.*
33 Young, 27.
34 F.O. 97/322.
35 *Ibid.*
36 *Ibid.*
37 *Journals,* 242.
38 Seaver, 426.
39 *Narrative,* 569.
40 Seaver, 433.

EPILOGUE

1 *Narrative,* 383.
2 *Ibid.*
3 Seaver, 439.
4 *Narrative,* 584.
5 Seaver, 442.
6 *Ibid.*
7 *Ibid.*
8 *Journals,* 386.
9 Blaikie, 285.
10 Coupland, 269.
11 Jackson Haight, 342.
12 de Lacerda, 10.
13 Stewart, 228.
14 *Ibid.,* 232.

Index